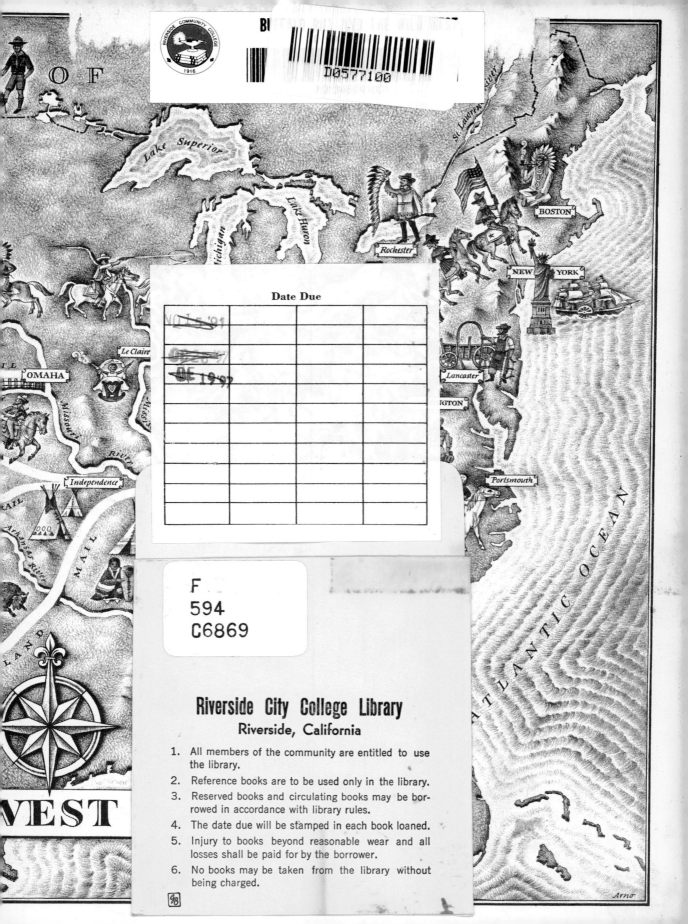

Date Due

NOV 5 '91			
DE 19 97			

F
594
C6869

Riverside City College Library
Riverside, California

1. All members of the community are entitled to use the library.
2. Reference books are to be used only in the library.
3. Reserved books and circulating books may be borrowed in accordance with library rules.
4. The date due will be stamped in each book loaned.
5. Injury to books beyond reasonable wear and all losses shall be paid for by the borrower.
6. No books may be taken from the library without being charged.

2 70/3rb+

BERTRAND SMITH
ACRES OF BOOKS
240 LONG BEACH BLVD.
LONG BEACH, CALIF.

BUFFALO BILL and the WILD WEST

Rosa Bonheur
1890

BUFFALO BILL AND THE WILD WEST

By HENRY BLACKMAN SELL

and VICTOR WEYBRIGHT

New York
Oxford University Press · 1955

Riverside City College Library
Riverside, California

F594 .C6869 1955
Sell, Henry Blackman.
Buffalo Bill and the Wild
West,

© HENRY BLACKMAN SELL and VICTOR WEYBRIGHT, 1955

LIBRARY OF CONGRESS CATALOGUE CARD NUMBER 55-10932

DESIGNED BY JOHN BEGG

PRINTED IN THE UNITED STATES OF AMERICA

THIS BOOK

IS DEDICATED

TO

Contents

ACKNOWLEDGMENTS

IT IS IMPOSSIBLE adequately to express our appreciation to the men and women, and in particular to members of the Cody family, who during the decades that we contemplated this life of Buffalo Bill contributed so much to our accrued knowledge of our subject. It is possible, however, to acknowledge our profound gratitude to the individuals (and institutions) consulted during the past year.

We are especially grateful to our principal research assistants, Horace Coon and E. J. Dingwall, who in the United States and Great Britain respectively found no trail in library, museum, or among old friends and acquaintances of Col. Cody, too much trouble to explore. Mr. Coon delved into the records at Cody, Denver, Chicago, New York, the Yale University Library, and elsewhere. Professor Dingwall explored the archives of the British Museum, the Continent, and the foreign press, including the records of her late Majesty, Queen Victoria, at Windsor. We have to record our dutiful thanks for special permission to make use of unpublished extracts from the journal of Queen Victoria in the Royal Library, Windsor Castle.

Mrs. Mary Jester Allen, Curator of the Buffalo Bill Museum, supported by the board of directors—especially by Mr. Ernest J. Goppert, president of The Buffalo Bill Memorial Association, nourishing body of the museum—generously made available hitherto unknown and unpublished material. Individual thanks are also due the following who assisted our research in Cody: Helen Cody Allen, Mr. and Mrs. I. H. Larom, Ned Frost, Henry H. R. Coe, Mrs. E. F. Shaw, Mrs. Pearl C. Newell.

At the Denver Public Library, Western History Department, special acknowledgment should be made of the helpful co-operation of Mrs. Ina Aulls, Mrs. Alys Freeze, and Mrs. Opal Harber; and, also in Denver, of the assistance of the Colorado Historical Society Museum; and of Mrs. Agnes Wright Spring; and of Mr. Robert Linneux, the artist who painted "The First Scalp for Custer!"

In Chicago, Miss Elizabeth Baughman, Reference Library of the Chicago Historical Society, was particularly helpful.

We are grateful to the Library of Congress, the Smithsonian Institution, the New York Public Library, and the Newark, N. J., Public Library for the extensive use of their archives, newspaper files, and reference material.

We are grateful to Carl W. Drepperd, Director of the Pennsylvania Farm Museum of Landis Valley, in Lancaster, for background on the origin and development of the Conestoga Wagon and "Prairie Schooner," and for his co-operation in preparing a photograph of one of the vehicles in that institution.

Mr. Archibald Hanna of the Western Americana Collection at the Yale University Library was consistently helpful in producing relevant material from the magnificent William Robertson Coe collection. Indeed, the late Mr. Coe, whose estate now owns the Rosa Bonheur painting of Buffalo Bill, has generously preserved Western Americana in the Buffalo Bill Museum at Cody as well as at Yale University and elsewhere. Every student of the frontier must be grateful to Mr. Coe's foresight and generosity; and also to the support Cornelius Vanderbilt Whitney has given to the Buffalo Bill Museum, which is adjacent to the equestrian statue created by his mother, the late Gertrude Vanderbilt Whitney, whose Cody papers are now generously available at the Whitney Museum in New York. We appreciate the co-operation of the Metropolitan Museum of Art in New York, and the Grand Central Gallery, which made pictures available. We also are indebted for permission to reproduce paintings of the Old West to C. R. Smith and to Brown & Bigelow.

Without the extraordinary collection of publications and other reference material in the British Museum in London, it would have been impossible to cover accurately the foreign tours of Buffalo Bill's Wild West Show.

Among individuals who have been especially helpful to us are the following: Gene Fowler, whose writings and recollections have been invaluable; the Honorable Robert D. Coe., Ambassador to Denmark, who graciously granted permission for the use of the Rosa Bonheur painting; Miss Mina Turner, who made available the remarkable photographs of the Sioux Indians on the Plains, and in the Wild West Show, by her late grandmother, Gertrude Käsebier; Marc Jaffe, associate editor of New American Library, and Miss Helen Herman who helped organize a vast flow of research material, photographs, and appointments for interviews; Robert F. Canaday, who studied and photographed the terrain of the Yellow Hand Duel; O. B. Marble, who provided much background from first-hand observation of Indian life; and hundreds of men and women whose memories go back to the time of Buffalo Bill and his circle of friends, show folks, and family connections. In the circle, for example, are the Rt. Hon. the Earl of Portsmouth, now in Kenya, who knew Buffalo Bill at the turn of the century in Wyoming; Lady Baden-Powell, who helped establish the authenticity of a sketch made by her husband from a photograph taken with Colonel Cody in Winnipeg; John Collier; J. Frank Dobie; Harry Hansen; the editors of the Cody *Enterprise;* and generations of our own families, particularly co-author Sell's great-grandmother Senna Markle Billings and grandmother Mary Elizabeth Billings Blackman, who made the Colonel very real, then and now.

The picture acknowledgments, on another page, will never do adequate justice to the zeal and co-operation of Jack Richard of Cody, Wyoming, or to the scholarly enterprise of Vincent Mercaldo.

To one and all, including Carroll G. Bowen, editor, and John Begg, designer for our publishers, our heartfelt thanks.

—The authors

x

BUFFALO BILL and the WILD WEST

The Foothills of Heaven

"GOD is my propertyman," said Buffalo Bill when he took his Wild West Show on the road. The Good Lord was eventually assisted by 529 highly trained performers, tent men, ticket collectors, advance agents, and a publicity staff of twelve. But the Prince of the Plains was right. God had set the stage. Colonel Cody was an actor in the last great Eden on earth: the Wild West, two thousand miles by two thousand miles of unspoiled virgin land. Buffalo Bill symbolized the later days of this modern Eden. Ten years from the time he was cooking his meals on the treeless plains over a fire of buffalo dung—*bois de vache,* as General Frémont delicately described it—he was dining with royalty at the first dude ranch, a social fixture of his

own elaboration if not actual invention, and was eagerly awaited in Washington by the President and in London by Queen Victoria and the Prince of Wales, later Edward VII. Stetson was soon to be making the Buffalo Bill hat, then as now the favored headgear in the West. Later, Rough Riders and Boy Scouts, whom he inspired, would carry on his frontier tradition of courage and chivalry.

He was as real as Washington or Lincoln, Davy Crockett or Andrew Jackson. He fulfilled his own dreams and those of millions of admirers, by doing what he wanted to do as a youth, and reliving those delightful boyhood days, amid applause and wealth, in maturity. He fixed the image of the Wild West in the world's mind

3

more vividly than Frémont the Pathfinder, Kit Carson the Army Scout, Custer the Indian Slayer, or their predecessors Dan'l Boone and Davy Crockett.

But Buffalo Bill was legend as well as man. Some eight hundred books have been written about him, all but a score of them dime novels of a day and age that is past. The heroism of a nation guilty of Indian fighting was wished on him. He would, if asked, acknowledge all the accounts of his derring-do as true. He was vain, but proud and generous too. Early in life he assumed support of his family, and when asked by his sisters for money, he replied, "Brave it out a little longer, girls." Within twenty years he had given them and his daughters thousands of dollars. He had faith in the future of the plains and those beautiful Wyoming hills, "the Foothills of Heaven." He had built hotels, developed ranches, financed the irrigation of thousands of acres of arid land in the Shoshone Valley of Wyoming.

Readers of this life story of an eternal American hero, will know why Buffalo Bill was more than a scout, or a showman, to the world. In fringed white buckskin jacket, his cavalier locks falling over his shoulders in a romantic fashion seldom matched since the Restoration of Charles II, he seemed Richard the Lion Hearted on the way to face Saladin. Only, unlike the great Crusader, Colonel Cody met, admired, and emulated the infidel chiefs who were presumed to be his enemies. Like all great scouts, he lived by taking on the color and attributes of the terrain and its denizens; and then portrayed them for all the world to see and understand. To this day his example has fixed so firmly the tradition of western novels, songs and ballads, films and dramas, that the Wild West itself must live up to the epic which he discerned and established.

The Great Plains and the slopes of the Rockies are no longer carpeted with buffalo grass. On top of Lookout Mountain in Colorado, the body of Colonel Cody lies, far from his sacred Wyoming where he wished to be buried, far from "the Foothills of Heaven" which Buffalo Bill, last of the great frontier scouts, made features of the terrain in everyone's heart.

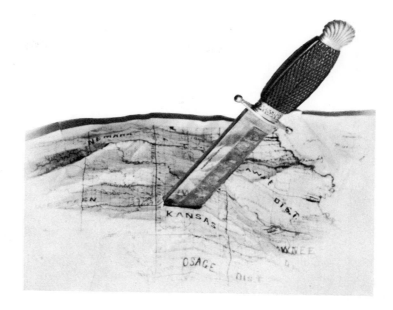

Chapter 1

The Hostile World of Reality

WHEN Buffalo Bill was born in Iowa in 1846 the West was being won by American troops in Mexico and by American negotiators in London. Soon California, Texas, and the Southwest, as well as Oregon and Washington, would complete the map of the continental nation of which the Founding Fathers (Thomas Jefferson in particular—through the Louisiana Purchase and the Lewis and Clark Expedition) had dreamed. A domain five times the area of western Europe awaited exploration, settlement, development.

Buffalo Bill's sister Helen remembered his birthplace in Le Claire, Scott County, Iowa, as a "pleasant, roomy farmhouse, set in the sunlight against a cool, green wood and mottled meadow." It was not far from Davenport, Iowa, which is on the Mississippi River, across from Illinois, over a hundred miles upstream from Hannibal, Missouri, where Mark Twain was born. It is said to be the place where Black Hawk and his warriors performed their last war dance, before the campaign which ended with the treaty between Black Hawk and General Winfield Scott. A famous half-breed Indian scholar and interpreter, Anton Le Clair, had built his cabin there and given the place its name.

William Frederick Cody was born on February 26, 1846, the fourth of eight

5

children. He had two older sisters, Martha and Julia, and an older brother, Samuel. Later he had three younger sisters, Eliza, Helen, and May, and a younger brother, Charlie. Not much is known about his mother, Mary Ann Leacock, except that she was well educated and that she believed her son William would some day be president of the United States. His father, Isaac Cody, was a restless, ambitious, energetic man who, like most of his generation, aspired to take his family to California. He had married Mary Ann in Ohio and started west soon afterward. He had Irish blood and legend has it that he was a descendant of Milesius, king of Spain, whose sons founded the first dynasty in Ireland. The first Codys came to America and settled in Massachusetts just one hundred years before Buffalo Bill was born.

Tragedy suddenly struck the Cody family when Bill was about six years old. His brother Samuel was riding a big mare when she reared without warning, flung herself

6

The only known picture of Buffalo Bill's mother, Mrs. Isaac Cody.

LITTLE BILLY CODY at the age of two, from an old tintype.

BUFFALO BILL'S boyhood home in Le Claire, Iowa, was moved to Cody, Wyoming, next to the Buffalo Bill Museum.

on her back, and crushed the boy who clung to her. Bill witnessed this, and never forgot it. His mother was so unhappy with the memory of the loss of her first son that Isaac Cody decided to divert her by moving from the scene of the fatal accident. They packed up the family possessions and started across Iowa with two big wagons carrying their household goods.

Young Will Cody—he was usually called Will by his family—enjoyed every minute of the thirty-day journey, for he rode beside the wagons on his pony pretending to be an Indian scout. They stopped at Weston, Missouri, where his uncle, Elijah Cody, kept a general store, before crossing into Kansas.

Buffalo Bill remembered that his father showed him Fort Leavenworth. He saw the blockhouse, the artillery rumbling over the parade ground, the westerners in buckskin and coonskin caps, and Indians of many tribes. It was his first glimpse of the dangerous unknown world just over the horizon. After this excursion, the Codys moved deeper into turbulent Kansas and settled in Salt Creek valley, about twenty miles from Leavenworth.

This part of Kansas was not the real West, but the Middle Border—between North and South, between established states like Iowa and Territories of the Great Plains not yet admitted to the Union. Seven years before the War between the States (the Civil War in which Kansas was to give one fifth of all her male population to the Union forces) it was a bloody fighting ground over the issue of

8

LEAVENWORTH IN 1856.

the extension of Negro slavery.

Here the dangerous foes to be faced were not wild beasts, or native Indians resentful of the encroachment of settlers. The real enemies were white men determined to prevent antislavery Abolitionists from gaining a foothold and control of the destiny of the territory that would eventually be a state.

Isaac Cody originally planned to continue moving westward to California and the newly discovered gold that was already making millionaires out of the few prospectors lucky enough to make a strike. But he liked the lush prairie around Salt Creek, and stopped there. Will Cody was then seven, an impressionable age in a hostile world.

Isaac Cody was against slavery. In his opinion the best way to make Kansas a free state, and to avoid friction, was to keep all Negroes—slaves and freedmen alike—out of the territory. But he was caught in the deep and violent struggle and, having

LAWRENCE, KANSAS, IN 1865.

9

staked out a claim as a settler, had to face the challenge of the southerners who threatened to drive him out of Kansas.

There was no real government.

"Govern Kansas?" said Wilson Shannon, the second territorial governor. "You might as well have attempted to govern hell!" After the President had declared it open for settlement in 1854, Congress decreed the settlers could vote either for slavery or against it. Northern Abolitionists hurried from Illinois to fight the proslavery Missourians rushing in from the South. They fought with gun and Bowie knife. Soon John Brown, God's angriest man, stormed amongst them with his sons, to murder ruthlessly in Pottawatomie.

A brutal and quarrelsome breed of men had followed the Codys into the valley. "If I had my way I'd hang every damned Abolitionist!" screamed an editor named Stringfellow from the Missouri side of the river. "And everyone born north of the Mason-Dixon line is an Abolitionist!" At his behest a mob of horsemen rode into the Salt Creek valley and declared that slavery was "thereby instituted in the Territory of Kansas."

During the summer of 1854 new settlers drove their heavy wagons through the tall grass, frantically staking out homestead claims. Four logs tied together in a square were called an "improvement," and evidence of legal settlement. The town of Leavenworth consisted of four tents, a steam engine, and a sawmill. It was proslavery; so were Kickapoo and Atchison. Border men galloped over the grassy limestone hills believing they saw fortunes under the fertile soil.

Desperate men from Missouri came with horses, wagons, plows, cattle, Negro slaves. In Washington Senator William H. Seward shouted, "Come on, gentlemen of the slave states! We will engage in competition for the virgin soil of Kansas, and God give victory to the side that is stronger in numbers as it is in right!"

"Stake out your claims!" answered a border newspaper. "And woe to the Abolitionist or Mormon who shall intrude upon it!" Every Saturday night rallies at the local grocery stores stirred the mob spirit around the whiskey barrels whose spigots poured a liquor said to have the strength of forty jackasses. Anti-abolitionist secret societies were spawned at these gatherings. A southerner waved a hundred dollars, boasting, "I just sold a nigger for that and I reckon that's my share for cleaning out them daggone Yankees!"

In this atmosphere Isaac Cody, though against slavery, usually kept his mouth shut. But, prudent as he was, he could not resist going to a rally at the Salt Creek trading post. The crowd wanted to know where he stood. Will Cody claimed a long time after that he remembered what his father said: "I was one of the pioneers of the state of Iowa, aided its settlement, helped organize it as a state. I voted it should be a *white* state, that Negroes whether free or slave should never be allowed to locate within its limits. I say to you now, and I say it boldly, I propose to exert all my power in making Kansas the

same kind of a state. And I shall always oppose the further extension of slavery. . . ."

"You black Abolitionist!" the crowd shouted. "Get off that box or I'll put you off!" a ruffian yelled. Another pulled out a Bowie knife and stabbed him in the back.

A neighbor rescued Isaac Cody and took him to his home. Cody asked to be taken to his brother's cabin across the Missouri River at Weston. Young Will Cody rushed home to tell his mother, and she hurried to Isaac's side. From then on Isaac was a hunted man.

Such incidents were common in Kansas in those days. Proslavery vigilance committees terrorized the territory, killing, lynching, tarring-and-feathering. An Abolitionist lawyer in Leavenworth, which was growing rapidly and now boasted a hotel, was seized by a mob, his clothes stripped from him, his head shaved, hot tar ap-

Border ruffians from Missouri invade Kansas before Civil War.

plied, and then he was ridden on a rail for a mile and a half and sold for a dollar and a half by a Negro auctioneer. A public meeting in Leavenworth endorsed this demonstration and called the victim a "moral perjurer."

Later a preacher in Atchison was tied to a raft and shipped down the Missouri while the mob threw stones at him. The proslavery newspaper, the *Squatter Sovereign,* warned, "the same punishment we will award to all free-soilers, Abolitionists and their emissaries." An orator in St. Joseph declaimed, "I tell you to mark every scoundrel among you that is the least tainted with free-soilism or abolitionism and exterminate him. Those having qualms of conscience as to violating laws, state or national, the time has come when such impositions must be disregarded. Vote at the point of the Bowie knife or revolver." They voted; the proslavery men won the first election in 1854.

Isaac Cody hid from the mobs. Once he escaped from his home disguised in a bonnet and shawl and lay in his cornfield while armed men surrounded his house and searched it. After three days he fled to Fort Leavenworth, where he joined a group of armed free-staters who set out to help a number of antislavery men then trying to cross the river at Hickory Point. Missourians turned out in force, and a pitched battle was fought in which several men were killed on each side. The free-staters went to Lawrence, Isaac returned home. Mrs. Cody was terrified lest the mob find out he was there, so he fled

again, this time to Grasshopper Falls, thirty-five miles west of Leavenworth, where he started building a sawmill.

Mrs. Cody soon got word that the proslavery men knew where he was and were planning to kill him. Since there was nobody else she could send, she dispatched young Will on a pony. It was his first great adventure and, as he told it afterward, he was in constant danger. He ran into a gang of his father's enemies. "As I galloped past," he wrote later, "one of them yelled, 'There's Cody's kid now on his way to warn his father. Stop, you, and tell us where your old man is!'

"A pistol shot, to terrify me into obedience, accompanied the command. I may have been terrified, but it was not into obedience. I got out of there like a shot, and though they rode hard on my trail my pony was too fast for them. My warning was in time."

Will and his father then went to Lawrence, where the free-staters had organized a legislature to draw up a state constitution. Isaac joined the group. Several times he visited his family at night. Once, according to Will, a drunken proslavery man came to the house and demanded a meal while, unknown to the visitor, Isaac lay ill upstairs. The intoxicated man showed the boy his Bowie knife, telling him that he was going to use it on Mr. Cody. Will ran upstairs, got a gun, and sat at the head of the stairs, ready to shoot the visitor if he made a suspicious move. However, the food made the strange caller sleepy, and after a nap he forgot his murderous inten-

12

tions and went off, stealing the boy's pony from the stable.

During the winter of 1854–55 the Codys were practically destitute. Isaac had no money to send them from his almost inactive sawmill and Mrs. Cody had difficulty running the small grocery store which they had bought. Proslavery customers ceased to patronize it. Mrs. Cody was pregnant; another boy was born in the spring.

Will did what he could by hunting rabbits and birds. They made their own flour by grinding their corn. Relatives urged them to move, but Mrs. Cody was a determined woman. She would not, she said, be driven out of the country in which they had chosen to live. Proslavery bullies visited them almost daily looking for Isaac. They helped themselves to whatever they fancied. Frequently they compelled Mrs. Cody to cook meals for them, hanging around the house and refusing to leave.

All America was agitated by the Kansas Question. In New England, New York, and Ohio emigrant aid societies recruited

THE STABBING OF ISAAC CODY.

13

settlers, helping them to move to the territory. And in the South groups were formed to tip the balance in favor of slavery. Isaac Cody was sent to Ohio by the free-staters to tell prospective settlers of the rich fields in Kansas where hatred smoldered along the rivers and creeks. Every man was armed. Northerners shipped by river steamer great boxes marked "Books" containing Sharp's rifles which were the latest type of firearm. Often they were called "Beecher's Bibles" because the famous preacher, Henry Ward Beecher, a brother of the author of *Uncle Tom's Cabin,* had recommended the Sharp's rifle as a better moral instrument than the Bible for the conversion of slave-owners.

The proslavery territorial legislature passed laws that meant jail sentences for residents caught reading free-soil newspapers. Armed bands of men with nervous trigger fingers roamed the countryside. Homes were burned, men shot. Personal animosities flared. A free-soiler, Charles Dow, took a swing at a proslavery neighbor, who shot him and fled. A mob wanted him hanged but he escaped.

Violence centered around Lawrence, where the free-staters entrenched themselves behind breastworks to repel threatened attacks of southerners. In Washington Senator Charles Sumner's oration on "The Crime against Kansas" was halted by blows from a heavy cane in the hands of Preston S. Brooks of South Carolina. Southerners brought cannon against the town of Lawrence, blew up the hotel, burned and sacked the free-state stronghold.

This outrage drove John Brown to retaliate. With a small group of followers armed with cutlasses he hunted for proslavery sympathizers, found what he thought were some near Pottawatomie Creek, not only killed them but mutilated their bodies, splitting skulls and hacking off hands and fingers.

Such crimes aroused the whole country. What effect they must have had upon young Will Cody, then ten years old and in the center of the region of violence, we can only guess. His father returned home in the spring of 1857 ill and exhausted. Will Cody always insisted that Isaac Cody never fully recovered from the Bowie-knife stab in his back three years before. In April his father died, which meant the end of Will's regular attendance at the little one-room schoolhouse at Salt Creek. After his father's death, young Will got occasional jobs herding beef cattle for settlers of sufficient means to own more animals than could be conveniently tethered for pasture.

The boy had learned to rough it in a hostile world where violence was all about him, where to survive men needed courage, cunning, strength, resourcefulness against fanatic enemies. Handling horses and guns became second nature to a boy growing up in this frontier. Survival demanded extraordinary skills; he knew with certainty what evil lay in the world around him.

14

Chapter 2

Wagon Trains and Pony Express

AT the age of eleven young Will Cody, conspicuous for his big brown eyes, his fine features, and his mop of blond hair, was a good rider, a crack shot, and the principal breadwinner for a family of six. He was no skulking orphan, but, because of his strength and sturdy build, a precocious, self-confident young frontiersman. He had spent his childhood among individualists, and did not know the meaning of self-pity. At Leavenworth he had seen and admired the glamorous cavalrymen from the U.S. Army post and the stately Indian chiefs, as well as the variety of people from all over the world who were traveling westward beyond Kansas to seek their fortunes in California.

The Gold Rush was on. From the moment in 1849 when gold had been found in Sutter's Creek in California, the whole world seemed to be moving westward. Some easterners sailed around Cape Horn; some attempted the sailing-vessel short cut, with a dangerous trek across the Isthmus of Panama; but most packed up all their possessions and attempted the Overland Trail. One of the greatest mass migrations in history passed through "Bleeding Kansas," giving young Will Cody contact with a more varied life than he would have

15

had as a poor boy on an obscure street in London, Paris, or New York. He was keen to learn, and he longed to join the westering multitude—venturing into the mysterious Great Plains of bison herds, Indians, endless grassy slopes, then the splendor of the Rockies, and the Pacific.

The movement of eastern Americans and European immigrants across the plains created a revolution in communications and transportation. It provided jobs for everybody, opportunities for all who knew how to take advantage of them. The frontier was pierced. Agriculture could advance across the plains with the prairie schooners, Kansas and Missouri could be linked with California. A whole generation suddenly realized that a great, rich new world lay beyond the Rockies, perhaps richer than the empire their fathers had discovered beyond the Alleghenies.

At first there had been only the dusty Santa Fe Trail over the mountains. Pack trains of horses plodded the interminable miles, followed soon by big, lumbering covered wagons carrying cotton goods to Colorado, and returning with beaver skins. After the triumphant war with Mexico this trade grew rapidly, multiplied by vast caravans organized by businessmen. At the same time the Oregon Trail, the longest wagon road in the world, from Independence, Missouri, to Fort Kearney, Nebraska, through Fort Laramie and South Pass, Wyoming, became the beaten track for journeys that took five months. And in the same year the Mormons, expelled from Illinois, made their historic trek to establish Zion in the remote fertile fields at Great Salt Lake, Utah.

Young Cody was a picturesque if junior participant in these historic movements of men, goods, horses. Of the travelers who sang and pushed their way through the Kansas mud, bound for California, more than forty thousand passed his mother's door. He could no more resist following them than a boy can resist following a parade. The stories of broken wagons, of cholera on the road, of hostile Indians, of dust, heat, and starvation did not discourage him. What could be more thrilling than the frontier in those days? Adventure and opportunity waited just over the horizon. Rough men, infatuated by their visions of sudden wealth, shouted "Pike's Peak or Bust!" and wrote it on their Conestoga and Murphy wagons.

ROLLING CARTS & WAGGONS, for the Amendment & Preservation OF ROADS. as they are now built by JAMES SHARP, of Leadenhall Street London.

THE CONESTOGA WAGON, basic freight vehicle of the transcontinental trails, was first made in the Conestoga Valley of Lancaster County, Pennsylvania, in the early 1700s.

Because it was so effective a freight carrier, wagon makers kept locating farther and farther westward, a typical one being Studebaker, who first made wagons in Adams County, Pennsylvania, next in Ohio, and finally in Fort Wayne, Indiana. The first travel across the Plains and Rockies was in the early type Conestoga Wagon. The Lagans, originally from Lancaster, made Conestoga Wagons at St. Louis and at Dubuque, Iowa, for the wagon trains to the coast. Studebaker modified the wagon somewhat and so did the war department, making a lighter vehicle for immigrant companies and army trains.

In the West the Conestoga Wagons were first pulled by oxen, later by Missouri mules, eventually sometimes by horses.

 All these wagons, and their variants, derive from the English road wagon adapted to American needs by Richard Carter, from Warwickshire, England, wagonwright and wheelwright, who built and established his wagons in the Conestoga Valley before 1750. He developed the medium-sized dished front wheels, and huge dished rear wheels, to throw the load forward and give more efficient drawbar pull. Left, the prototype of the freight wagon—the seventeenth-century English "rolling cart."

17

As the travelers drove West they demanded letters, newspapers, express, freight, the amenities as well as the necessities of life. A stage line began running from Independence to Santa Fe in 1849, and later a monthly overland stage to Salt Lake. In 1854 the government began paying John Butterfield eighty thousand dollars a year to carry mail by the southern overland route from St. Louis to San Francisco by way of El Paso.

In the autumn of that year Senator William Gwin of California traveled by stage to Missouri on his way to Washington. Riding the same stage was B. G. Ficklin, who worked for Russell, Majors, & Waddell, a new firm in fast-growing Leavenworth which had established a big and highly profitable freight service, using high-wheeled Conestoga wagons which could carry three and a half tons of merchandise. Ficklin and the Senator talked about ways of getting faster service, how to set up a speedier letter express. A year later Mr. Russell was called to Washington to discuss contracts.

It was with Mr. Russell's firm that young Will Cody got his first steady job. Alexander Majors, pioneer in the business, began in 1848 to operate the fleets of wagon trains which carried stores for the Army to the outposts in New Mexico, Colorado, and Utah. In 1855 he went into partnership with Russell and Waddell. Contracts with the Army made necessary more stations and warehouses along the line, for it was no small operation: 16 million pounds were shipped in one year, requiring 3,500 wagons and teams, 4,000 employees, 1,000 mules, 40,000 oxen.

A typical wagon train consisted of twenty-five big covered wagons, each drawn by twelve oxen in six yokes or pairs. A caravan of this size would also have twenty to thirty extra oxen in case of accident or lameness. When the train camped at night, or stopped for a noon rest to allow the cattle to graze, a corral was formed by the wagons, the tongues turned out and a chain of poles extending from the hind wheel of one wagon to the front wheel of the next, making a solid pen except for gaps at each end. The entire train usually numbered 320 head plus four or five mules for the riders who herded the cattle and carried messages along the line, which would often be strung out for four or five miles.

At the head was a wagon master or his assistant, followed by teamsters, a man to look after the extra cattle, and several extra men in reserve. They traveled twelve to fifteen miles a day, although sometimes they made twenty miles, a distance they could average easily with empty wagons on the return trip. If properly driven, the oxen could do two thousand miles during the season from April to November, living upon the grass along the route. To operate efficiently a train of twenty-five prairie schooners needed organization and discipline, each individual performing his duty in the place assigned to him. Confusion meant delay. One recalcitrant could hold up the whole train.

Alexander Majors periodically timed

his teamsters. "In sixteen minutes from the time they commenced," he said, "each man had yoked six pairs of oxen and had them hitched to their wagons ready to move." The men were formed in messes, six or eight in a mess, each with a cook appointed from among the group. "We never left the cattle a day or a night without a two-man guard," Majors declared, "the teamsters taking their turn so that each man was on guard two hours out of the twenty-four." The average salary was a dollar a day and expenses. The chief annoyance on the road was rattlesnakes.

Sometimes two men went ahead of the caravan, with whips to frighten the reptiles out of the trail ahead.

When eleven-year-old Will Cody watched these wagon trains made up in Leavenworth, he longed to join one of them. He begged his mother's permission until she accompanied him to see Mr. Majors, known as Uncle Aleck to the Cody family. The boy could go along as a messenger, she said; Majors agreed reluctantly, warning of the dangers in taking dispatches from one wagon to another along the weary march.

Overland stagecoach of the 1858 period.

19

Will enthusiastically asserted that he could ride as well as a man, which was true. He received forty dollars a month and food, the salary to be paid his mother. Like every other employee of Majors, Cody signed the pledge he required: "While I am in the employ of A. Majors, I agree not to use profane language, not to get drunk, not to gamble, not to treat animals cruelly, and not to do anything else that is incompatible with the conduct of a gentleman. And I agree, if I violate any of the above conditions, to accept my discharge without any pay for my services."

Although it is doubtful that Will killed his first Indian on this trip, as his autobiography and other accounts suggest, the journey was packed with excitement for him, and he improved upon it in the retelling. Near Fort Kearney, he said, he was

tired and dragging behind the train, clinging to his old Mississippi Yaeger rifle, a muzzle-loader that carried a ball and two buckshot, when ahead of him he saw the moon rising, and on its face was the figure of an Indian, wearing a war bonnet of feathers. He raised his rifle and fired. One of the men from the wagons rushed back to find out what was happening. When the boy told him the man exclaimed, "Little Billy's killed an Indian all by himself!"

The story was so good it was later published in a Leavenworth newspaper. So Will acquired the reputation as "the youngest Indian slayer of the plains." The same year he asked to go on another, longer trip. Majors referred him to Lew Simpson, a tough character who was to be wagon master of a train headed for Salt Lake. Simpson was amused by the young-

20

YOUNG WILL CODY asking Mr. Majors for work.

ster. "We need Indian fighters," he told him, and gave him a job to ride a mule and herd the extra cattle.

This train was to take supplies to General Albert Sidney Johnston, who later made a reputation as a Confederate commander. For some time there had been increasing bad temper between the U.S. government and the Mormons. United States authority had little standing in distant Utah. Federal officers and judges, sent out to Utah from Washington, commanded little respect from the independent Mormons who were determined to found their own inland empire. President Buchanan ordered an army detachment to make a show of force to re-establish federal prestige. The excursion was not successful: the Mormons cut and burned his supply trains, and General Johnston had to retreat.

Again there were many adventures for Will Cody, in an attack by stampeding buffalo, the first he had ever seen, a threatened attack by Indians, and then one by Mormons. The warlike Mormon group, known as the Danites or Destroying Angels, were reputed to be responsible for at least one wagon-train massacre.

As the Simpson party approached Mormon territory they stopped one day at noon to water the cattle at a nearby creek. Cody was at the stream with Lew Simpson when a group of bearded men appeared over the hill and ordered them to throw up their hands. As they did so they noticed that the wagons were already surrounded by a considerable force and that

BUFFALO BILL REPORTS FOR WORK.

21

the teamsters had been rounded up. Simpson was told he could have one wagon with oxen if he agreed to take his men back to Missouri.

"Can we have our guns?" Simpson inquired.

"No, nothing but food and blankets," he was told.

The Mormons watched while Simpson's men loaded a wagon with cornmeal, bacon, coffee, blankets, and clothing. Then the Danites set fire to the wagon train. It meant that Cody had to walk a considerable part of the thousand miles home. He learned then, he said, that the thicker the soles of your shoes, the easier it is on your feet on a long hike over rough territory.

Will went back intermittently to school at Salt Creek during the winter, but by

BUFFALO BILL at the age of twelve and at the age of fifteen, taken from a small locket.

spring he was anxious to go out on the road again. Simpson gave him a job as a general utility man, so that he rode a horse on this trip and also got a chance to be a relief driver, or bull-whacker, on the wagons. Cody tells us that Simpson believed that oxen were faster than mules, so to heighten the interest he arranged a race with a wagon master who used mules on his wagon trains, to see who would reach Fort Laramie first. Although most bulls couldn't do much better than fifteen miles a day with heavily loaded wagons, Simpson's selected animals, according to Cody, could do twenty-five.

The mule train was defeated by the River Platte, where it became mired in the soft muddy banks, while the bulls plunged in, through the mud, and swam or wallowed across, with the tightly constructed Conestoga wagons floating behind them. The Overland Trail, two thousand miles without a bridge, sometimes represented a primitive amphibious operation when streams had to be crossed at deep fordings

A TYPICAL SIOUX VILLAGE: tepees were made of buffalo skins, with sides that could be rolled up from the ground in hot weather for ventilation, and were kept warm in winter with fire in center, smoke vent at top.

22

through, stopped to rest, to buy supplies, or to wait for others to catch up. Forty-niners had hurried by feverishly; army detachments had been outfitted here and then staggered back, exhausted and wounded, to escape the blizzards or the blinding prairie sun. Missionaries halted briefly. Frémont's expedition tarried in 1844 for a time; Brigham Young led his dedicated band by in 1847.

and ferry-rafts were impossible to construct for lack of timber.

Young Cody later reported on his first vision of old Fort Laramie. This magnificent bastion of the Old West stood eighty air miles to the northeast of the present city of Laramie. Before Cody saw it, thousands of emigrants had already passed

Surrounding the adobe walls was a peaceful settlement of several thousand Indians—Sioux, Arapaho, Cheyennes—many of them sleeping in the sun while their naked children ran up and down the hillside. Blockhouses stood at each corner and there was a fortified tower over the main gate. Inside the walls there was a self-sufficient village, complete with stores,

OLD FORT LARAMIE.

KIT CARSON, the famous scout, from a photograph taken when he visited St. Louis.

houses, a blacksmith shop, the whole fortress built to resist a siege. Established as a fur-trading post in 1834, it was bought by the Government in 1849 and used as a center for the meeting of white men and Indians, the place for pow-wows and the making of treaties.

The famous scouts, Kit Carson and Jim Bridger, were there during the summer of 1858; and twelve-year-old Will Cody was immediately attracted to both of these established heroes of the frontier. Amid the rich atmosphere of the old fort, teeming with the sights and smells of a wilderness caravansary, the small, quiet Carson was an example of modesty and discretion. Bridger, the seasoned mountain man, then in his fifties, represented everything that was thrilling and heroic to young Will.

Kit Carson, in his fiftieth year, had already lived through the great moments of his career, and made his home in Taos, New Mexico, with frequent trips up to Laramie. He was the man who had guided the headstrong General John C. Frémont across the Nevada desert and the California mountains, through regions known only to trappers such as himself. His resourcefulness had saved the lives and reputations of both General Frémont and General Phil Kearney; his hunches and endurance, indeed, had helped to create a national reputation for Frémont that took the latter within a hair's breadth of the White House. Years later Cody named his only son for the incomparable scout.

Bridger was the epitome of the mountain man who needed no maps and whose mind could visualize a wilderness to the smallest detail; he taught young Cody that you could love a mountain as intimately and passionately as a man could love a woman.

The boy sat for hours and watched these men talk to Indians in a sign language which he tried to learn; he also picked up a working acquaintance with the speech of the Sioux, an accomplishment of lifesaving importance later on. Bridger at that time was a veteran of many tough expeditions into the Rockies and battles with the Mormons. Marveling at the frontier prowess of these two celebrated men, and at the awe in which they were held by whites and Indians alike, Will Cody decided that he would be a scout.

24

JIM BRIDGER, mountain scout and guide.

Will had to go back to Missouri with Simpson, however, so he had to put such dreams to the back of his mind for the time being. On the way he ran into many adventures with hostile Indians, once having to hide in a cave filled with Indian skeletons. Back in Leavenworth he collected his pay, which was nearly a thousand dollars.

In 1898, on Cody Day at the Trans-Mississippi Exposition at Omaha, he recalled the pride he felt that time. "Ain't it splendid, Mother, that I can get all this money for you and my sisters?" he remembered saying as he spread the silver coins on the table. Then, carried away by the memory and the intoxication of the moment, he added, "And I've been spreading it ever since!"

Alexander Majors told the same audience how young Cody learned to write, practicing all along the route of the wagon train, for Majors had found "Will Cody," "Little Billy,' "Billy the boy messenger," and "William Frederick Cody" written with the burnt end of a stick upon tents, wagon covers, and all tempting places; and carved on wagon bodies and wherever he could find suitable wood for his penknife was the name he would make famous.

After this trip Cody tried going to school for a few weeks, but in his imagination he relived those days at old Fort Laramie. He decided to try a season as a fur trapper and trader. With a friend, Dave Harrington, from Salt Creek he set out for the Rockies with a yoke of oxen, a wagon sheet, wagon, traps, and poison for the wolves. About two hundred miles from home they found a likely spot on Prairie Creek and built a dugout in the hillside, roofing it with brush, long grass, and dirt. A rude earthen fireplace served for heating and cooking. Their success in trapping was soon undone by a series of catastrophes typical of such a wilderness occupation. As Will reported in one version of his life story, first an unusually ferocious bear attacked the boys' camp and killed their oxen. Moreover, a few days later Will broke his leg, so Harrington had to hike for help 125 miles away. Worse yet, a band of Indians looted the cabin of the helpless, lonely boy. Fortunately they spared Will's life because he had been a playmate of the braves' children at Fort Laramie. Snowed in, surrounded by howling wolves, Will waited twenty-nine days before Harrington returned to rescue him.

Meanwhile the firm of Russell, Majors, & Waddell was getting into the pony-express business, against the best judgment of two of the partners. Mr. Russell spent the winter of 1858–59 in Washington, where he talked with Senator Gwin about a fast mail service to the Pacific Coast. The Butterfield route had its disadvantages, they agreed, for it went from San Francisco to Los Angeles, across the Colorado River and up the valley of the Gila, then by way of El Paso and Texas, crossing the Arkansas River at Fort Gibbons, thence to St. Louis.

This route was not only too long, but it could easily be cut if there should be a war between the states. A direct route, further

north, seemed imperative. Since Russell, Majors, & Waddell ran a daily stage from the Missouri River to Salt Lake City, in addition to their freight service, the California senator asked Russell if his company could not start a pony express, following the route of the stagecoach to Salt Lake and then north to Sacramento, across both the Rockies and the Sierras. Russell said he would take up the matter with his partners.

Both Majors and Waddell declared that such an undertaking could not pay its expenses. They estimated that it would cost $100,000 to equip such a line, $30,000 a month to maintain it. What other expenses might come to they could not conjecture.

Certainly they would need more than 400 of the best horses procurable, 190 stations along the line, 400 station men and assistants, 80 riders—the costs leaped astronomically. Even at five dollars for each half ounce for letters, plus a government subsidy, it did not seem feasible.

However, Russell felt that he had committed himself. Although Senator Gwin admitted that all previous attempts had failed, he was nevertheless determined. Other senators cited the impassability of the mountains in winter. Some favored the southern route. Gwin argued that it was necessary to get somebody to demonstrate that a central route was practicable. If Russell and his partners would attempt it, he

INDIANS ATTACK AN EMIGRANT TRAIN; the Cavalry rides to the rescue.

PONY EXPRESS RIDER READY TO CHANGE
HORSES AT STATION IN THE ROCKIES.

said, he would use all his influence to get a subsidy for them.

Reluctantly the partners agreed to gamble on the hope of a subsidy, and began building stations every ten miles from Salt Lake City to Sacramento. Within two months they were set up and ready to start. Advertisements in the New York newspapers announced the first trip. Letters were sent by fast train to St. Louis, then up the Missouri River by steamer to St. Joseph, where a boy waited, his pony saddled. The minute the steamer arrived he was off. On the same day, April 3, 1860, Harry Roff, on a bronco, started eastward from Sacramento.

Until then the record for carrying a message between San Francisco and New York was twenty-one days, made over the Butterfield line. Russell's ponies did it in ten days. This became the established schedule. But the early estimates on cost proved correct: between 400 and 500 horses were needed, 190 stations, 200 stationkeepers, 80 riders. Each rider averaged a little less

28

than thirty miles riding three ponies in relays at full gallop. In emergencies they did greater distances. Messages were written on the finest tissue paper, five dollars per half ounce for the 3,000-mile transcontinental trip, paid in gold. Usually, of course, the messages were urgent. A California lecture manager wrote Artemus Ward a single line: "What will you take for one hun-dred nights?" The humorist replied in three words: "Brandy and water."

Will Cody asked his friend Lew Simpson to help him get a job on the pony express. Simpson introduced him to Mr. Russell, who gave the boy a letter to Alf Slade, sometimes known as "the terrible Slade" for his monumental rages and his bad habit of shooting men who disagreed

PONY EXPRESS RIDER SEES TELEGRAPH LINES BEING ERECTED.

with him. In spite of his reputation for homicide, however, he was an efficient superintendent for the pony-express division between Julesburg and Rocky Ridge, which had headquarters at Horseshoe Station. Young Will went out there, thirty-six miles beyond Fort Laramie, on a wagon train. At first Slade objected to putting him on because Cody was so young, but he agreed to give him a trial on the road from Red Buttes to Three Crossings.

One day as Cody was leaving Horse Creek, fifteen Indians tried to catch him in a ravine eight miles west of the station. He dug his spurs into the sides of his pony, and lying flat on his mount's back, escaped unscathed. Another time he galloped into the station to find that the man who was to carry his mail had been killed in a drunken fight the night before. Will promptly selected a new pony, plunged on eighty-five miles, to Red Buttes, the next station. Then he turned back and rode to his starting point. He made the trip, 320 miles, in 21 hours and 40 minutes.

On one occasion on one of his days off, fourteen-year-old Cody hunted sage hens. He was cooking them when he was interrupted by a band of outlaws who asked him for his horse. He started to lead two of them to the animal, tethered a short distance away, taking with him one of the hens. By a clever stratagem he dropped the bird; the outlaw stooped to pick it up; Will thereupon cracked the man over the head with the butt of his revolver, shot the other outlaw, jumped on his horse, and got away.

Soon afterward Alf Slade decided to lead a group of drivers, express riders, and stock tenders against a party of Indians who had been harassing the stagecoaches and stealing horses. With the Slade crowd was Wild Bill Hickok, the famous crackshot marshal, who was also working for the pony express. They found the Indians in a large encampment, many more than they had expected. Although the whites were outnumbered four to one, Wild Bill insisted that they fight. They waited until late at night, divided their group. While half of them made a dash for the corral to get the horses, the others rode into the camp, shooting down the Indians as they came out of their tents. They not only got the stolen horses but many more besides.

This was the first occasion on which Will had seen Hickok in action, although he had known him earlier. In his story about the thousand-mile hike, Cody said Wild Bill accompanied him, but Hickok's biographers do not mention the long walk. However, the famous sure-shot marshal did drive an overland stage. He was about ten years older than Cody, a tall handsome blond with long hair, a long curly moustache, sharp blue eyes, and tremendously broad shoulders. His body tapered to a narrow waist and exceptionally small feet. He was later described by General Custer as one of the most perfect types of physical manhood that soldier had ever seen. A very quiet man, Hickok was a virtuoso with a Colt revolver. Already he was known throughout the West for the McCanles affair, in which he killed three desperadoes

Wagon train, pulled by oxen, crossing the mountains.

single-handed. Apparently every man was proud of his marksmanship and anxious to demonstrate. Why so many challenged Wild Bill may perhaps be explained by the nervous temper of those days. Whenever a man reached for his gun, Hickok shot him through the head. Reaching for a gun was a universal, automatic, habitual, involuntary gesture.

Cody ardently admired anybody dexterous with firearms, and Hickok had no superior. Cody worshipped him, became his inseparable companion. Hickok had high ideals as well as calm nerves. Born in Troy Grove, Illinois, of a Presbyterian family who intended him to be a preacher, Wild Bill sought adventure in Kansas with the Abolitionist Red Legs, who accepted him when he demonstrated miraculous marksmanship. Once when an angry man hurled a rock at him, Hickok stopped the missile with a bullet. On another occasion, he is said to have stood between two telegraph poles with a pistol in each hand; firing simultaneously he hit both poles at spots he had marked. He could cut a chicken's throat at thirty paces without breaking its neck, and could hit a dime at fifty paces.

After their pony-express experiences Wild Bill took his young protégé with him to St. Louis, where they bet all their cash on a horse race. Cody's horse, Old Mountain, was pretty fast, but not as speedy as a little black mare from Peoria which made Old Mountain look as if he were standing still. The gamblers returned broke to their respective homes.

However, the two men met many times before Hickok was shot from behind at a bar in 1876. Cody liked to tell the story of how Wild Bill would fake drowsiness at a poker game, catch a crooked player off guard, and then suddenly demand that he show the cards he was hiding. Hickok was also skillful with a Bowie knife, once killing a she-bear in a fierce encounter in which he was badly mauled. Hickok is sometimes reputed to have killed the famous Indian chief, Black Kettle, with a knife in 1869. That was when Cody and he were often scouts together. Later Buffalo Bill persuaded Hickok to go on the stage with him, but Wild Bill had little taste for anything that was merely make-believe.

The rapid development of the telegraph made the pony express obsolete in less than sixteen months. Majors, Russell, and Waddell were temporarily ruined, but their stagecoach and freight service continued. Before they stopped, the riders were carrying seven hundred letters a week and the rates had been reduced to a dollar per half ounce. Only one mail pouch was lost. These pouches were small, covered with oilskins, and locked into a compartment in a saddle bag. Once a horse drowned swimming a river, but the rider and his mail escaped. Indians killed one rider, but the pony got away with the letter pouch. It was a glorious experience for the riders in which the whole nation shared vicariously. Few chapters in the history of transportation or communications are more exciting.

Chapter 3

War and Marriage

IN 1861, when Kansas was admitted to the Union as a state without slavery, life on the Oregon Trail to the west was infinitely more peaceful than it was on the Missouri border. The valley of the Kaw and of Salt Creek echoed with the voices and the gunfire of violent men when young Cody returned from his adventures on the wagon trains and the pony express. New settlers were pouring into Leavenworth and Lawrence, most of them rough, tough characters for whom gunplay ended most arguments.

Fanatical John Brown had taken his bloodthirsty sons to Harpers Ferry and martyrdom, leaving behind a bitter tradition of cruelty, torture, and murder. As soon as the War between the States commenced in the spring of 1861, the roving, gun-toting bands rode out again into the night to shoot, lynch, burn their ancient enemies on the other side of the Missouri River.

Everywhere men talked about secession, about Abraham Lincoln, about Fort Sumter. Throughout Kansas they talked more ominously about three notorious ruffians who dominated that troubled area. Biggest and most powerful was James H. Lane, a veteran of the Mexican War, a politician who had killed a man in what he called self-defense. His lean haggard sinewy figure, his sarcasm and invective, his harsh raspy voice, tyrannized his friends as well as his enemies. He later became a U. S. Senator.

The moment the news of Fort Sumter reached Jim Lane, he went to Washington to compel President Lincoln to give him a commission as a brigadier general. He succeeded in a fashion characteristic of him. With a hastily gathered gang of followers he bivouacked in the East Room of the White House until he got what he wanted. Then he returned to Kansas and recruited three regiments.

Lane's chief lieutenant was Dr. Charles R. Jennison, who had been a devoted disciple of John Brown. He considered every Missourian a natural-born enemy. As a leader of the outlaw Red Legs, he seemed to enjoy burning houses, stealing horses and cattle, terrorizing the countryside. He boasted that "Missouri mothers hush their children to sleep by whispering the name of Doc Jennison." It was in Jennison's regiment that Will Cody finally enlisted.

Opposed to these terrorists was an even more notorious character, Will C. Quantrill, who lived for a time in Kansas, where he taught school under the alias of Charlie Hart. A somewhat smaller man physically than Lane or Jennison, he habitually wore an angry expression on his heavy, coarse, brutal face. He was unforgettable also for his mass of tow hair and his huge hooked nose. A man given to sadistic rages, Quantrill was at one time or another on all sides of every public question, instinctively using every controversy for his own advantage. Originally from Ohio, he had stolen, cheated, and murdered his way West. Kansas disliked him and he was run out of the town of Lawrence.

On the Missouri side of the border he led a marauding band of outlaws which, during the war, killed several thousand men, almost always from ambush. On August 19, 1863, he invaded Kansas with three hundred men and the next morning attacked Lawrence, burning homes and stores, killing nearly two hundred citizens of the settlement in four hours. Hearing that a body of Union troops were coming after him, Quantrill and his men retreated, escaping over the Missouri border.

It was to this violent society and atmosphere that young Cody returned from the western caravans. It is possible, but has never been proven, that he may have joined one of the Red Leg bands in marauding the territory of proslavery sympathizers. Such primitive expeditions were considered legitimate guerrilla warfare by the men who had come under the influence of John Brown's example. The Kansans

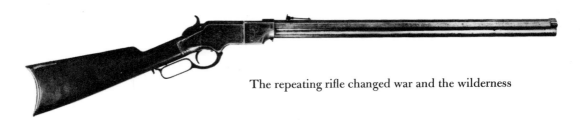

The repeating rifle changed war and the wilderness

were known as the Jayhawkers and the Missourians as the Bushwackers. There are many inconsistent explanations of the origin of these terms, which had such dramatic currency at the time. Both were a sort of land privateering, or freebooting—horse stealing in patriotic guise. A Missouri historian noted that Jayhawkers "never robbed or hung anybody who had the same political opinions, professing to rob, burn out and murder only Rebels."

Will Cody was only fifteen when he came home in 1861 with ideas about enlisting in the Union Army. His mother

begged him not to. He took a succession of temporary jobs, carrying dispatches again on the wagon trains, working as a teamster, making one trip to Denver, and serving also as a scout in western Kansas. In the fall of 1863 his sisters called him home. His mother, who had been running a boarding house since Isaac Cody's death, was dying of tuberculosis. She died in December of that year.

Will could not enlist at once, obviously because he had to earn some money for the family, so he took a job with another wagon train. It was at this time that his orphaned sisters asked him for financial help. His oldest sister, Julia, had married A. J. Goodman, a man of limited means. She took care of the household. Helen and May, the younger sisters, were dissatisfied with the clothes they had been given after their mother's death, and they appealed to their older brother. He answered, "My dear sisters: I am sorry that I cannot help you and furnish you with such clothes as you wish. At this writing I am so short of funds myself that if an entire Mississippi steamer could be bought for ten cents, I couldn't purchase the smokestack. I will soon draw my pay and I will send it, every cent, to you. So brave it out, girls, a

JOHN BROWN, who stirred violence in Kansas when Buffalo Bill was a child.

GENERAL JAMES H. LANE, KANSAS FIGHTER AND POLITICIAN.

little longer. In the meantime I will write Al. Lovingly, Will."

Al was, of course, his brother-in-law. Will Cody did as he had promised, sending all his earnings, a characteristic gesture which grew into a habit later in life when his Wild West show became profitable.

Finally, in February 1864, when he was just eighteen, he enlisted in the Seventh Kansas Regiment. Doc Jennison was then in Leavenworth calling for volunteers. Will gave his occupation as "teamster," described his eyes and hair as "brown," complexion "fair," height five feet ten inches (which is somewhat shorter than

36

WILLIAM C. QUANTRILL, troublemaker in Kansas, who led forces which burned Lawrence.

he was described by those who saw him in his later elegant days).

Since Isaac Cody had been an active Abolitionist who, in a sense, had given his life to the cause, young Will unquestionably held the same convictions. But he could not have had any comprehension of the deep political issues that split the people of North and South along the eastern seaboard. To him the war was a nuisance, a distracting incident which interrupted the great drama of western expansion.

To young Cody, as to most young men, the rigid life in the Army was vexatious, irrelevant to his main interests in life. His heroes were the individualists—Carson, Bridger, Hickok. He, too, aspired to be a scout on the open plains. He understood and enjoyed life on the real frontier, and had a growing appreciation of the Indian as a foe and as a friend.

Missouri stood between Kansas and the East, blotting out the eastern horizon with political confusions and regional hatreds. Washington, Virginia, or South Carolina seemed very distant. Even Illinois, Kentucky, and Tennessee were far away from the western banks of the Missouri, especially when a man had to walk. What happened in the trans-Mississippi territory was

important—important not only to Will Cody but also in the major decisions of the war.

If Missouri, which was a slave state, had gone with the Confederacy, the whole course of the war might have been different. The Jayhawker raids were not arousing any enthusiasm among Missourians for the Union cause. Quite the contrary; such murdering of civilians and burning of their homes led many people on the east of the border, who might have favored the Union, to turn against it. Many were Confederate sympathizers who owned slaves. They

37

were incited to fury when Kansas raiders stole their property, or kidnapped their Negroes.

Exactly what Will Cody did in the war has never been described in detail by his biographers or by himself. Since he evidently served as a scout, his ultimate press agents eventually manufactured romantic adventures along the familiar lines of hairbreadth escapes in which he was saved by his astonishing skill and ingenuity. Guerrilla warfare was easy for him to master. According to some accounts he was also a Union spy in Confederate territory.

Soon after the young teamster enlisted, his regiment was shipped to Memphis, where it joined the command of General A. J. Smith, who was organizing to fight the Confederate General Forrest in southern Tennessee. In Tennessee Cody was picked, on the basis of his experience as a plainsman, to scout the position of Forrest's forces, thought to be about two hundred miles south of Memphis.

Disguised as a Tennessee farm boy and riding a farm horse, he followed a wagon road south. Since he tried to imitate a southern accent whenever he encountered anybody this experience might be regarded as perhaps the first of his theatrical roles. He told a detachment of Confederate troops that he was a country boy looking for his father and brother who, he thought, were with General Forrest. Thus he penetrated the enemy lines, and by a similar tale—wanting to get back again—he escaped and reported to General Smith the location of the Confederate troops.

On another scouting expedition Cody stopped at a beautiful plantation where there were, as might be expected, two attractive young ladies. In great alarm for his safety they asked him if he did not know that the Yankee army was expected along this road shortly. All their menfolks, they told him, were hiding in the woods.

"The Yankees will go right through this house," the mother of the household said. "They will break up the piano and every stick of furniture. They will be sure to kill or take you prisoner."

A moment later the advance guard of General Smith's forces came down the road. A group rode up to the house. Cody requested them to leave the place alone. Much to the astonishment of this southern family, the Yankee soldiers obeyed. Will told the mother of the young ladies that he could not keep the Federals out of her chicken house or her smokehouse, but that he could, and would, keep them out of her home.

By then the southerners had decided he must be a Yankee. Grateful for his protection, they spread out a meal, urging him to eat quickly before the men of the family returned. If they found a Yankee in the house they would shoot him. As the southern woman spoke, three men rushed in the back door. They had seen from their hideout in the woods what Will had done and they thanked him.

This anecdote, though the facts may be embroidered, illustrates Cody's chivalry, which was one of his outstanding qualities from a very early age. It also reveals his ex-

tremely attractive personality, a gift for making people like him. It is, however, one of the few experiences in Tennessee which he later found worth relating. Once, during a skirmish, he was rebuked for fighting from behind a tree, Indian fashion. By a strange coincidence, he met the officer who rebuked him years later on the Great Plains with Custer, and the officer acknowledged then the expediency of such concealment when fighting Indians.

After the battle of Tupelo in Mississippi, Cody's regiment was sent back up the river. A Confederate army of fifteen thousand men under General Sterling Price, which had been assembling in Arkansas, moved to invade Missouri and threaten either St. Louis or Kansas. The troops under General A. J. Smith, among others, were there-

fore sent into Missouri to defend Pilot Knob, the chief fortified point in the state.

Cody, then with the Ninth Kansas Cavalry as a dispatch rider, passed around and through General Price's army a number of times. On September 27, Price's men made a bloody assault on Pilot Knob but they were repulsed with a loss of about fifteen hundred men by Union troops under the command of General Thomas Ewing, and retired, planning to attack again at daybreak. That night, Ewing, who was vastly outnumbered, spiked his cannon and moved away, blowing up his powder magazine. He delayed Price for several days while St. Louis was reinforced and fresh federal forces gathered. Later the Confederates were decisively defeated at Westport. After Price retreated to Arkansas, Smith's army moved into St. Louis, late in October. That was the end of the fighting for Will Cody. He was then detached for hospital duty.

Cody was serving as a hospital orderly in St. Louis when he met Louisa Frederici. One description of this first encounter includes a rescue from a runaway horse when Louisa's bridle rein broke and young Will caught the frightened animal. Another story, told by John M. Burke in his later years, has perhaps more semblance of the

39

truth. Some drunken soldiers in the streets of St. Louis were making loud comments about a group of schoolgirls, teasing them and making advances. When Cody saw what was going on he ordered them to stop. While the men argued with him, all the girls ran away except one, who was too frightened to move. This was Louisa. Will escorted her home and they promptly fell in love. When asked how they met, Louisa replied, in later days when romance had evaporated, that they were introduced by her cousin. On that occasion she said, Cody made a remark which she misinterpreted and she slapped his face. However they met, after a brief courtship in the spring of 1865 she consented to marry him. The wedding had to be delayed, however, until he could earn some money. Honorably discharged in April after fifteen months of service, Will Cody went home to his sisters. At Leavenworth he found a job with an old friend, Bill Trotter, driving a stagecoach.

Cody relates in his autobiography, however, that before starting the stagecoach-driving job he traveled across the plains as a dispatch rider with General William Tecumseh Sherman, who was on his way to a conference with Indians at Council Springs. This was on the Arkansas River about sixty miles beyond old Fort Zarrah, or Zara, and three hundred miles southeast of Leavenworth. The guide for the party, Dick Curtis, lost his way. The maps of the territory were inaccurate. Sherman called in Cody, who told him they should be going due south instead of due west. For twelve miles, he said, he rode with Sherman. "I found he knew my father well and remembered his tragic death in Salt Creek Valley." Cody thereupon became Sherman's scout, taking him to Bent's Fort, to Fort Laramie, and back to Leavenworth.

There are several inconsistencies in this story. A council meeting was held with the Indians in 1865, but it was with Generals Harney and Sanborn, not with General Sherman, who conferred with Sitting Bull two years later. That Sherman ever knew Cody's father is exceedingly doubtful. Years later the general wrote a testimonial letter to Cody: "You guided me honestly and faithfully in 1865–66 from Fort Riley to Kearney." On the basis of that letter, the showman's press agent apparently elaborated the anecdote about Council Springs.

How the young stagecoach driver outwitted some holdup men is a famous persistent story. Bill Trotter, just as he was about to start on one of his last trips, handed him a package which Cody knew, without being told, contained a large sum of money. Among his passengers were two ruffians who had aroused Bill's suspicions. Acting on impulse he jumped off the driver's seat of the coach, opened the door, and asked the men to hand him a rope that was under the seat.

As they did so Cody whipped out his revolvers. Automatically the men put up their hands, asking, "What's the matter?"

"I just thought I would get there first," he answered.

"You're a cute one," they growled as Will ordered one to tie up the other's

BUFFALO BILL, ALREADY A FAMOUS SCOUT AT TWENTY-TWO.

LUXURY MISSISSIPPI-MISSOURI RIVER STEAMERS. THE CODY HONEYMOON SHIP "MORNING STAR," RIGHT.

hands. Then he threw out their guns and completed the job of trussing them. As he did so the talkative outlaw remarked, "You'll find your match down the road."

At the next relay station he turned the pair over to the stocktenders. Carefully he cut out one of the stagecoach seat cushions and hid the package with the money. Farther on, at a ford, the holdup men he had been expecting set upon him.

Will was very calm. "Sorry, gentlemen," he greeted them, "your pals got ahead of you. They got the boodle first. If there's anything you want you're welcome to it."

"Where's your strongbox?" they demanded.

Will opened it, proving that it was empty.

"Where did they hold you up?"

"About seven or eight miles back. They didn't have any horses. Maybe you can catch them."

"Come on, let's go!" The leader wheeled his horse around and the gang hurried back down the road.

Cody urged his horses on at a fast clip to the end of the run with his precious package. On the return trip he picked up his prisoners and took them to Fort Kearney, alert and apprehensive lest the gang be out looking for him.

Meanwhile Louisa was writing to him, impatiently insisting that he give up his wild life and come to St. Louis. Since he had saved some money he made no objection when she suggested a wedding date: March 6, 1866.

The simple ceremony took place at the home of the bride at eleven in the morning. The young bridegroom, just twenty years old, had begun to let his hair grow in the style of the western scouts he admired. It hung down over his shoulders, and he had also started a moustache and goatee. Dressed in what he called "western fashion," he must have been conspicuous even for St. Louis, the gateway to the West, a metropolis which attracted many strange characters from the plains.

When the happy honeymoon couple boarded the luxurious river steamer *Morning Star* at two in the afternoon for the trip up to Leavenworth, they attracted much attention. The resentment against Kansas Jayhawkers had not been forgotten, and it is quite possible that this bizarre bridegroom was identified as one of Jennison's band. Cody carried the story considerably further in his later accounts, for he related that his new father-in-law became excited and threatened to take his daughter home, away from this outlaw. Cody said that an armed party was waiting to seize him at the next stop, but the steamer backed out into the river before his enemies could get

aboard, while he buckled on his belt with two large revolvers, which did little to calm the nerves of his bride. She later asserted there was no truth in this story. Once they arrived at Leavenworth the Cody's high spirits revived when they were greeted by a crowd of the bridegroom's friends and relatives.

Even though they were very much in love, conflicts inevitably developed early in their marriage. Their personalities and interests were diametrically opposed. Louisa, a prim, properly brought-up French girl, was rigidly conventional in her ideas. She had been thoroughly trained in the domestic virtues and was a good dressmaker. She loathed being made conspicuous. Highly volatile and emotional, exceptionally beautiful, she had the vanity of a spoiled daughter. She expected flattery and constant attention. When her husband's imagination strayed into the mountains, she grew resentful and jealous.

All her life Louisa displayed a quick, sharp temper. She would take violent and seemingly irrational dislikes to Cody's friends and showed her feelings without restraint. When things did not go as she wished, she became moody and considered herself unfairly treated. This side of her personality Will Cody could not comprehend. He did everything he could think of to please her. Reluctantly he had promised her that he would abandon what he cared most about: the western plains and mountains. It was a promise he could not possibly have kept.

In an attempt to prove to Louisa that

43

he could settle down to a conventional life he set himself up in the hotel business at Salt Creek. He took the old boarding house his mother had conducted and called it "The Golden Rule Hotel," promptly inviting his sisters and friends to move in. He was a magnificent host, but his qualities of generosity prevented him from becoming a successful hotelkeeper.

From Louisa's point of view, it is easy to see how he might have been, on occasions, irritating. He was egotistical, already exhibiting in his dress qualities which later made him a great showman. He liked to tell tall stories, which distressed her. He was full of grandiose and impractical dreams of glory, which alarmed her. Because he had such self-confidence in his ability to make money, he never knew what it was to be thrifty. Money was for pleasure; it was to be spent joyously and lavishly. No wonder he could not adapt himself to her wishes or her ideas or that she found it impossible to discipline him to her ways. Not to act naturally, buoyantly, generously, was to deny his basic nature. To try to do so made him restless and miserable—for Cody was the prototype of the primitive natural man who scorned conventions and who could never be domesticated no matter how much he loved the wife who tried to tame him.

A TYPICAL WESTERN SETTLEMENT.

44

Chapter 4

Indians, Buffalo, and the Railroad

To understand the West which Cody loved and eventually portrayed, one must know how it came about that the winning of the West by the white man was so tragic an affair that ever after his final victory the white man has been trying to recapture the unspoiled atmosphere of the primeval plains as they were before he despoiled them. Cody—the buffalo hunter and Indian fighter—became a conservationist, game-preserve exponent, and, above all men of his time, a friend of the Indian. He adopted his half-Indian costume of fringed buckskin, and the long hair that challenged scalpers, to set himself apart as a scout—not a uniformed soldier—without quite knowing at the time the reason for his imitation of a white version of an Indian chief.

As he grew older he saw the contradictory nature of his dual role as the destroyer and the reincarnation of the West. But not even his Wild West Show could ever reflect the deeper drama of American history in which he was conspicuous. Hence, a glimpse at the highlights of the history of the Indians, especially the Indians of the plains, is essential to understanding Cody and his West.

For a thousand years and more before the white man invaded the North American continent, the Indian lived in idyllic

harmony with his environment. All living things played their roles in perfect balance with one another. All the Indian wanted was space, health, and strength. He adjusted himself to the rhythm of the seasons, surfeit or want.

On the Great Plains he found space, and from the fertile soil and its creatures he derived health and strength. His diet was ideal, for few foods are more nourishing than that of high-protein buffalo meat. A soil-grass-Indian relationship established for the native American of the Great Plains a happy economy, in which the buffalo provided food, fuel, clothing, and shelter, the latter the tepee. Without the buffalo the circle weakened, and the whole Indian civilization crashed.

When the white man came to the East Coast there were about one million Indians in the territory now the United States. Today there are about four hundred thousand. Before Columbus about six hundred different tribes lived in comparative contentment, each in its own environment perfectly adapted to forest, plain, desert, rivers, or lakes, as well as to the animal life. Few sought outright conquest or

domination over the others; they were for the most part moderate; they did not increase their population beyond what their own resources could support. They feared only the elements: drought, flood, storm, disease. The Indian disciplined himself to overcome such dangers; from that discipline he developed wisdom.

For two centuries the Indian welcomed the white man to his bountiful homeland. But he could never comprehend the white man's greed for land, his race prejudice, his reckless destruction of nature's resources, his insensitivity to all that made life for the Indian beautiful, pleasurable, peaceful. To destroy for no discernible reason the environment that supported him, and would support all reasonable life, seemed to the Indian outrageous, a violation of all that was sacred—an affront to the Great Spirit.

The fertile land of the Indians lured the colonists from the moment they first debarked on American shores. Year after year the pioneers blazed trails, cleared valleys, fought their way inland, frightening off game, forcing the Indians from their villages and hunting grounds. The white men

A BISON HERD ON THE MOVE ACROSS THE PLAINS BEFORE THE DAYS OF THE WHITE MAN.

worshipped different gods; created new heroes for themselves. As they mastered the wilderness, they developed self-confidence, courage, hardihood, energy. They grew more acquisitive and impatient to plunge westward. Rugged new individuals emerged as leaders; the frontiersmen personified the new western civilization.

Once the pioneers had crossed the Alleghenies, they found that the middle western rivers helped them to hasten their pace and provided an easy access to bigger farming areas. It was not long before men built canals to carry more goods and people. For half a century they drove on in

greater numbers regardless of obstacles, building new roads deeper into the continent.

Against such pressure the Indian could not stand. He was overwhelmed by sheer numbers. The white population doubled every twenty-five years. Treaties were made which the settlers often had no intention of keeping. They made promises only to salve their consciences. They were eager to get the land. Let somebody else take care of the Indians who claimed that land. The tribes retreated, learning as they did so how treacherous were the whites. And the whites manufactured

RUSSELL'S "INDIANS HUNTING BISON WITH BOW AND ARROW."

Copyright Brown & Bigelow, St. Paul, Minn.

stories to justify themselves. When they made an enemy out of the Indian they decided, of course, that he was evil.

When Georgia, one of the first states which tried to eliminate the Indians entirely, demanded Cherokee lands, President Monroe recommended that as soon as agreements could be made, the troublesome tribes be moved to the West and Northwest, the limits of the new Louisiana Purchase. So began a policy of colonization by force and of removal to new homes provided by the government, usually on lands of other tribes. Although treaties pledged that the Indians would not be moved without their consent, and that the whites would stay out of Indian territories, such promises were never kept. No mere word of honor could stop the surging tide of American expansion.

Settlers reaching the Mississippi over the lands which the Sauk and Fox tribes had given up in 1804 eyed the rich prairies beyond. When the Indians saw

INDIANS HOLD UP THE U.S. OVERLAND MAIL.

them march over the graves of their ancestors, they fought back. Panic threatened the frontier during the hopeless Black Hawk War, the last struggle for the fertile plains of the Middle West. After that, in 1832, an office for Indian Affairs was established in the War Department; new treaties provided for new migrations. So the Northwest began to open up. Easterners speculated in public lands, drew new routes for transportation, projected future railways from those already begun. By the 1840s steam packets plied a route from Pittsburgh to Keokuk. Those who said, "The Indian must go!" had their way.

During and after the Civil War it was said that the restlessness and hostility of the Indians were caused by the machinations of Confederate agents. But as the Indian was pushed west toward the Rockies he became less reconciled to the white conquest. He continued to resist the effort to occupy his lands. Trappers, hunters, prospectors pursued him. Surveyors planned railroads through his forests. Farmers and ranchers built homes along the Santa Fe Trail. Indians knew what portended as more and more covered wagons and stagecoaches rattled West across the Great Plains.

By August 1864, Ben Holladay's coaches and freighters had been attacked so frequently and disastrously that he was nearly driven out of business. Indians destroyed his stations, burned farms, massacred small groups struggling along the trails. At Ewebank a family of ten was massacred. At Plum Creek ten persons were murdered. For nearly four hundred miles almost every ranch along the stagecoach route had to be abandoned. Only strongly armed coaches could get through. From Colorado settlements came demands that something be done.

Major Jacob Downing thereupon went out from Denver against the Cheyennes with forty men. He found an Indian village near Cedar Bluffs. "We commenced shooting; I ordered the men to commence killing them. They lost twenty-six killed and thirty wounded. I burnt up their lodges and everything I could get hold of. We captured about one hundred head of stock, which was distributed among the boys." The Indians retaliated by burning, scalping, and mutilating a family within twenty miles of Denver. This aroused Governor Evans of Colorado to say that there was no hope for peace on the plains until after "severe chastisement." A general war threatened. Proud, eloquent, diplomatic Black Kettle, chief of the Cheyennes, stepped forward. Although he was a mighty warrior, he declared his readiness to make peace if all the tribes were included.

On September 28, 1864, Black Kettle of the Cheyennes and White Antelope of the Arapaho met Governor Evans in Denver at the invitation of Major E. W. Wynkoop, military commander at Fort Lyon, who was trying to avoid an open Indian war. Black Kettle spoke: "All we ask is that we may have peace with the whites. You are our father. We want to hold you by the hand. We have been traveling through a cloud. The sky has been dark ever since the war began. These braves who are with me are willing to do what I say. We want to take good tidings home to our people, that we may sleep in peace. I want you to give all these chiefs of the soldiers here to understand that we are for peace, and that we have made peace, that we may not be mistaken for enemies."

The Governor would give the chiefs no assurance. It was war, he said, and they would have to come to terms with the Army, which would not be satisfied with mere peace agreements but demanded complete submission. Major General Curtis at Fort Leavenworth said, "I want no peace until the Indians suffer more." Governor Evans had raised volunteers for battle. "What shall I do with the regiment?" he asked. "They were raised to kill Indians and they must kill Indians."

Black Kettle and White Antelope, under the impression that peace had been achieved, led about five hundred of their tribes, mostly women and children, to a camp near Fort Lyon to spend the winter. Colonel J. M. Chivington, a gigantic, ruthless man, once a Methodist preacher, impatient for battle, took a force of seven hundred men, including mounted troops and howitzers, on November 29 and surrounded Black Kettle's camp. On the way he told his half-breed guide, "I haven't had an Indian to eat for a long time. If you fool with me, and don't lead us to that camp, I'll have you for breakfast."

Black Kettle hurriedly ran up an American flag on the lodge pole in front of his tepee with a white flag beneath it, shouted that they would not be harmed for they were under the protection of the U.S. government. Just then Chivington's men began firing. "We killed as many as we could," Chivington reported. "The village was destroyed and burned." Black Kettle, against his will, was carried off by his young warriors. White Antelope stood before his tent, wrapped in his blanket, folded his arms and sang his death song as the soldiers beat him down and shot him.

Chivington's troops chased the Indians up Sand Creek. An interpreter who witnessed the killing wrote, "All manner of depredations were inflicted on their persons; they were scalped, their brains knocked out; the men used knives, ripped open women, clubbed little children, knocked them on the head with their guns, beat their brains out, mutilated their bodies in every sense of the word."

Some people of the frontier said that this was the only way to treat the Indians. Old Indian scouts Kit Carson and Jim Bridger were indignant, and warned of swift and terrible retribution. Horrified people in the East could not understand such a massacre; editors in New York denounced it; but nobody was ever punished by the government, though the Indians were its wards.

Cheyenne chiefs sent a war pipe north. Their northern brothers smoked it, and so did the Sioux, among them Sitting Bull, who got his revenge eleven years later on Custer at the Battle of the Little Big Horn. In January 1866 the Cheyennes began striking at ranches and the stage line. Three wagon trains were looted. The Indians raided Julesburg, a fort, and burned it. During the summer a wagon train near Platte Bridge was attacked; a battle grew in dimensions as more Indians and soldiers joined in. Among the Indians was a great warrior named Roman Nose. After an all-day fight he rode alone around the corral of wagons. Everybody was dead or badly wounded. He motioned to his Cheyennes. They leaped forward and killed all who showed a sign of life.

The greatest sport for the Indians was to wreck a railroad train. They discovered this pastime late in the summer of 1867. First they derailed a handcar. That was easy. Then they pulled the spikes from a rail, bent it, and waited to see what would happen. At last they saw the headlights of the locomotive. It roared toward them, struck the loosened rail, jumped off the track and turned over. This was hilarious. Screaming with delight, the Cheyennes fell upon the wreck. Only one trainman had survived. They killed him, looted the train.

Meanwhile trouble simmered among the Sioux in the north. Pioneers had been blazing a new trail in the Northwest from Fort Laramie through the Indians' best

ND CREEK near Denver, Colonel Chivington led forces which surprised and massacred a Cheyenne village.

hunting grounds. This was the Powder River road to Montana, to the mines just opening near Bozeman. Sioux Chief Red Cloud, a lifelong implacable foe of the whites, refused to yield or even to discuss the use of this road. As the Army started building forts along it, Indians who were believed to be Red Cloud's warriors but who actually were led by Chief Crazy Horse surrounded Fort Phil Kearney, sniping at everybody who entered or left. In five months they killed 154 persons.

Early in December the Indians attacked a wagon train hauling wood to the sawmill. Colonel H. B. Carrington, in command of the fort, sent Captain W. J. Fetterman with a column of men to relieve the wood train. In a skirmish several were killed on each side and the Indians retreated.

Another wood train was attacked on December 21 and again Fetterman was sent out, this time with eighty-one officers and men. The wood train returned, unharmed, but not one of Fetterman's men came back alive. He had boasted that if he had eighty men he would ride through the whole Sioux nation. Evidently a handful of warriors had tantalized Fetterman into an ambush, closed in on him, and, joined by a force of two thousand, cut his men to pieces.

The Indians used bows and arrows for the most part in these battles. Only six of Fetterman's men died of bullet wounds. The easiest way the Indians could get rifles was to capture them in raids upon white men. However, about this time the Indian Department began to issue rifles and ammunition to the Indians, explaining that since they were expected to live chiefly on game, they needed rifles with which to shoot it. Indian agents explained the Fetterman fight by saying that the Indians were simply hungry and the War Department had refused to issue guns. What the Indian agents did, in effect, after that, was to supply the tribes with arms with which to fight the U.S. Army. By doing so they transformed the Indian from a savage warrior to one of the finest fighting soldiers in the world.

Since the whole country was aroused about the Indian problem, Congress established a peace commission to treat with hostile tribes. It met at Fort Laramie in September and at Fort Larned in October, obtaining much information but achieving small results. One difficulty was in communications: how to reach the chiefs and persuade them to attend a conference. After all, it was not practicable to write them letters, send them telegrams, or serve subpoenas. Red Cloud had said that he was making war against the whites to save the valley of the Powder River, "the only hunting ground left to his nation." When the military garrisons were withdrawn, the war on his part would cease.

In the end the commission had to accede to his demands. Yet not until the Army showed good faith by actually withdrawing did the chief agree. The flag was hauled down at Fort Kearney and the Cheyennes occupied it as the soldiers marched out.

The Army sent new generals out to the frontier. General Hancock took his command marching for hundreds of miles with-

52

HOLDING THE FORT.

53

GENERAL SHERMAN COMMANDED THE ARMY FIGHT-
ING THE INDIANS AFTER THE CIVIL WAR.

out finding a hostile Indian. General Sherman went out with the peace commission,
formed his own conclusions. "We have
now selected and provided reservations for
all [Indians] off the great roads," he said.
"All who cling to their old hunting grounds
are hostile and will remain so until killed
off. We will have a sort of predatory war
for years, every now and then be shocked
by the indiscriminate murder of travelers
and settlers, but the country is so large,
and the advantage of the Indians so great,
that we cannot make a single war and end
it. From the nature of things we must take

chances and clean out Indians as we encounter them." The chief accomplishment
of the peace treaties of 1867 and 1868 was
to open up the continent for the railroads.
The Union Pacific was the first to take advantage of it.

General Philip Sheridan became the new
commander of the Department of the Missouri. At the same time General George
Armstrong Custer arrived on the frontier,
eager for blood and glory. A handsome,
daring, popular "boy general"—he was
only twenty-nine in 1868—he had made
a distinglished reputation in the Civil War
as a cavalry officer with General Sheridan.
Now he was determined to make a big
name for himself as an Indian fighter. It
was with Custer that Will Cody served as
a government scout in 1868.

When Cody found he was not suited to
make a success of the hotel business, he
went to Salina, Kansas, to look for a job
on the Kansas Pacific Railway, then building to join eventually the tracks of the
Union Pacific. At Junction City, Cody met
Wild Bill Hickok, who was working as a
scout out of Fort Harker. Wild Bill told
Cody scouts were needed. That was the
job Will Cody really wanted. He was
hired temporarily at Fort Larned, sixty-five
miles west. Reporting at daylight, he found
Custer already in the saddle. Custer glanced
disapprovingly at Cody's mule.

"This is one of the best horses at the
fort," Cody explained.

"That isn't a horse at all," Custer said.
"But if it's the best you've got, we shall
have to start."

54

Cody's mule had a fast walk, holding the General's horse at a half trot. The mule continued its lively pace. Once Cody suggested an easier gait out of consideration for the horses, but Custer insisted on pushing ahead. As the day wore on it was evident that the horses were tiring. At a ridge overlooking the fork in the roads, the scout gave Custer directions and offered to go on ahead to Fort Larned with dispatches. Custer repeated the instructions to the captain with him, then said he would continue on with Cody. "I'm ready for you and that mouse-colored mule."

The untiring mule continued to set a fast pace. At the fort Custer stayed with the officers while Cody went to the scouts' quarters. After an early breakfast, Cody and his mule were ready, waiting for Custer. The General appeared out of sorts.

"I'm not in good humor this morning," Custer remarked. "My horse died during the night."

Cody said he was sorry the animal got into too fast company the day before.

Custer looked grim. "Well," he replied, "hereafter I will have nothing to say against a mule."

Cody returned to Fort Hays, where he was ordered to accompany the Tenth Cavalry, a Negro regiment, as scout to find a band of Indians which had raided the railroad, killing five or six men. They met a larger body of Indians than they had anticipated and had to retreat after a sharp fight in which several men were wounded. They had brought along a mountain howitzer which had to be abandoned when they retreated to the fort. Custer extricated the command from a critical situation during the night and led them safely back.

RAILROAD BUILDING in western Nebraska at time Buffalo Bill supplied fresh meat for the workers.

After this scouting experience Cody engaged briefly in land speculation, and then he obtained the job which made him his reputation as the world's champion buffalo killer. His adventure as a real-estate promoter was repeated later in his life when he tried to make money quickly in investments. He was inclined to be gullible about financial transactions; he jumped impulsively into propositions which glittered with promise, and was likely to overlook an essential factor that led to disaster. If an idea looked good, his natural enthusiasm carried him away.

Opportunities for real-estate promoters abounded all over the West, especially along the railroad lines. The promoters would pick a spot along a main line, hire surveyors, lay out a town, stake out lots, build a store, and start selling the lots. Sometimes they would build a hotel. That is what Cody started to do with a town site on the west side of Big Creek, a mile from Fort Hays.

With a partner named Rose, who had a grading contract with the railroad, he planned a town to be called Rome. They donated lots to anybody who would build on them, reserved for themselves corner lots to be sold at $250 each. Cody figured that he was worth $250,000 on paper, wrote to Louisa to come at once with their newborn baby daughter, Arta. He met his little family at Ellsworth, about a hundred

56

miles from Rome, with three wagons filled with furniture, and a carriage for his wife and child. He did not tell Louisa that hostile Indians in the neighborhood made it a dangerous trip.

A band of immigrants accompanied them. The first night Cody formed the men into squads to patrol the boundaries of the camp while the others slept. When he went out to inspect his guard Louisa complained. He did not tell her why he went out, or why he slept with his guns close by. She grew uneasy about this ideal life on the plains.

At Rome the gambling and dance halls closed to welcome their arrival. That night Louisa was startled by shots outside the window.

"What is that?" she asked.

"Just a serenade," Cody assured her.

"Are they blank cartridges?"

"Of course not. Nobody carries blank cartridges in their pistols. Everybody in town is armed."

"Why?"

"To keep law and order."

This was something more than she could understand. Why couldn't policemen maintain law and order as they did in St. Louis? Her husband told her that policemen wouldn't last very long in a town like Rome. That was even more puzzling.

The next day Cody met a handsome stranger named Webb who wanted to go buffalo hunting. Cody obliged, showed him how he did it, galloping alongside a buffalo and shooting it. The man was de-lighted. Cody took him to dinner, and after some conversation about the wonderful location of Rome, the man made him a proposition.

"I'll give you one eighth of this town site," Mr. Webb informed him.

The nerve of offering Cody a share of his own town site took him off his feet. He laughed, saying he had no time to discuss a proposition like that. The next day Cody went out after buffalo meat for the railroad workers. Three days later, as he came back he stopped at the ridge overlooking the town.

Something odd was happening to Rome. It was being torn down and carted away. Everything seemed to be moving east. When he got into town he found out that Mr. Webb, who had offered him one eighth of his own town, was president of the town-site company for the Kansas Pacific Railway. After Cody had gone to get the meat for the railway workers, Mr. Webb had invited the people of Rome to come over to see where the new railroad division town of Hays City was to be built. Everybody went. Here Mr. Webb showed them where the repair shops would be, how the town was to be laid out. He began to sell lots at once. Then he loaned them government wagons to bring their goods and chattels over. Immediately there was a general exodus for the new town. Nothing was left of Cody's dream of Rome except his own little house and a few dug-outs.

His partner was leaning against the house, whittling.

"What happened?" Cody asked.

Before Rose could answer Louisa reminded her husband, "You wrote me you were worth $250,000."

Cody answered that he had no time to talk about that just then; he wanted to know why his town had moved.

Louisa said he should have taken that offer from Mr. Webb. Rose then explained that Mr. Webb was in charge of building the division site for the Kansas Pacific Railroad. That was why everybody had moved over there.

Louisa inquired again about that $250,-000.

"I still have time to make it," Will told her. He turned to Rose: "How does it feel to drop from a millionaire to a pauper?"

"It's quite a fall," the partner admitted. "I haven't got over it yet."

Rose went back to his grading contract and Cody returned to his profession as buffalo hunter. As soon as the hotel was moved to the new metropolis of Hays City, he installed his wife and child there and resumed his former job. Sooner or later, he knew, another big idea would come along.

His reputation as a buffalo hunter had spread. Hunters who had passed through that country had hired him as guide and marveled at his skill. Goddard Brothers, who had a contract to feed the men who were working on the railroad, now advanced to the western end of Kansas, hired Cody for five hundred dollars a month to supply them with buffalo meat.

For his buffalo hunting Cody used the first of his famous horses, Brigham—named

BUFFALO BILL HUNTING BISON.

for Brigham Young, the Mormon leader—
an animal that knew as much about buffalo
as any man. A Ute Indian who had once
owned the horse had named him, and
Cody was pleased to continue the name.

Before he went to work for Goddard
Brothers, Cody met a group of officers on
the plains looking for buffalo. Their leader, a captain, didn't think much of Brigham. "Can you catch buffaloes on that
Gothic beast?" he inquired.

Cody said he could. They went out together. A number of bison in the distance
were making for the creek. Cody started
toward the creek to head them off. Suddenly a herd rushed past him, not a hundred yards away. Cody pulled the bridle

off Brigham. The horse set off at top speed,
running alongside the rear buffalo. Raising
his old gun, "Lucretia Borgia," Cody killed
the buffalo with one shot. Brigham went
on without stopping to the next; as soon
as the bison fell the horse was beside the
next one, running so close Cody could
almost touch the huge beast. In a few minutes he had killed eleven animals with
twelve shots. As the last one dropped,
Brigham stopped; he knew his job was finished. Cody had explained that if he didn't
get a buffalo with two shots, the horse
would go on anyway to the next. Brigham
figured his rider could get his game with
two shots. If he couldn't, he wasn't worthy
of consideration.

59

In the seventeen months Cody worked on the job of supplying meat for the railroad workers, he killed 4,280 buffalo. From that time on he was known as "Buffalo Bill." There had been others with the same nickname, but once it was fastened on Will Cody it stuck for life. Again and again he demonstrated how he did it: riding to the head of the herd, pressing the leaders, and bringing them down one by one. The herd then went off to the left, and were soon circling, so that he could pick them off one at a time as each beast started away from the circle.

At the height of his fame as a buffalo hunter Cody was challenged by Billy Comstock to a contest. Comstock was the chief of scouts at Fort Wallace. His friends wanted to see who could win in an actual contest between the two hunters. It was agreed that they would hunt one day for eight hours, beginning at eight in the morning, betting five hundred dollars. The contest took place about twenty miles east of Sheridan. A crowd turned out, including a special excursion from St. Louis. Louisa and the baby came. There were plenty of buffalo available in the vicinity. Comstock and Cody agreed that they would ride into the herd at the same time and make their runs, each killing as many as possible. A scorer followed close behind each hunter.

Cody felt confident, for he believed he had the best buffalo horse in the country. And he had perfect faith in Lucretia Borgia, his needle-gun, a breech-loading Springfield rifle of .50 caliber. Comstock had a Henry rifle, which could fire more rapidly but did not have the power of Lucretia.

As they rode in, Comstock took the left bunch, Cody the right. Soon Cody had the animals running in a beautiful circle. He killed thirty-eight. Comstock kept his buffalo on a straight line. He killed twenty-eight, scattered over a distance of three miles. Cody's were all in one place, con-

PIONEERS HUNT BUFFALO FOR FOOD, DRY THE MEAT AT ONCE.

venient for the butcher to pick up. After the first run some of the visitors from St. Louis sent Cody a bottle of champagne. It was his first. He thanked them, telling them that champagne was an excellent thirst quencher for the Kansas prairie. At the end of the day the score was Cody: 69, Comstock: 46.

Buffalo Bill presented the heads of the beasts to the railroad company, which had them mounted. Eventually they found their way to railway-station waiting rooms, hotel lobbies, restaurants, and bars.

The American bison multiplied prolifically for so many hundreds of years that the Indians could not imagine a time when there would be no great herds wandering the prairies. Year after year the rich soil provided the finest grazing. But the beasts were stupid; they wandered over cliffs and into quicksands. They could not protect themselves against wolves; they froze to death in winter. Hence the vast herds did not outgrow their food supply. They seemed to exist for the sake of the Indian whose horses took naturally to the chase. These horses were descended from the mounts brought over by the Spaniards, and obtained by purchase or theft in Old Mexico or sometimes caught and tamed from herds that had escaped and gone wild in what is now New Mexico and adjoining states. They were perfectly suited for buffalo hunting. Skilled Indian hunters

61

could bring a bison down with bow and arrow. Sometimes the beasts were stampeded over cliffs to pile up in acres of meat.

Originally the several species of bison ranged from the Great Slave Lake in Canada to Chihuahua in Mexico; they wandered as far as northern Nevada and eastern Oregon. Most of them grazed not too far from the Mississippi, but sometimes in pre-Columbian days they strayed into the grasslands of Tennessee, Kentucky, and even Ohio. Perhaps a few walked as far as the shore of Lake Erie in New York, possibly into Pennsylvania.

As settlers invaded their grazing lands, their range shrank, and they were frightened west with the Indians who exploited them for their skins. White men did not hunt them much before 1850. Somehow the idea did not appeal as a sport until it was introduced by Buffalo Bill and perhaps by a few other scouts who hunted for the same reason as he did: to supply meat for the railroad workers. It was in the 1870s that the big slaughter really began, and it was to continue unremittingly until the bison were almost extinct on this continent. In the early 'seventies it was possible to travel through herd after herd, and in one day see from half a million to twelve million bison moving in scattered herds.

Yet such a mighty multitude was exterminated quickly. By the end of the 'seventies buffalo were scarce. The Indians could not believe they had gone; they expected to see them return each springtime. What had once been sixty million head had disappeared. Less than a thousandth part of their meat was ever used. Yet it was a wonderfully rich food. Indians and mountaineers never tired of it. A regular daily allowance for an employee for the fur company was eight pounds. The early inhabitants of the plains never wanted or needed bread or vegetables as long as they had buffalo meat. The tongue was a special delicacy.

Extermination of the buffalo meant the decline of the Indians. When the white man realized this, he continued his slaughtering with renewed vigor, although a few questioned the morality of civilizing the Indian by starving him to death. Yet that, if not the deliberate policy of the U.S. government, was what happened. Seldom did the slaughtering contain any element of sportsmanship. It became a war measure against a whole race, a deliberate policy of genocide, carried out as cold-bloodedly as moral hypocrisy would permit.

Europeans were highly curious about the American bison, for it seemed to them somehow a romantic beast. Buffalo were a big attraction when Cody later took some of them to England and the Continent with his Wild West Show. The beasts did not prosper there, but Buffalo Bill by his showmanship kept the memory of the animals alive. He perpetuated the legends about them as he perpetuated the legends about the Indians and the cowboys. He gave thousands of people a vivid glimpse and a memory of what it once meant to see these great herds roaming the prairies in that idyllic, Arcadian era before the whole magnificent life cycle was destroyed.

Chapter 5

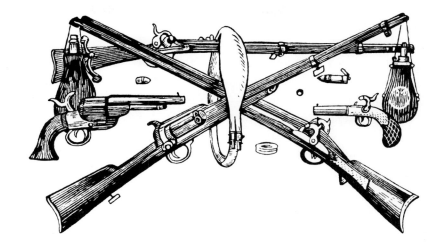

Chief of Scouts

IT is sometimes alleged by detractors of Buffalo Bill—prejudiced against him by his later years of glorified showmanship—that he was never, as advertised, Chief of Scouts. The official records offer easily consulted evidence to the contrary. He was employed by the Army in his early twenties under circumstances that appear in dispatches, without elaboration, and which reveal his professional as well as personal relationships with Generals Sheridan and Custer.

The problem of the U.S. Army on the western frontier in the years immediately after the Civil War was staggering. General Phil Sheridan's command, the Department of the Missouri, included an area of about 150,000 square miles in western Kansas, eastern Colorado, Oklahoma, and New Mexico. Most of this territory had been mapped by military expeditions, but was known in detail only by Indians and trappers. To patrol the whole area Sheridan was allowed 2,600 men: 1,200 cavalry and 1,400 infantry. The cavalry was the Seventh and the Tenth (Negro) Regiments; the infantry the Third and Fourth Regiments, and four companies of the Thirty-eighth Regiment. With these he had to garrison twenty-six army posts at great distances from each other. He was also expected to furnish troops quickly when any of the settlements were attacked.

Four thousand or more—nobody knew

how many—nomadic warriors and their families wandered over the trackless plains and hills. These Cheyenne, Arapaho, Comanche, Kiowa, and Wichita tribes were self-sustaining; they could live as they pleased, do as they pleased. No treaties could bind them, no laws restrain them. They took orders from nobody, had nothing but contempt for the white man and his ways. They could live somehow in a semi-arid country, protect themselves from blizzards and sand storms, find their way in what was to them familiar, gully-corrugated hills. Eating was an individual, not a mass, problem. The Indians, certainly not squeamish, could live on jackrabbits, terrapins, packrats, and even snakes.

Sheridan's troops were a motley, poorly disciplined, badly paid rabble. The soldier's sixteen dollars a month did not leave him much, after deductions, for the whiskey on which he usually spent it. Most of them were lonely and bored and, like their officers, constantly bickering among themselves. With such a lot Sheridan was supposed to keep the settlements safe, the ranches from being molested, the roads and trails clear so that the transcontinental railroads could be built without interruption.

At a meeting at Medicine Lodge in October 1867 of such chiefs as could be persuaded to attend, the Indians were told that they must become sedentary and conform to the white man's ways of living. A reservation of three million acres between the Red River and the Washita was offered the Comanche and Kiowa, and another

GENERAL SHERIDAN.

4,300,000 acres to the Cheyenne and Arapaho. They were to live on government rations of beef, flour, coffee, and sugar. In time they were to have homes, farms, agricultural implements, and instructors to teach them how to make the best use of the land.

Satanta, the most powerful and eloquent of the chiefs present, rose and said, "The white chief seems not to be able to control his braves. He sometimes gets angry when he sees the wrongs his people commit on the red men, and his voice is as loud as the roaring wind; but like the wind, it soon dies away and leaves the sullen calm of unheeded oppression. The white man grows jealous of his red brother. He once came to trade; he now comes as a soldier. He once put his trust in our friendship and wanted no shield but our fidelity; but now he covers his face with a cloud of jealousy and anger, and he tells us to be gone as the offended master speaks to his dog. You know what is best for us; do what is best. Teach us the road to travel and we shall not depart from it forever. For your sakes the green grass shall not be stained with the blood of whites; your people shall again be our people and peace shall be our mutual heritage."

Five thousand Indians in their rags, deerskin leggings, and vermin-covered blankets watched the final ceremonies. Into the cottonwood grove came the peace commissioners in Prince Albert coats and silk top hats. The Indian chiefs in breechcloths, leggings, and moccasins appeared for this occasion with their hair braided and wrapped in otter skins, and their necks were decorated with wampum, their arms with bracelets, and their heads with war bonnets.

Congress had granted them, they were told, liberal funds for subsistence. What was more to the point was the generous

Frederic Remington's "Cavalry Charge."

distribution, on the spot, of flour, beef, coffee, and sugar. And even better were the presents given on the side: whiskey, guns, and ammunition. In return the Indian was expected to revolutionize his ways, his habits, his entire mode of life overnight. Satanta could speak for himself and perhaps for his tribe, but he could not speak for all the Indians. Nearby white settlements offered tempting bait for Indian raiders. Soon after the meeting Indians were saying the conditions laid down were too difficult for the tribesmen to live up to.

Indian agents and army officers disagreed violently about government policies toward the Indians. The questions raised at Medicine Lodge were vigorously debated in the press of the eastern cities. When Sheridan arrived at Fort Leavenworth in the spring of 1868 he discovered that although the head men among the Indians had agreed, "many of the young men were bitterly opposed to what had been

SCHREYVOGEL'S "BREAKING THE CIRCLE."

done, and claimed that most of the signatures had been obtained by misrepresentation and through proffers of certain annuities, and promises of arms and ammunition to be issued in the spring of 1868."

"This grumbling," he continued in his personal memoirs, "was very general in extent, and during the winter found outlet in occasional marauding, so, fearing a renewal of the pillaging and plundering of an early day, to prepare myself for the work evidently ahead the first thing I did on assuming permanent command was to make a trip to Fort Larned and Fort Dodge, near which places the bulk of the Indians had congregated on Pawnee and Walnut creeks. I wanted to get near enough to the camps to find out for myself the actual state of feeling among the savages, and also to familiarize myself with the characteristics of the Plains Indians."

Fort Larned he found too close; for his proximity invited, it seemed, unnecessary talks. Fort Dodge, he decided, was more to his liking; but it took him only a few days to discover the great discontent about the Medicine Lodge treaties, "to see that the young men were chafing and turbulent, and that it would require much tact and good management on the part of the Indian Bureau to persuade the four tribes to go quietly to their reservations."

A delegation of prominent chiefs wanted a conference, but Sheridan refused because he felt that Congress had delegated to the peace commission the whole matter of treating with them and a "council might lead only to additional complications." His

refusal left them without hope of obtaining better terms, or delaying matters longer, so henceforth "they were more than ever reckless and defiant. Denunciations of the treaty became outspoken, and as the young braves grew more and more insolent every day, it amounted to conviction that, unless by some means the irritation was allayed, hostilities would surely be upon us when the buffalo returned to their summer feeding-grounds between the Arkansas and the Platte."

The principal sufferers, Sheridan foresaw, would be the settlers in middle and western Kansas who, "entirely ignorant of the dangers hanging over them, were laboring to build up homes in a new country. Hence," he wrote, "the maintenance of peace was much to be desired, if it could be secured without too great concessions, and although I would not meet the different tribes in a formal council, yet to ward off from settlers as much as possible the horrors of savage warfare, I showed, by resorting to persuasive methods, my willingness to temporize a good deal. An abundant supply of rations is usually effective to keep matters quiet in such cases, so I fed them pretty freely, and also endeavored to control them through certain men who, I found, had their confidence."

No trouble developed until midsummer. In July the tribes began moving to new locations north of the Arkansas instead of toward the reservations to which they had been assigned. A party of Cheyennes had made a raid on the Kaws, a tribe of friendly Indians near Council

Grove, and stolen their horses. They also robbed several white settlers nearby. This was the beginning of the Indian war of 1868.

The Comanches and Kiowas then went to Fort Larned to receive their annuities, expecting also to get the arms and ammunition promised them at Medicine Lodge. However, when the Indian Department heard of the raid at Council Grove, the issue of arms was suspended. This angered the Indians, who refused to accept annuities unless they also got guns and pistols. They retired to their camps for war dances and pow-wows with their medicine men.

Some of the chiefs then went to see Brigadier General Alfred Sully at Fort Larned and convinced him that the Indians responsible for depredations were only a few bad young men who would be held in check if the agent would only issue arms and ammunition. With that understanding arms were issued. It was a serious mistake, for as soon as the Indians obtained the arms they began raiding. Two hundred Cheyennes, with a few Arapaho and Sioux, fell upon homes in the Saline Valley, then went on into the Solomon Valley, stealing as many horses as they could find.

Sheridan called upon General William Tecumseh Sherman at St. Louis for help, and Sherman ordered his commanders to do their utmost. The policy of the peace commissioners had failed miserably, he decided, and he wrote his brother, Senator John Sherman, in Washington, that these outbreaks were a direct result of the government's not having kept its treaty promises. General Sherman's letter led to a furious argument with the Indian Bureau, whose agents accused him and Sheridan of planning a war of extermination.

General Sherman replied angrily, "As to extermination, it is for the Indians to determine. We don't want to exterminate or even to fight them. At best it is an inglorious war, not apt to add much to our fame or our personal comfort; and as for our soldiers, to whom we owe our first thoughts, it is all danger and extreme labor, without a single compensating advantage. To accuse us of inaugurating or wishing such a war, is to accuse us of want of common sense. . . . The injustice and frauds heretofore practiced on the Indians as charged, are not of our making; and I know the present war did not result from any acts of ours."

To Indian agent Tappan General Sherman wrote, "Either the Indians must give way, or we must abandon all west of the Missouri River and confess that forty million whites are cowed by a few thousand savages. . . . I have stretched my power and authority to help them, but when they laugh at our cordiality, rape our women, murder our men, burn whole trains with their drivers to cinders, and send word they never intended to keep their treaties, then we must fight them. When we come to fight Indians, I will take my code from soldiers and not from citizens."

Sheridan, after studying the problem, concluded that it was hopeless to try to stop marauding bands with small detach-

ments of cavalry. The only way to fight
the Indians, he decided, was in the winter, when he could fall upon them relent-
lessly because their ponies would be thin.
If they were without strong ponies to help
them move about, the troops could overtake them, he felt sure. He planned for it
carefully. One necessary ingredient in his
plans was to have experienced scouts.

Hays City, Sheridan noted in his memoirs, "was filled with so-called 'Indian
scouts' whose common boast was of having slain scores of redskins, but the real
scout—that is, a guide and trailer knowing

the habits of the Indians—was very scarce
and it was hard to find anybody familiar
with the country south of the Arkansas,
where the campaign was to be made. Still,
about Hays City and the various military
posts there was some good material to select from, and we managed to employ several men, who, from their experience on
the plains in various capacities, or from
natural instinct and aptitude, soon became
excellent guides and courageous and valuable scouts, some of them, indeed, gaining
much distinction.

"Mr. William F. Cody ('Buffalo Bill'),

Sɪᴏᴜx Iɴᴅɪᴀɴs capture a Union Pacific freight train in 1868, unroll bolts of cloth.

whose renown has since become world-wide, was one of the men thus selected. He received his sobriquet from his marked success in killing buffaloes for a contractor, to supply fresh meat for construction parties on the Kansas-Pacific Railway. He had given up this business, however, and was now in the employ of the quartermaster's department of the army, and was first brought to my notice by distinguishing himself in bringing me an important despatch from Fort Larned to Fort Hays, a distance of sixty-five miles, through a section infested with Indians. The despatch informed me that the Indians near Larned were preparing to decamp, and this intelligence required that certain orders should be carried to Fort Dodge, ninety-five miles south of Hays. This too being a particularly dangerous route—several couriers having been killed on it—it was impossible to get one of the various 'Petes', 'Jacks', or 'Jims', hanging around Hays City to take my communication.

"Cody, learning of the strait I was in, manfully came to the rescue, and proposed to make the trip to Dodge, though he had just finished his long and perilous ride from Larned. I gratefully accepted his offer, and after four or five hours' rest he mounted a fresh horse and hastened on his journey, halting but once to rest on the way, and then only for an hour, the stop being made at Coon Creek, where he got another mount from a troop of cavalry. At Dodge he took six hours' sleep, and then continued on to his own post— Fort Larned—with more despatches. After

OLD INDIAN FIGHTER, GENERAL GEORGE CROOK.

resting twelve hours at Larned, he was again in the saddle with tidings for me at Fort Hays, General Hazen sending him, this time, with word that the villages had fled to the south of the Arkansas. Thus, in all, Cody rode about 350 miles in less than sixty hours, and such an exhibition of endurance and courage was more than enough to convince me that his services would be extremely valuable in the campaign, so I retained him at Fort Hays till the battalion of the Fifth Cavalry arrived, and then made him chief of scouts for that regiment.

"The information brought me by Cody" —General Sheridan continues his narrative—"on his second trip from Larned indicated where the villages would be found in the winter, and I decided to move on them about the 1st of November. Only the women and children and decrepit old men were with the villages, however—enough, presumably, to look after the plunder—most of the warriors remaining north of the Arkansas to continue their marauding. Many severe fights occurred between our troops and these marauders, and in these affairs, before November 1st over a hundred Indians were killed, yet from the ease with which the escaping savages would disappear only to fall upon remote settlements with pillage and murder, the results were by no means satisfactory."

After the famous ride described by General Sheridan, Cody was attached to the Fifth Cavalry, which was sent against the so-called "Dog Soldier" Indians in the Republican River region. They got their name from "Cheyenne," which is derived from *chien*, the French for dog. They were a band of fighting Cheyennes and other unruly groups who would not be bound by any treaties. They refused to go on a reservation.

The Dog Soldiers had formed themselves into a kind of fighting fraternity and won a reputation as being among the fiercest fighters in the whole history of the plains. They were bound together by strict discipline, attracted some of the bravest warriors, who in battle staked themselves to one spot and never retreated. Their chief, Tall Bull, exercised an absolute control over them.

While the famous cavalry regiment marched toward Beaver Creek early in October, Buffalo Bill supplied them with buffalo meat, driving the beasts toward the camp and slaughtering them within sight of the men, thus saving transportation, as he had done for the railroad workers. General E. A. Carr, one of the outstanding Indian fighters of his day, soon took command, and brought with him Frank North's Pawnee Scouts, a band of Indians who had proved themselves as wily in battle as the Cheyennes. Buffalo Bill welcomed them, for he was aware of their cunning, but he was Carr's chief scout and impressively demonstrated his ability to find his way and to lead the regiment to water when the whole territory appeared arid.

At Fort Lyon they refitted for a winter campaign on Sheridan's order, then set out, following the trail of General Penrose, who had gone ahead with three hundred men. Although it was difficult to find his trail and to keep on it, Cody managed to do so. When they reached the Raton Mountains, Cody showed them how to get down to a valley to camp by putting chains on the wheels of the wagons so that they could be slid down the steep slope. Eventually they caught up with Penrose's command, which was being guided by Wild Bill Hickok. Hickok had heard that there was a wagon train coming from New Mexico with a quantity of Mexican beer. The two scouts lay in wait for it and then "requisitioned" (perhaps hijacked is more accurate) it for General Carr's troops. The weather was cold, so they warmed the beer with picket pins heated red hot. It was a powerful brew.

Their celebration led to an argument

WILD BILL HICKOK ON THE FRONTIER.

and then to a fight between the Mexican scouts and the Americans. A feud had existed for some time. Stimulated by the beer, Cody and Hickok evidently decided to settle matters by cleaning up the Mexicans. At any rate, General Carr decided that Cody and Hickok started the fracas, and suggested they work off their excess energy by a few days of antelope hunting.

In the spring of 1869 Buffalo Bill visited his family for several weeks on a leave of absence. On the way to rejoin his command, he became involved in a misunderstanding about some mules which he had

left with a friend named Perry, a hotel-keeper at Sheridan. A quartermaster's agent seized the animals, believing they had been unlawfully sold to Perry. This led to a fight between Cody and the agent, who accused Bill of selling government property. Cody's answer was to knock him down, and out. General Bankhead, jumping to conclusions, sided with the quartermaster and threw Cody in jail. When the scout tried to wire Sheridan and Carr what happened and where he was, Bankhead refused at first to allow the messages to go through. But finally he gave in and the matter was settled amicably.

Buffalo Bill in his autobiography tells another mule story concerning an earlier incident at Fort Dodge. He had asked for a horse to take him to Fort Larned, but there was only an old reliable government mule. He took the mule and followed a creek instead of the main road since the creek would be both shorter and safer. Once he stopped for a drink of water; the mule jerked loose and went on down the road by himself. Cody followed him, hoping he would catch his foot in the bridle rein and stop, but he made for the main road and proceeded in a jogtrot just too fast for the scout to overtake him.

Cody had his gun in his hand and was tempted to shoot him, he was so angry, but that might have brought the Indians down on him. So Bill trudged after the old mule, mile after mile, cussing him and the whole mule family and never getting close enough to catch him, for he was always just out of reach. By the time they reached

Fort Larned, Bill was out of patience and thoroughly fagged out. "Now Mr. Mule," he said, "it is my turn," and he shot him.

When Cody rejoined his regiment General Carr sent him out to catch some horse thieves. He followed their trail down the Arkansas River to Denver. Government horses and mules, obviously animals that had been stolen, were being auctioned off. Cody caught the leader and his accomplice,

had them arrested. They were desperate characters, however, and escaped when he tried to bring them back to Carr's camp. After a fight he recaptured one of them, but the other got away.

On a march to the Platte River country Cody, while scouting, discovered a large force of Indians on the move—thousands of them. He notified Carr, who pursued them so closely that the Indians had to discard most of their supplies, camp equipment, and furniture. It was Tall Bull and his Dog Soldiers heading north. This time he got away, for even with tepees, women, children, dogs, and everything else, his band could travel fifty miles a day.

At Fort McPherson, Carr's regiment was reinforced again by the Pawnee scouts, who had been up north fighting the Sioux. One of these Indian scouts had a horse which Buffalo Bill fancied. By trade and a few additional presents, he thus obtained the second of his famous horses, Buckskin Joe, a big yellow horse known as a buckskin because of his color. Much bigger than most Indian ponies, he was one of the greatest long-distance horses of his day.

As soon as Cody got him he demonstrated how he hunted buffalo. After that he rode Buckskin Joe on all his scouting and hunting expeditions. He would often ride another horse, but take Buckskin along to use when the work was dangerous or in case he had to run for his life. The horse was almost human in his ability to scent danger, and the longer the chase the more the animal seemed to enjoy it. Later in his career a terrific ride of 195 miles from the headwaters of the Republican River to Fort McPherson was too much for the faithful animal, and he went blind. Joe was sold, but a friend bought him and presented him to Cody, who kept him on his ranch until the animal died of old age. A tombstone was inscribed, "Old Buckskin Joe, the horse that on several occasions saved the life of Buffalo Bill by carrying

him safely out of range of Indian battles, died of old age, 1882."

In the spring of 1869, General Carr learned that the Cheyennes were camping at the headwaters of the Republican River. They were raiding settlements almost daily, in May and June, killing civilians, abducting women, and had stolen more than five hundred horses and mules. On July 1, Carr set out with five companies of the Fifth Cavalry and the Pawnee Scouts. The Pawnees picked up the trail and had a short, sharp fight with some of the Cheyennes. Again the Cheyennes showed extraordinary speed in getting away.

Tall Bull, the wiliest and toughest of the Indian chiefs and a close friend of Roman Nose, was contemptuous of the white man and overconfident. He tried to

GENERAL E. A. CARR, COMMANDER OF THE TENTH CAVALRY.

confuse his pursuers by scattering his people, disguising his trail. At one point a heavy trail went off to the right, a light one to the left. Carr was not fooled. The dim trail grew heavier. Furthermore, the Indians had captured two white women and made them walk and the Pawnees detected the print of their shoes.

In one day Carr's regiment made a 65-mile march in intense heat toward Summit Springs. About noon on July 11 a Pawnee reported the Indian camp only a few miles ahead. The Dog Soldiers were taking it easy, smoking and talking in Tall Bull's village. Seeing them in the valley at the foot of some bluffs, Carr ordered the charge sounded. The excited bugler forgot the notes of the call. The general repeated the command, which flustered the bugler even more. Quartermaster Hays then seized the bugle and sounded the call himself, threw the instrument away, drew his pistol, and went into the fight.

The Pawnee Scouts had already stripped their horses, for they always rode into battle bareback. Every horse leaped into the camp, the Pawnees yelling. At first the Dog Soldiers advanced to meet the attack, then saw that they would be overwhelmed. A white woman ran from a tepee, a Cheyenne after her. "Lie down!" shouted the cavalrymen. She obeyed, the horses sprang over her, but she had already been shot through the breast. The other white woman, a Mrs. Alerdice, who had been captured in Kansas, ran out. A warrior seized her, brained her with a tomahawk.

Tall Bull saw he was beaten. His favorite fast horse had been tied beside his tepee. Putting his wife and daughter onto its back, he jumped up behind them and hid them in a gulch, then returned to the battle, resolved to die. Carr's men had already killed 52, captured 117, but the fight was not entirely over. He ordered all the tepees, buffalo robes, and camp equipment burned. Mrs. Alerdice and the other white woman were buried. While this was going on some of the Sioux warriors, who had been with Tall Bull's Dog Soldiers, came back for another skirmish.

At the same time Buffalo Bill noticed Tall Bull riding his big bay horse, ordering his warriors back into the battle, shouting that they had lost everything and that they might as well die fighting. As the chieftain passed the head of the canyon, Cody shot him at less than thirty yards. Tall Bull tumbled from the saddle, his horse continuing on its way, galloping toward the soldiers. One of the cavalrymen dismounted, caught the animal, and found on its back the war bonnet from the head of the dead chief. The sergeant handed the horse over to Buffalo Bill, who had been searching for him. The sergeant had seen Cody shoot the chief and knew he wanted the horse.

Later this horse proved to be one of the fleetest west of the Mississippi. Buffalo Bill named him Tall Bull and often told how he had killed the chief and captured the animal. Cody liked to ride him bareback, holding on to his mane and jumping to the ground and up again, often repeating the performance seven or eight times.

Ever since the battle there has been heated controversy regarding who killed Tall Bull. This is Cody's version, although his latter-day press agents have provided several other versions, and Cody himself once said Lieutenant Hays did it. Many historians give Major Frank North credit, for instance Stanley Vestal in his description based on George Grinnell's book *The Fighting Cheyennes*. One account even says Cody wasn't there at the time of the battle. But Buffalo Bill re-enacted it as a part of his Wild West Show. Major North played in the show and did not directly contradict Cody's story.

Actually, probably nobody knew with certainty who shot Tall Bull, for in the excitement of the battle many men were firing and it would have been difficult to determine even at the time whose bullet hit the chief. The only certainty is that Tall Bull was shot by *somebody*. Nearly all accounts place Cody there, in the thick of it, and it might as surely have been Buffalo Bill as Major North or any of his scouts.

This battle cleared the hostile Indians from the middle of the continent. Two months earlier the golden spike had united the tracks from East and West on the Union Pacific. White civilization had triumphed.

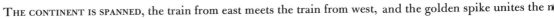

THE CONTINENT IS SPANNED, the train from east meets the train from west, and the golden spike unites the n

Chapter 6

Dudes, Buntline, and the Stage

THE real turning point in Buffalo Bill's life came in the early 1870s. Although he was at first only partly aware of it, it was during those years that he was changing the pattern of his career from that of a "hired man on horseback" to that of a celebrity. He was broke most of the time, and was often looking for a job, but at the same time he was finding his vocation, and realized in part where and in what direction his innate talents would lead him.

Louisa, an adept seamstress, now tailored his ornately fringed and beaded buckskin coats. She had become a nagging wife, and frequently a jealous one, as her handsome 25-year-old husband gained renown. He didn't chase women—but they had begun to chase him, attracted by his picturesque charm, his grace of body, and his ever cheery art of conversation. Men sought his company, too, not only because he was known to have no fear of wild horses, desperadoes, or Indians, but because he looked the part of a hero more dashing than Hickok, Custer, or an Indian chief. He could outdrink them all without getting drunk; he could play poker all night and start out on the trail at dawn as fresh and colorful as the purple sage; and he could outride and outshoot all competitors. He was the Wild West.

Then—more to his own surprise than to that of any of his comrades of the saddle —suddenly he became a national figure. With the discovery of the true magic of his personality, his ego expanded and he gained self-confidence in rich new worlds of sophisticated society that he had scarcely heard about before. He changed from a typical frontiersman to an elegant man of the world, from a local border scout to an actor behind the footlights of theaters in Chicago and New York. One week he was looking for a job as a coachman or even as a driver of fire engines; the next he was catapulted onto the stage and was soon to be one of the greatest showmen the world has ever known. It was a stroke of fate that the role he was to play was himself—Buffalo Bill, scout of the western plains.

Two curiously different impresarios were responsible for his wider fame. The first was the paunchy little Civil War general, Phil Sheridan, who had acquired a taste for high society, and who rightly guessed that Buffalo Bill was destined to enchant the ladies and gentlemen of the East. The second was Ned Buntline, a dime-novel writer of unsavory reputation

who lived from hand to mouth and from tongue to pen, by turns a beggar, an actor, a jailbird, and a promoter, as well as a drunkard and a temperance lecturer.

Energetic General Sheridan was a busy man in the years after the Civil War. President Grant and General Sherman had directed him to quiet the Indians. At the same time Sheridan was in demand by New York, Washington, and Chicago society. He was a bachelor, a war hero, likable and popular. Sheridan was always the

78   Ned Buntline at the time he found Buffalo Bill and made him hero of dime novels.

center of attention when he was invited to the White House or to dinners at Grant's summer home at Long Branch, New Jersey. He liked rich food so much that one friend commented that he began to look like a "low comedy man," and General Crook referred good-humoredly to Sheridan's "bloated little carcass."

It was at Long Branch that Sheridan met Commodore James Gordon Bennett II, who was soon to inherit his father's New York *Herald*. The naval title was earned at the New York Yacht Club. The little general regaled the adventurous-minded newspaper proprietor with colorful stories about the West. This was a subject Bennett had come to know through the columns of his own newspaper. The Indian campaigns had been well covered by his special correspondents, who had written many lively features about them in the enterprising New York *Herald*. Bennett had heard about Buffalo Bill and wanted to meet him.

When Sheridan suggested a buffalo hunt in western Kansas, with Buffalo Bill as leader of the sporting expedition, the Commodore jumped at the idea. Unfortunately the party could not be organized in the summer of 1870 because President Grant had asked Sheridan to go to the European battlefields as a military observer in the Franco-Prussian War. Sheridan was delighted, and asked his friend General Forsyth to come along. They sailed the end of July, met Bismarck, Napoleon III, and the outstanding military men of the time. The buffalo hunt had to be post-poned. When Sheridan returned to his command in September 1871, one of the first things he did was to make arrangements with Buffalo Bill to look after the party of eastern society men on their forthcoming buffalo shoot.

British sportsmen had already discovered the thrills of hunting in the West. Sir George Gore went out in 1855 to Colorado, taking one of the largest parties that had roamed the Rockies up to that time: forty retainers, fourteen hounds, 112 horses, six wagons, twenty-one carts, and twelve yoke of oxen. The story is that he killed three thousand buffalo, forty grizzly bear, as well as many antelope and deer. This smacks of a western tall story, yet the yarn adds that Sir George's party slaughtered so wantonly that the Indians feared for their food supply and threatened to slaughter the nobleman in turn. When the American Fur Company demanded an exorbitant fee to transport his hides, Sir George burned all the hides and the wagons, and dumped the remains into the river.

The Earl of Dunraven hunted buffalo and bear in the Rockies in 1871. He had already been a yachtsman, explorer, author, and war correspondent in Abyssinia in 1857 and during the Franco-Prussian War. Estes Park was named for another Englishman, Joel Estes, who built a cabin on Fish Creek in 1860. When two other families homesteaded nearby he moved out, complaining of "too many people."

The New Yorkers, led by Lawrence R. Jerome, the oldest member of the group, were Leonard W. Jerome, Jerome's son,

Commodore Bennett, Carrol Livingston, John G. Heckscher, and General H. E. Davies. General Sheridan also invited a number of military men: General Fitzhugh of Pittsburgh, an old Civil War crony; Colonel J. Schuyler Crosby; Captain M. Edward Rogers, of a prominent Philadelphia family; General Rucker, who soon afterward became Sheridan's father-in-law. Sheridan's personal surgeon, Dr. Asch, also went along to be useful in case of emergencies.

They left New York on the Hudson River Railroad by sleeping car for Chicago, where they spent several days being entertained. One of the things they did was to make a special trip to the Lincoln Park Zoo to take a look at a real, live buffalo so that they would know what their ultimate quarry looked like. Sheridan entertained them at his mansion, where he maintained bachelor quarters with his younger brother, Colonel Michael V. Sheridan.

After changing from the Northwestern to the Union Pacific Railroad at Omaha, as a special privilege several of the group were allowed to ride on the cowcatcher of the locomotive. Over coffee and cigars on the train they decided to offer two trophy cups: one for the first buffalo killed by a member of the party and one for the first elk.

General Emory of the Fifth U.S. Cavalry, commander at Fort McPherson, met them at the North Platte station, then practically a ghost town since the railroad had been finished and the workers had moved on. General Carr had taken a part of the Fifth Cavalry with him to Arizona. Sheridan sent him special instructions not to take Buffalo Bill with him since he wanted the scout to guide his party of dudes.

Camp was established at once near the fort. Each camp was named after a member of the party. The first was Camp Rucker. Lieutenant Hayes was quartermaster of the expedition and had assembled the supplies and equipment, which included six wall tents and a hospital tent to be used as a mess hall. The tents were equipped with floors and carpeting, and regular beds with comfortable mattresses.

Lieutenant Hayes had also obtained three four-horse ambulances for the expedition's guns, personal baggage, and other equipment. Among the passengers in one of the ambulances were five greyhounds, to be used for coursing antelope and jackrabbits. Two wagons were set aside to carry ice and wine. The party ate full-course dinners cooked by a French chef brought from New York, and were served by waiters wearing full-dress suits. China dishes and silverware were also brought from New York.

The dudes had heard much about Buffalo Bill since one of Ned Buntline's stories had appeared in the New York *Ledger* just before they left. The young scout met them at the camp, which he designated as a "dude ranch" or "dude wigwam." He dressed for the occasion in a white buckskin suit fringed in white leather, complemented by a brilliant crimson shirt, which Louisa had designed and made. He rode a

As they became better acquainted and he told them stories of the great West around the campfire, they began to realize the richness of his personality. He was, they decided, a fascinating individual. He, in turn, seemed to grow in stature as he achieved a new conception of himself, in the mirror of their admiration. They constituted a new and strange audience for him, wonderfully appreciative and responsive. Their comradely feeling of social equality and frank acknowledgment of his leadership supported his self-confidence. He saw himself through their eyes in a fresh vision of self-recognition.

The party, protected from hostile Indians by three hundred men of the Fifth Cavalry, started south at 5:00 A.M. the second day after their arrival. Already Buffalo Bill had introduced them to what he told them was an old western custom: a good shot of bourbon before breakfast, which they agreed was "more refreshing than brushing the teeth." Buffalo Bill led the dudes across the high prairie, following a trail well worn by herds of buffalo through cottonwood-bordered canyons. They noticed that the buffalo grass was yellow and short. Cody told them that it was wonderfully nourishing for cattle and that horses relished it. This was country that had been described to the New Yorkers as the "great American desert." They made seventeen miles the first day and camped at Fox Creek without seeing any game.

That night Buffalo Bill told them stories around the campfire. The bugle sounded at three-thirty in the morning. Breakfast

snow-white horse. The dudes were much impressed, surprised that he was not the desperado he had been pictured but a mild, agreeable, well-mannered, strikingly handsome man, with a magnetic baritone voice.

BILL CODY AS A SCOUT.

was at four-thirty, and they were in their saddles long before sunrise. As they rode along, Cody told them how the buffalo hunters often cut off the tails of the slain beasts as trophies. The old buffaloes, he said, the bulls who were too old to fight and maintain their authority over the herd, stayed together as a kind of club, "like old gentlemen do in the cities." So when they sighted a group of elderly bison they knew that the main herd could not be far away. The dudes were amused by the large number of prairie dogs, most of them sitting inquisitively to stare at this odd party of easterners. General Davies, who later wrote an account of the trip for private distribution among the members, explained that the prairie dog was something like a woodchuck or European marmot. Cody told them the dogs lived in holes which they shared with owls and rattlesnakes. Their meat, he added, tasted much like that of rabbit.

Soon Buffalo Bill sighted the herd he had been expecting. He divided the party, taking Lawrence Jerome, Livingston, Heckscher, Fitzhugh, Rogers, and Crosby with him to a canyon beyond the herd, to windward of them, while the remainder of the party made a detour, staying on the crest of the hill to get a good view. Cody led the charge on the buffaloes at full gallop, then relinquished his place to Fitzhugh, who rode up alongside the rear buffalo, firing at him and wounding him. Another shot brought the beast down. Crosby then dashed by them and dropped another animal, while Livingston shot a third. So

Fitzhugh won the buffalo cup. Heckscher's horse caught his foot in a prairie-dog hole, fell, and rolled over on the gentleman, who, fortunately, was not seriously hurt.

As soon as the buffalo were killed a recess was declared for the purpose of celebrating the event with champagne, a beverage Buffalo Bill, who had tasted it only once in his life, told them he particularly enjoyed. For years afterward, he noted, the sites of their camps were marked by the abandoned bottles. General Davies commented that some future scholar may some day explore the West and decide that it was inhabited by a civilization which had a curious ritual: drinking out of black vases which bore the names of Mumm or Roederer. "We are the Mumm tribe, all right," said Buffalo Bill.

The following day the party split up again so that some of the sportsmen could look for elk. They did so without success. Lawrence Jerome took a fancy to Buffalo Bill's horse, Buckskin Joe, and asked if he could ride him. The scout graciously permitted him this honor. When they came upon the buffalo, Mr. Jerome dismounted to get a steady shot. As he did so he let go of Buckskin, who promptly scampered off by himself at the herd, racing far ahead of them. Not until three days later did Buckskin Joe return to Fort McPherson.

That night the party rested at Camp Cody—"a real dude ranch"—celebrating with a special dinner which included game shot by the party. The menu began with buffalo-tail soup. The fish course was broiled cisco, a fish something like perch,

82

which General Sheridan had caught. The entrees were salmi of prairie dog, stewed rabbit, filet of buffalo with mushrooms, accompanied by vintage claret. The dessert consisted of tapioca pudding, followed by frappe champagne, whiskey, brandy, and ale, with coffee and Havana cigars afterward.

During the next several days General Sheridan shot two buffalo with a new gun of the Ward Burton type. The party tried out the greyhounds on a herd of antelope, but the hounds couldn't overtake them. Later some of the party shot antelope by following Buffalo Bill's directions—standing perfectly still so that when the animals sighted the hunters they would come toward them curiously until within easy range. Heckscher shot some wild turkey. Johnston got a black-tailed deer. General Stager stalked and killed an elk. Wilson brought down some mallard duck. One night a porcupine ventured into the camp; he was caught and put in a cage, but escaped later by gnawing through the bars of wood. General Sheridan got several jackrabbits. General Davies reported that the ears of the rabbits were six inches long.

The whole excursion was so delightful that the dudes invited Buffalo Bill to visit them in New York. Cody probably learned as much from the dudes as they did from him. They discovered the Great West; he discovered the potentialities of Buffalo Bill. The outlines of his new role grew clearer and stronger. The easterners returned with a powerful impression of a vivid, unique personality, a favorite topic of their conversation for years afterward as their anecdotes about him grew with the telling. The clubmen reassured their fellow members, "That fellow Cody is all they say he is and more. Let me tell you about . . ." And thus the stories multiplied.

Buffalo Bill conducted several other dude parties, and regaled his friends with tales of them. He later told with special relish how he played a practical joke on a visiting Britisher named McCarthy. With the co-operation of Major Frank North a number of Pawnees were persuaded to wrap themselves in blankets and pounce suddenly on the hunting party just as Buffalo Bill was riding alongside McCarthy, telling him about the hostile Indians. The Pawnees rushed out of the woods firing their guns in the air and war-whooping. As they appeared, the scout asked the Englishman casually, "Shall we run or fight?" McCarthy's response was instant flight. He turned his horse around and raced back to the camp, losing his gun and dropping his hat. Since he would be certain to report that the Indians had attacked him, Cody followed and explained to the commanding officer that it was all a practical joke on the Englishman. The officer saw the humor of it.

Buffalo Bill also told of another British gentleman—one whom he greatly admired —who insisted on paying all checks, all the bills for everybody. Cody described him as a fine sportsman and a splendid shot. When the party ran out of liquor during the hunt, they rode thirty miles to the nearest saloon. When the Briton inquired the price of the tavern, he was told it could be purchased for five hundred dollars. He thereupon bought it—the house, the bar, the stock of wine and spirits, everything—and presented it to the man he had brought along on the party as the official bartender. That was the kind of grandiose gesture that Buffalo Bill enjoyed, and the kind he often made himself later on when he was in the big money.

Buffalo Bill's growing fame as a host to eastern dudes was not neglected in the press. Meanwhile, parallel to the reports from men of wealth and position, the first of Ned Buntline's Buffalo Bill books were becoming best sellers in popular paperbound form. More amazing than the dime novels, however, was Buffalo Bill's first royal guest, who came to America in 1872 when Cody was just twenty-six years of age. The royal guest set the final stamp of approval by the wealthy society of the East upon the young plainsman, and soon placed him on the register of New York's exclusive Union Club. The visitor was Grand Duke Alexis of Russia—a charming young man whose trip to the United States was inspired by the White House.

Late in the autumn of 1871 a squadron of the Russian Imperial Navy sent by Emperor Alexander II steamed into New York harbor. On board one of the warships was Grand Duke Alexis, the Emperor's third son, sent to pay his respects to the United States. After the American purchase of Alaska in 1867 relations with Russia had

THE GRAND DUKE ALEXIS OF RUSSIA at time he hunted buffalo in party conducted by Buffalo Bill.

soared to a high plane of felicity. Emperor Alexander II wished to reciprocate the tender regard of America for Russia which was reflected in many newspaper articles of the period. At the same time, Americans tried to outdo themselves in expressing their admiration for the Russian royal family. At a dinner for Alexis soon after his arrival in Washington, General Sheridan told the Grand Duke about the buffalo hunt with Cody. The Duke immediately expressed a desire to go to the plains and shoot these wonderful beasts under Buffalo Bill's tutelage.

Sheridan then had to go to Chicago to take charge of the city following the Great Fire. After that emergency duty he was notified by General Sherman to make preparations for the royal hunt to take place early in January. Army circles vibrated with excitement. Everybody wanted to get in on the expedition. Sheridan wired Major General Pope to find out at once where the bison would be likely to be spending the winter. He notified his staff, General Forsyth, Major W. H. Brown, Lieutenant Hayes, to go the limit on expenses to procure the best food and the best cook. He appointed General Innis H. Palmer to take charge of the royal party and directed General E. O. C. Ord to furnish Palmer with all the supplies he might need. He officially requested Buffalo Bill to act as head scout, and invited Generals Custer and Fitzhugh to accompany the party. Dr. Asch was also informed that he would be the official surgeon.

As an added feature, Sheridan arranged for the famous Sioux warrior, Spotted Tail, to accompany the party with some of his tribal colleagues. This was a touch which Sheridan thought correctly would appeal to the Grand Duke and incidentally also flatter the Sioux chieftain, who might appreciate being included in such high royal society.

General Sheridan, accompanied by Cody, met the royal party at North Platte and conducted them to Denver, where a formal grand ball was planned. Sometime after midnight, when the ball was at its height, a telegram arrived. The musicians stopped playing while it was read. It announced that a buffalo herd had been spotted in Kit Carson County, Colorado. On Cody's advice Sheridan had alerted some of his best army scouts with instruc-tions to wire him at once when the bison were sighted. The ball broke up as suddenly as the one in Brussels had ended the night before the Battle of Waterloo. The hunting party, in full dress, rushed to the special train which had been held in readiness. At the last moment one of the musicians, violinist Chalkley Beeson, lay down his fiddle, followed the hunters, and got aboard the train.

Neither the musician nor Sheridan joined in the action of the hunt itself. Watching from a nearby hill, Beeson noticed a young calf had left the herd, staggering away wounded toward where Sheridan was standing. "Catch him by the tail," the General ordered Beeson, "and I'll put him out of his misery." The violinist did so while the breathless little general shot the animal with his pistol.

Years later Beeson headed a cowboy band in Chicago and attended a dinner at which Sheridan described the royal hunt. "I was on that hunt," Beeson remarked audibly.

Annoyed at the interruption, Sheridan glared at the musician. "I don't remember you," he said.

"You should," Beeson retorted loudly. "I'm the man who held the buffalo by the tail while you shot it!"

The eyes of the nation were on the hunt. Headlines announced on January 14, 1872, that Sheridan had officially informed Secretary of War Belknap, "The Grand Duke killed his first buffalo today in a manner which elicited the admiration of the party with me." When the buffalo fell, the Duke stopped his horse, let out a whoop, and waved his hat. This was a signal to his suite to open a large basket filled with bottles of champagne. Everybody obligingly and with proper courtesy drank a toast to the great hunter.

Buffalo Bill was noticeably uneasy about the presence of Spotted Tail, who was one of Sitting Bull's best warriors and later a leader in the massacre of Custer and his men at the Battle of the Little Big Horn. The scout was doubtful about the wisdom of permitting the Indian to carry a loaded rifle, because, as he said, he didn't know for certain in which direction the warrior might shoot. He thought Spotted Tail would probably observe with dignity the amenities of a guest, but feared lest some of the other warriors might recall old grudges and forget the proper courtesies.

Buffalo Bill loaned Buckskin Joe to the Grand Duke for the occasion and also let him use his old gun, Lucretia Borgia. First the Duke tried to hit a buffalo with his pistol, but with no success. He then raised Lucretia; Cody flicked Buckskin Joe sharply with his whip. The horse galloped into the herd. The scout shouted to the Duke to shoot; he did so and his first bison fell. The champagne ritual lasted so long after each foray that it took the Grand Duke three days to kill eight buffalo. The Duke wanted to see how the Indians brought down bison with their bows and arrows. Spotted Tail and Buffalo Bill arranged an exhibition. An Indian named Two Lance drove an arrow clean through the body of a bull, then ceremoniously presented the arrow to Alexis as a souvenir.

After the hunt Buffalo Bill demonstrated to the Duke his accomplishments as a stage driver. The only available vehicle was an old-fashioned Irish dogcart. It was drawn by four spirited cavalry horses. With Sheridan and Alexis as his passengers, Cody held the reins as they raced across the prairie. Sheridan wanted more excitement. "Shake 'em up a little, Bill," he said.

The scout cracked the whip, the horses responded, and they flew over the ground toward a steep hill. The four horses leaped down the hill. Buffalo Bill could not hold them back. The dogcart, which had no brakes, bounced from side to side while the General and the Grand Duke held the sides of their seats, pretending to enjoy themselves.

Later, safely at North Platte, the Russian prince invited his colorful stage driver into his private car, and offered him a wad of bills, but Cody said he could not accept the money. The Duke then handed him a small jeweled box. He also gave the scout a magnificent fur coat, which he accepted. When Alexis reached New York he arranged with a jeweler to have made to order for Buffalo Bill a set of cuff links and a scarf pin. The pin was studded with diamonds and rubies in the form of a buffalo head. Buffalo Bill wore these on special occasions for years.

Alexis asked Sheridan what he could give Spotted Tail as a present. The Gen-

GENERAL GEORGE A. CUSTER, left, joins party of GRAND DUKE ALEXIS, right, in famous buffalo hunt.

eral told him it was not necessary to give the Indian anything expensive—a couple of red blankets would be sufficient. Before the Duke left, the Sioux staged a ceremonial war dance and a sham duel. General Sheridan offered Cody a commission in the Army in recognition of his services on the hunt, but the scout declined, declaring he preferred to remain on the plains. There were no more hunting parties at that time, however, and Cody soon began to worry about a job. Happily, it was at this moment that Commodore Bennett and his Union Club friends sent Cody a second urgent invitation to visit them in New York.

Possibly the most fascinated reader of the newspaper accounts of the battle of Summit Springs was a dime-novel writer, E. Z. C. Judson, who wrote under the name of Ned Buntline. In spite of an incredibly adventurous career in the Civil War, at sea, and many romantic entanglements in both glamorous and sordid surroundings, Buntline had run out of material for paperback fiction. If ever a man lived by his wits, Buntline did. Always broke, always in trouble, constantly in and out of jail and matrimony, adept at almost anything including inciting to riots, he felt the need in 1869 for fresh adventures which he could process quickly into lurid fiction. Most of the reports of the victory over Tall Bull gave much of the credit to the Norths, Frank and Lute. Here, thought Buntline, were two characters made to order for the kind of story he wrote.

When Buntline found Frank North, however, the leader of the Pawnee Scouts was not interested in becoming a fictional hero. Buntline talked to him at Fort McPherson, explaining his need for such a hero. North seemed amused, and pointed to Buffalo Bill asleep under a wagon. "There's the man you're looking for," he said, probably imagining that he was thereby playing a joke on his old friend. Buntline went over and woke the 23-year-old scout.

By his extraordinary creative talent for transfiguration, the writer made Buffalo Bill famous almost overnight with a story in Street and Smith's *New York Weekly* entitled, "Buffalo Bill, The King of the Border Men," published in December 1869. He subtitled it, "The Wildest, Truest, Story I ever Wrote." It was a terrific success, apparently just what the public had been waiting for. It fastened indelibly in the minds of millions the image of Buffalo Bill. And it was only the first of many romances in which Cody was glorified. Three followed immediately: "Buffalo Bill's Best Shot, or the Heart of Spotted Tail," "Buffalo Bill's Last Victory, or Dove Eye, The Lodge Queen," and "Hazel Eye, the Girl Trapper."

On his way to New York in 1872, Buffalo Bill stopped in Chicago, where none other than Colonel Michael V. Sheridan entertained him. One of the first things the Colonel did was to take the handsome scout to Marshall Field's for a complete outfit, including a new dress suit. When Cody saw himself in it his impulse was to get his hair cut; he felt conspicuous with his long light brown hair spread over his shoulders. General Sheridan wouldn't hear of such a thing. Instead, he suggested a silk hat. Buffalo Bill thereupon announced that he would go to the party being given for him in Chicago in a western-style Stetson or not at all. He went, but after one dance the Beau Brummel of the plains decided such affairs were not for him. He escaped from the ballroom to the bar, where he remained comfortably for the rest of the evening.

J. G. Heckscher and Schuyler Crosy met Cody at the station in New York. They took him to the Union Club, which was then on Fifth Avenue at fashionable Twentieth Street. They disapproved of his Chicago clothes, and insisted that he go with them to Heckscher's New York tailor. His first night in town they took him to the theater to see *The Black Crook.*

Buntline, meanwhile, was in New York delivering his famous temperance lecture between drinks. Although Cody's Union Club friends tried to monopolize him, he escaped from them long enough to go to Niblo's Garden with Buntline to see the dramatization of the dime novelist's story. It was called *Buffalo Bill.* Cody was impersonated by J. B. Studley, a popular and versatile actor whose recent big hits had been *A Dream of Destiny, Money and Misery, The Irish Outlaw,* and other melodramas, in which he appeared almost continuously at Niblo's, the Bowery Theater, Hooley's, or the Olympic in Brooklyn.

The dramatic critic of the New York *Herald* described the drama of Buffalo Bill as rewritten for the stage by F. G. Meader: "J. B. Studley played his part to perfection. The laudable desire he exhibits to avenge the murder of his paternal ancestor and the coolness he displays when encompassed by dangers and difficulties is superb. Rounds of applause greeted him when, finding himself surrounded by Indians, he slipped like a snake into a hollow log; which log the redskins presently added as fuel to the campfire; but the trapper soon found it grew uncomfortably hot, so he threw his powder horn into the fire. There was a grand explosion and the Indians went yelling skyward, while the hero escaped unscathed.

"This, as might be expected, was warmly applauded by the 'gods,' but the highest pitch of excitement was reached in the third act when Jack McKandkess, a noted border ruffian, meets Buffalo Bill and a terrific hand-to-hand conflict with Bowie knives three feet long ensues. The audience were spellbound, breathless, during this fierce encounter; but when it was brought to a conclusion by the death of the villain and the victory of Buffalo Bill, the burst of enthusiasm that followed would have rivaled the roar of Niagara."

This masterpiece ran for four weeks and then was frequently revived in Studley's customary repertoire. New York newspapers carried notices of it for the next two years.

What might have been in Buffalo Bill's mind as he saw himself portrayed on the stage? It must at first have seemed like an

90　　　　　　　　　BUFFALO BILL VISITS NEW YORK, BUYS FINE CLOTHES.

incredible nightmare that such a distorted version of his life should be the subject of a play and that such a drama would appeal to New York audiences. He had seen in print the first of the romances which Ned Buntline had concocted about him. He could hardly visualize what effect this dime novel—and others which he knew were to follow—would have upon him, his career, or his fortune, but he had fervent hopes that such stories would aid him financially. He needed such help badly. Not only did he have a wife and daughter to support; he now also had a son, Kit Carson Cody, born in November 1870.

Ever since he had guided those fashionable hunting parties he had been a man waiting for a miracle; and this trip to New York seemed to be such a miracle. It was incredible enough to see himself the hero of a printed book; to see himself dramatized as an unbeatable hero on the stage was even more astonishing.

Whatever his contemporaries may have said about Buffalo Bill, all agreed that he was intensely practical—not about saving his money, but about getting ahead, about getting out of predicaments. A man had to be practical and realistic to survive in the frontier world. Money was not easy to earn, but men all about him were trying, by get-rich-quick schemes, by gold prospecting, by land speculation, to make money easily. It was a part of the western tradition, and very much a characteristic of Cody, to spend money recklessly. But he always had an eye for the main chance, and a new faith that opportunity would turn up on the other side of the next hill.

In the civilization in which Buffalo Bill grew up to the age of twenty-six a man did what he could, whatever was handy, whatever offered itself, and he made the most of his opportunities. That is what Will Cody had done, from job to job, from bullwhacking to scouting, selling his skills in a competitive market. He had learned that there were some things, such as the drudgery of hotelkeeping, for which he seemed to have no aptitude. His dreams, ambitions, the things he liked to do, lay upon the prairies and the Rocky Mountains. His career must be in an outdoor setting. Yet civilization, eastern civilization, was devouring the world he had known. Scouting, hunting, trapping did not seem to promise as big a future as they had when he was a boy.

Now, in 1872, he was suddenly transported to cities, to the East of the Gilded Age, to the New York of Jim Fisk and Boss Tweed, to the world of Barnum and Broadway. Most amazing, most miraculous of all, here was he, Will Cody, now glorified as Buffalo Bill, in the very center of this theatrical world. It was a kind of magic, the kind of experience the young frontiersman had never seen or imagined—but, and in this he was only human, he enjoyed the "spotlight." Nothing, it would seem, could be farther from his tastes or talents, for here was a universe of intangibles. Everything suddenly became a fantasy, created by the imagination and not by nature.

William F. Cody had always displayed fertile imagination. He could take a simple story and turn it into a wild adventure. Never before, however, had it occurred to him that the world of imagination could be exploited in such a fashion as this, or that he, as a character and a personality, could be exploited. The dudes had opened to him a world of wealth and splendor, of luxury and pleasure, a whole society in which nobody ever seemed to worry about money. Naturally he longed to enter such a world and become a part of it.

Mysteriously and miraculously Ned Buntline presented him with the key that would open the magic doors. How he could use this key he did not immediately grasp. But Buffalo Bill was perceptive enough to realize that if Buntline could exploit him, then there must be some way in which he could exploit himself. He was being led along a strange trail; it behooved him to study this new trail thoroughly. If other people could make money pretending they were Buffalo Bill before a paying audience, then perhaps he could make money by being himself.

The idea of going on the stage at first repelled him. When the spotlight was turned on him at the Bowery Theater he was becomingly shy, yet he kept his nerve and tried to make a short speech. He couldn't imagine himself, just then, behind the footlights, play-acting to a theater full of people staring at him, waiting for him to make a fool of himself. His first reaction was to reject such a possibility, to refuse to try to become an actor. Yet he was of-

fered five hundred dollars a week by the manager of the Bowery Theater, the most he had ever made in a month shooting buffalo for the railroad workers.

The transformation of the frontiersman into an actor was at first painful. It took him several years, although the revolution in his personality and the change in his career *seemed* to happen almost overnight. The first step occurred that night when Buntline took him to the Bowery Theater, for then it entered his mind for the first time that such a step was possible for him. It took longer for him to become aware that he had been playing a romantic role from boyhood, a role that he would improve upon the rest of his life. He was a born actor, capable of playing only one part: Buffalo Bill.

That whole six-week visit to New York early in 1872 had the quality of a dream —a confusing experience because of the many ideas and sensations which overwhelmed him. It was his nature to do whatever his generous hosts suggested, particularly when it seemed glamorous. It was also his nature to live up to others' expectations. He quickly sensed what was expected of him, what kind of character his admirers imagined he was, and instinctively he played that role. He played it for all he was worth while the dudes clamored for the privilege of escorting him in New York society and introduced him to their friends. He knew how to adapt himself quickly to new and strange situations, whether it was an attack by Indians on the prairie or the flattery of New York society.

92

JAMES GORDON BENNETT, II.

Moreover, Buffalo Bill sensed that one of his attributes was that he had never hesitated at any time to accept a challenge. He was always ready to take a chance on a horse race, a shooting match, or a roulette wheel. If the chance offered danger or risk, he was all the more eager. He would gamble on anything, and it was in the spirit of a great gamble that he finally went on the stage.

When the spotlight was turned on him at the theater during the intermission of the performance of *Buffalo Bill,* the audience suddenly realized that here in the flesh was the real man whose adventures they had just witnessed on the stage. The whole crowd immediately rose and cheered. Instantly Cody sensed his whole future career. The same thought occurred to Ned Buntline. In fact, that great rascal had already planned to get Cody onto the stage.

During the highly publicized New York visit Buffalo Bill's fame spread throughout the nation. Not only Bennett's New York *Herald* but other newspapers also found out what good copy he made. When Commodore Bennett took him to the theater, the audience rose to give Buffalo Bill an ovation. When August Belmont gave him a sumptuous dinner, Cody remarked, "I see you are determined that I shall not run short of rations while I am in New York." When he was late for another dinner, which James Gordon Bennett had planned for him, Buffalo Bill explained his confusion about the time by saying he "had got lost and gone out on a scout." These were anecdotes that were to be repeated by all the social gossips of the period. This fellow Cody was a "natural," the lion of the season.

As a climax to his visit, a masked ball was held at the Academy of Music. A pageant in his honor featured a team of Russian bears dragging an enormous snowball into the hall. The cotton snowball opened majestically and a gentleman dressed to represent the Grand Duke Alexis stepped out. Buffalo Bill gave the simulated Duke a greeting of warm recognition and the two embraced. Here was another big story for the New York papers. Everyone in fashionable society who missed that event regretted it for many social seasons.

Before Cody left the city Buntline arranged a reception at which a long-range rifle was presented to Buffalo Bill. To the delight of the reporters he remarked that this rifle would shoot so far that he would have to load it with rock salt or else the meat of the slain animal would spoil before he could get to it. Another story relates how he invited his wealthy friends to dinner at Delmonico's. He thought that fifty dollars would cover the bill. It was a great joke as well as a source of embarrassment when he found out what a short way fifty dollars would go in New York, even in the 'seventies. He was quoted as saying he could have gotten a dinner like that at home for the price of a bullet.

During this visit East, Buffalo Bill went to see a relative of his mother, Colonel Henry R. Guss, who lived in West Chester, Pennsylvania. He took his friend Buntline with him. The accounts they gave of the excursion are not very reliable, but Cody's story has the charm of a Mark Twain yarn, for he tells with relish of his predicament at riding to foxhounds. He saw the humor of the situation, made fun of himself, "promoted" his kinsman to the rank of general and all the neighbors to the hunting gentry. It is clear that his equestrian fame had preceded him and that he appreciated in full the irony as well as the drama of the role he played as a "hossy" character and hero from the plains, riding in a scarlet coat to hounds in pursuit of a "varmint" fox.

While Buffalo Bill was in Pennsylvania, General Sheridan wired him to return for more scouting of hostile Indians. Before his departure, Cody promised Buntline to meet him in Chicago the following fall and to appear with him in a stage show. He would bring some real live Indians with him, and Buntline was to have the play ready for rehearsal.

Chapter 7

Buffalo Bill Behind the Footlights

STORIES of Buffalo Bill's high life in New York spread across the prairies to his old friends in the West. By arrangement, a party of "old pards" met him at Omaha with the intention of entertaining him, and having him entertain them, while he waited half a day for the train for North Platte. They had heard about his evening dress clothes and insisted on seeing them. Glad to oblige his old companions, Cody went to the Paxton Hotel with his baggage and put on his formal evening attire. The transformation was so astonishing that it called for another round of drinks, following the initial whiskey to celebrate his arrival.

By the time Cody was ready for his display the party had increased to fifty friends. After the sartorial exhibition and toasts, they put Cody on the train for the frontier, but no one remembered to bring the scout's trunks and suitcases from the hotel. Consequently, after the farewells at Omaha, Buffalo Bill sped over the plains in the

THE POSTER THAT BROUGHT THE CROWDS.

train, wearing his tailcoat and his new silk top hat. With his long hair tucked under the hat, he would have been elegant on Fifth Avenue after dark, but was not suitably turned out for the Indian fighting that awaited him at the end of his journey.

One of his oldest friends, a scout known as "Buffalo Chips" White (who was later killed while scouting for General Crook), awaited Cody at Fort McPherson with his horse, Buckskin Joe, ready to join General Reynolds and his command just beyond the fort. "Buffalo Chips" was astonished and almost angered by Cody's costume, but he was quieted by the bottles of champagne Bill had brought along from the Omaha send-off. As the bottles were passed around among the other welcomers, the more comical Buffalo Bill appeared, especially when he sat astride his horse popping corks and pouring wine like an eastern dude.

Buffalo Chips, doubtful about the reception his formally clad friend would receive at the camp, followed him to General Reynolds' headquarters.

"Who in thunder are you?" demanded the General.

Cody took off his silk hat and let down his hair with a graceful bow. The effect was almost as comical as the display he had made in Omaha, save that there was no more champagne. Derision soon turned to affectionate ribaldry. Texas Jack Omohundro and the other scouts were actually delighted to see Buffalo Bill in his full eastern glory. They soon found an old buckskin suit for him and a Stetson hat. Better

yet, they also found his gun, faithful Lucretia Borgia. Seated once more on his horse in a western outfit, Buffalo Bill was at last happily at home on the plains again.

"Texas Jack," a familiar name for cowboys then and since (many cowboys in the old days did not reveal their last names because they feared they might be posted by a sheriff under the heading, "Wanted"), actually was from Texas. Six feet tall, with the long hair customary to his profession, he carried several tattered Indian scalps on his belt to prove his prowess as a scout. According to the dime novels, Buffalo Bill met Texas Jack during the Civil War, but it is more likely that they met at a bar several years after the war when they were scouts together on the frontier. Texas Jack enjoyed a reputation for hospitality, and often bought a drink for all present when he entered the door of a saloon because, as he said, somebody might be insulted if he didn't.

The two scouts were sent ahead by General Reynolds to find a party of Indians that had been making trouble. Cody guided a small detachment toward the Indian camp, getting within fifty yards before he was discovered. He quickly pursued six mounted Indians fleeing down the river and captured two of their horses.

In Buffalo Bill's later account he said he rode Buckskin Joe into the Indian camp and charged upon the warriors, who tried to run to their horses on the other side of a creek. There was a brief pitched battle, during which an Indian was killed and Buffalo Bill suffered a head wound, the

BUNTLINE, BUFFALO BILL, AND TEXAS JACK AS THEY
APPEARED IN THEIR FIRST STAGE SHOW AT CHICAGO.

only time on record that he was ever wounded, at least while he was attached to the Army. They captured 250 Indians. It was in this minor skirmish that Buffalo Bill showed such bravery that he was recommended for a Congressional Medal of Honor—in those days a less rare decoration than it has since become.

After this battle there was little for Cody or any of the scouts to do. Although Cody was notified he had been elected to the Nebraska legislature, he had no intention of taking his seat. He accepted the honor as a compliment, and as justification for using "Hon." before his name, rather than as an opportunity to enter active politics. He dallied with the idea of running for the U.S. Senate or for Governor, but something much more lucrative was in the offing.

Meanwhile, Ned Buntline wrote him regularly, reminding him of the theatrical engagement in Chicago. Cody was reluctant; but Texas Jack persuaded him, and a compact of "I'll go if you'll go with me" was agreed upon. When Cody reached Chicago he was reminded that he had forgotten all about his promise to bring Indians with him. Instead he had brought Texas Jack, on whom he relied for sympathy and support in his first scheduled venture behind the footlights.

The improvident Buntline had earned his way to Chicago as a salesman for a fire-insurance company. On his arrival he told Jim Nixon, the manager of the theater, that two genuine scouts and twenty Indians were on their way. When the scouts arrived without Indians, Nixon was furious.

No matter how bad the show might be— and he had small expectations that it would be a hit—Nixon believed that Chicagoans would pay to see real Indians on the stage.

Ned Buntline assured him that they could hire ten down-and-out actors from the part of the city known as Blue Island, dress them in tan-colored costumes, and nobody would know that they were not true Indians. Doubtful of this, Nixon asked to see the script.

"I haven't written it yet," Buntline confessed.

"But this is Thursday. The opening is Monday!" Nixon canceled the contract on the spot.

Then, as Buntline later told the story, he asked Nixon, "How much rent do you want for your theater next week?"

"Six hundred dollars."

Ned recalled that he thereupon counted out the dollar bills. It is unlikely that Buntline ever had six hundred dollars in cash in his life before he met Buffalo Bill, and the chances are that he persuaded Cody and Texas Jack to back their own show.

However it may have been arranged, Buntline took Buffalo Bill and Texas Jack to a cheap hotel room, where he started to write the play. He boasted that he wrote the show in four hours. What he did was to reproduce from memory as much of Fred Meader's drama, *Buffalo Bill,* as he could,

ITALIAN-BORN MLLE. MORLACCHI, who had a weakness for scouts in "Scouts of the Prairie," later married to Texas Jack.

99

except that he added another character, Cale Durg, to be played by himself. He called the opus *Scouts of the Plains*.

He hired an obscure Italian actress, known as Mlle. Morlacchi, to play the only feminine role, that of Dove Eye, the Indian maiden. The Chicago *Tribune* reported that she had "an Italian accent and a weakness for scouts."

The opening, December 16, 1878, was a sellout, grossing $2,800. As the curtain rose the three scouts—Buffalo Bill, Texas Jack, and Buntline—dressed in fringed buckskins, were discovered standing somewhat uneasily behind the footlights.

The first line was to be spoken by Buffalo Bill. But the seasoned scout, loquacious among his friends, now stared out into space in frozen silence. For the first and probably the last time in his life he was tongue-tied. He had told his friends several days previously that it would take him seven years, with good luck, to memorize his part. Now he couldn't remember a word of it. The three intrepid cavaliers of the prairie stood helpless.

Buntline suddenly rose to the emergency. He recalled that a man named Milligan, who had recently been guided by Cody, was in the audience. "You've been off buffalo hunting with Milligan, haven't you?" he inquired of Buffalo Bill.

Cody, prompted to be himself, began to comprehend where he was and what was expected of him. The script disappeared from his consciousness. But the question made sense. He started an informal description of the buffalo hunt with Milligan. The play was composed anew, ad lib, on the stage, as they went along. The audience perceived that this was real scout talk.

Without knowing it, the actors were creating a new formula, a new style in entertainment, that years later reached its peak in the cowboy monologues of Will Rogers.

Having no further worry about the lines written for him, Buffalo Bill talked naturally about hunting and scouting. Encouraged, Texas Jack slowly recovered from his stage fright, dimly understood what was expected, and helped Buntline to feed the novice star new cue lines, mainly questions, to keep him talking.

As Buntline saw his hastily written dialogue lost forever, he was at his wit's end how to bring the curtain down on the first act. Finally he signaled into the wings for the phony Indians. They came in screeching, looking like badly made-up tramps from the railway yards. Following their mentor's example, Buffalo Bill and Texas Jack seized their guns and pretended to shoot the hostiles. One by one the stage Indians went down, to the very last man. Never was there a show like this. As can happen in the theater, a play intended to be serious was taken as a rollicking comedy. What the audience beheld was an adolescent's fantastic dream of the Wild West.

In the second act a half-hearted attempt was made to revive the plot. One critic said it was "a three-cornered fight between the scouts, the Indians, and some characters

Riverside City College Library
Riverside, California

HE-NU-KAW. (The first born.)

to do they leaped at one another and yelled. Coached by Buntline, they tied the author-villain to a stage tree with the evident notion of burning him alive. The audience cried with delight. Before his demise, however, Ned Buntline thought the element of suspense could be enhanced by the technique of delay, so he launched into one of his interminable temperance speeches. Thereupon the audience demanded that he be promptly conflagrated. As the torch was applied the second curtain came down amid riotous applause.

The third act was a rehash of the first and second, with resurrected Indians and constant shooting. Encouraged by shouts from the audience, which threatened to join in the battle at any time, the actors found lariats which had been overlooked before, and lassoed each other. Cale Durg died again, to the delight of the spectators, who felt he couldn't die too often. For weeks afterward it was said that dazed playgoers would shout, "The Indians are upon us!" and explode in maniacal laughter.

The Chicago *Tribune* critic reported next day that Buffalo Bill "speaks his lines after the diffident manner of a schoolboy, fidgeting uneasily when silent, and when in dialogue, poking out the right hand and then the left at regular intervals."

The extemporaneous composition performed before their eyes drove all the drama critics frantic for words to describe their disapproval. They had never seen anything so awful by theatrical standards. It was unbelievable—and yet there it was,

supposed to be whites" led by the lugubrious Cale Durg, "a human nightmare who managed to keep drunk for several hours without a drop of anything." Bits and pieces of the speeches came back to them. Incoherently they addressed the dew, the clouds, and decried the baseness of the white man.

When the actors did not know what else

POSTER FEATURING FEMININE LEAD.

101

a hit! The incredible lines went over triumphantly with the audience.

The Chicago *Times* reporter wrote, "It is not probable Chicago will look on the like again. Such a combination of incongruous dialogue, execrable acting, renowned performers, mixed audience, intolerable stench, scalping, blood and thunder, is not likely to be vouchsafed to a city for a second time—even Chicago."

The tireless Buntline promoted the show to capacity with special matinees for the ladies, at which photographs of Buffalo Bill, Texas Jack, and himself were autographed. He sensed that he had a matinee idol on his hands but was uncertain how to make the most of such good fortune. Through this preposterous extravaganza Buffalo Bill was learning a number of things that were invaluable to him when he later staged his Wild West Shows. He acquired some ideas about what audiences wanted, what they would take, how to put a show over. Chicago would have patronized the show for weeks, but Nixon wanted his theater back; so the troupe moved on.

December 23, 1872, was a bitterly cold night, but the St. Louis Grand Opera House was packed. Louisa Cody came with her family to see the show which, of course, was never quite the same on two consecutive nights. The more the actors extemporized, the better the audiences liked it. Buffalo Bill suddenly saw Louisa in the third row. Struck with honest remorse at the spectacle he was making of himself, he called out, "Oh, Mama, I'm a bad actor!" That brought the house down. The crowd cheered and yelled their agreement—and they loved him for it.

No critic knew quite what to make of it all. Newspapermen speculated how long the show's composition had required and, when told, wondered how it could have taken so long. One critic declared, "Buffalo Bill is a beautiful blonde, and wears the Alexis diamond in his shirt, whose fastenings are in the rear." Those who saw *Scouts of the Plains* never forgot it, or forgot Buffalo Bill.

A few days after the opening in St. Louis, Buntline was arrested, not for the dramatic crime then playing to packed houses, but for jumping bail many years before. The play's cash receipts were attached, but the wily rascal worked his way out of this predicament by changing the title of the play to *Scouts of the Prairie*, protecting himself legally by a fictitious new title, ownership, and management, and continued his tour.

At Cincinnati one of the actors died from injuries received during a performance. No explanation was ever made of this casualty. The troupe went on to Albany and Boston, in the East, where Buntline talked grandiloquently of staging the whole affair on horseback with perhaps a hundred extras, including more and genuine Indians.

Finally the *Scouts of the Prairie* reached Niblo's Garden in New York. The *Herald* reported: "Buntline represented the part of Cale Durg as badly as possible for any human being to represent it. The Hon. William F. Cody, otherwise known as Buffalo Bill, occasionally called by the refined people of the eastern cities 'Bison William,'

RITTEN EXPRESSLY FOR W.F. CODY (BUFFALO BILL) BY MAJ. A.S. BURT, U.S.A.

is a good-looking fellow, tall and straight as an arrow, but ridiculous as an actor. Texas Jack is not quite so good-looking, not so tall, not so straight and not so ridiculous. Ned Buntline is simply maundering imbecility. The applause savored of derision and the derision of applause. Everything was so wonderfully bad it was almost good. The whole performance was so far aside of human experience, so wonderful in its daring feebleness, that no ordinary intellect is capable of comprehending it."

The writer for the New York *World* had a flash of prescience. "As drama it is very poor slop," he wrote, "but as an exhibition of three remarkable men it is not without interest. The Hon. W. F. Cody enters into the spectacle with a curious grace and a certain characteristic charm that pleases the beholders. He is a remarkably handsome fellow on the stage, and the lithe, springy step, the round western voice, the utter absence of anything like stage art, won for him the good will of an audience

POSTER FOR ONE OF BUFFALO BILL'S GREATEST STAGE SUCCESSES.

that was disposed to laugh at all that was intended to be pathetic and serious."

It was apparent that Buntline was not the man to manage Buffalo Bill, to guide him in his stage career, and to exploit to the best his real talents and potentialities. Cody was aware of this, and was disappointed that his small part of the tour's savings came to only six thousand dollars.

The impresario who sensed the potentialities of Buffalo Bill as a hero portraying himself, without benefit of a concocted dramatic plot, appeared miraculously from a stock-company theater. John M. Burke saw Cody, and idolized him for the rest of his days. Burke had the imagination to see the place that Buffalo Bill should occupy in show business. He dreamed of the Wild West Show in a grand style, and he lived to be an indispensable element in attaining those dreams. Near the end of his life Burke wrote in *Billboard* about his first meeting with Cody:

"For once realization excelled anticipation. Physically superb, trained to the limit, in the zenith of his manhood, features cast in nature's most perfect mold, on a prancing charger that was foaming and chaffing at the bit, and in his most picturesque beaded buckskin garb, he was indeed a picture.

"When he dismounted I was introduced to the finest specimen of God's handiwork I had ever seen, and felt that for once there was that nearest approach to an ideal human, a visual interpretation given to the assertion that man was indeed a replica of His Maker."

The quotation indicates the devotion with which Burke served Buffalo Bill as partner, friend, manager, and press agent for forty years. Not even Nate Salsbury, who became a partner in the Wild West Show at a critical period and contributed to its vast financial success, did more to create and establish the imperishable legend of the great scout and showman as an embodiment of the frontier.

"Arizona John" Burke had started as a character actor in repertoire theaters. Born in the District of Columbia, he was known as "Arizona John," though he had never seen Arizona. He had done everything in the theater. When he could not get a job on the stage he worked occasionally on newspapers, the best preparation possible for a potential press agent. He ultimately came to know every important newspaperman of his time by his first name. Burke not only admired Buffalo Bill, but he was drawn to the show by Mlle. Morlacchi. However, the Italian actress spurned the rotund, homely Arizona John and married handsome Texas Jack.

Buffalo Bill and Burke agreed on the elements that promised success in show business. They sensed the need for stars, and decided that if they couldn't sign the big names they would develop obscure characters and make them famous. Cody followed that principle in his first season on his own. In place of Buntline he persuaded Wild Bill Hickok, whose newspaper fame matched his own, to join the *Scouts of the Prairie*.

Hickok had already experimented disastrously with an early Wild West Show in a fashion that taught Buffalo Bill an important lesson. Hickok dreamed up a show with Indians and wild buffalo. Securing co-operative Indians was not too difficult, but capturing wild buffalo was a much more perplexing problem. Hickok accomplished this, however, and then transported the animals to Niagara Falls, where his show was to open in the spring of 1870. The enterprise failed spectacularly because he had not solved the logistics of presenting the show outdoors and charging admission. Getting the buffalo into the Hickok arena at Buffalo, near Niagara, almost started a riot. The beasts got away from the Indians, who chased them through the streets while noisy dogs and youngsters followed in high glee. As if that was not tribulation enough, a grizzly bear which Hickok had caged for a sideshow also got loose from the railroad car, sniffed some hot dogs and rushed for them. The audience saw the accidental buffalo hunt for nothing. Wild Bill had to sell the buffalo —which were eventually herded into a dead-end street—to raise train fare to get himself and his Indians back to the plains.

Wild Bill was not reliable as a dramatic trouper. Unable to resist a practical joke, he would fire his pistol at close range at the legs of the extras in order to see them jump. The supers, needless to say, objected to this coy persecution. When Hickok was in an impish mood he prolonged the play with such exercises. Apprehensive of the plainsman's whims, the supers kept jumping and dancing, and refused to lie down and die at the point in the script which called for their demise.

At one performance, while the scouts sat around the campfire telling stories and passing a whiskey bottle around, Wild Bill rebelled at the cold tea in the bottle. He took a swig, threw the bottle away, and shouted, "You think I'm the worst fool east of the Rockies. I can tell whiskey from cold tea. I can't tell my story unless I get real whiskey."

Although the audience thought this was amusing, such behavior had a demoralizing effect on the play and the cast. Buffalo Bill tried to induce Hickok to behave by supplying him with real whiskey. This tended to make Wild Bill Hickok amorous, however. He grew fonder of the heroine on the stage than was stipulated in the script.

When Wild Bill came to New York to join the show, Cody told him to meet him at the Brevoort Hotel, adding instructions for him to take a hansom cab from the station but on no account to pay more than two dollars for the ride. The driver demanded five dollars. Bill refused. The cabby looked over the Hickok finery: cutaway coat, flowered waistcoat, ruffled shirt, pepper-and-salt trousers, a string tie, high-heeled boots, broad-brimmed Stetson, his light brown hair falling becomingly over his shoulders.

"Give me five dollars, you backwoods dude, or I'll tan your hide for you."

These could have been the cabman's last words. Hickok simply picked him up and mopped the gutter of Lower Fifth

Avenue with him, as if he were a stable broom.

At the first New York performance the stagehand directing the spotlight thought it would be amusing to follow Bill with the light as he moved around the stage. Hickok endured this for a while, but when he discovered that the audience was delighted, he mistook their admiration for mirth. He hurled his pistol at the spotlight in the gallery and smashed it to pieces.

But the theater soon bored Hickok. Standing in the wings one night watching Texas Jack play a love scene with Mlle. Morlacchi, he asked, "Aren't they foolish? What's the sense in getting out there and making a show of yourself?" Soon after that he quit and disappeared. Because his name drew audiences, a rival producer used his name without his permission, billing an actor as "Wild Bill Hickok." The shooting, fighting marshal reappeared one night at the theater, jumped on the stage, and beat up the actor who was impersonating him.

Under Burke's astute management Buffalo Bill made money with this show, yet he still longed for the plains, the mountains, and the outdoor life. He was restless. He took time out to act as guide again for wealthy sportsmen. Yet he also knew that there was no longer a career for him in the role of hired escort for dudes. Nor was there any future in scouting; the Indian wars appeared to be over. Cody rightly deduced that if he was to make show business his principal employment, he would have to spend more time in the more thickly populated eastern states. So he moved his family—Mrs. Cody, his two daughters Arta and Orra, and his son Kit—to Rochester, New York. Louisa Cody liked the stability, respectability, and security of settled life,

BUFFALO BILL'S ONLY SON, little Kit Carson Cody, in Rochester, New York, just before he died.

107

and Rochester seemed to be the kind of place she preferred.

Since his theatrical season was prosperous, Cody set out to improve the company with the inclusion of real Indians. Everything went well until one night in April when a telegram was handed to him as he was about to go on stage in Springfield, Massachusetts, for the first act. It was from his wife, informing him that their son was seriously ill with scarlet fever. He must come at once. He called Burke, told him he would play the first act and then catch the train for Rochester. Burke stepped into the part and finished the performance.

Kit Carson Cody was a handsome child, with his father's eyes and hair, extremely sensitive, with an almost poetic look. Little Kit loved the stage. He enjoyed sitting in a box and watching the house fill with people. The moment the curtain rose and his father appeared, he would cry out, "Good house, Papa!" The audience was moved by this greeting, and so was the proud father. When Louisa Cody had curled his hair in long ringlets, the thirty-year-old father had insisted on cutting off the curls. This hair cut, Louisa said later, caused the chill which led to his last illness.

By the time Cody reached Rochester the delicate youngster was clinging desperately to life. The doctors said there was no hope. Buffalo Bill took the child in his arms and held him through the night. There Kit died. The child, not yet six years old, was buried in Mount Hope Cemetery in Rochester on April 24, 1876.

Kit's death was the great personal tragedy in Buffalo Bill's life. He loved all children, but above all his only son. He eventually spoiled his daughters with sentimental generosity, and he always liked to have children visit him in his tent when he was on tour.

Chapter **8**

The Duel with Yellow Hand

BROKEN-hearted over the death of his only son, Buffalo Bill resumed his tour with his show for only a few weeks before departing on the final and most widely publicized mission in his career as a scout—taking the first scalp in revenge for Custer's massacre.

The news was ominous. The Sioux in the North—in the Black Hills, and in what is now Wyoming and Montana—had never willingly submitted to the treaties of 1868. The Indians who had gone to the reservations usually forsook the prescribed areas in the summer. They were then pushed by the Army from place to place, retreating belligerently, seething with resentment, waiting for word from their wise and crafty chief, Sitting Bull, the medicine man who they believed knew what was best for his people.

A TYPICAL POSTER FOR A NEW DRAMA.

To complicate the problem, prospectors had found gold in the Black Hills, and Sitting Bull had declared that the Indians owned those hills and would never sell them. No offer could move him to change his mind. Settlers and miners went in anyway. When the Indians showed signs of hostility, the white population demanded protection by the U.S. Army.

A general Indian war was inevitable somewhere along the vital Powder River that to the Sioux represented sacred ground. General George Crook, a picturesque officer who parted his beard in the middle and braided the sideburns when he was on the march, commanded the troops in this area. He attempted vainly to follow the orders of General Sheridan to make war on the Indians in the winter, but frequent temperatures as low as sixty below zero made efficient operations impossible. Nevertheless, he sent Colonel J. J. Reynolds out to the Powder River. On March 17, Reynolds attacked an Indian village, suffered severe losses, and was forced to retreat while the Indians escaped.

General Crook ordered Reynolds court-martialed, and personally assumed command of the troops. Sheridan had told him to contain the Indians. Crook growled, "Let's see one soldier surround three Indians." The plan was to have General Terry, with Custer's Seventh Cavalry, circle around to the northeast, and attack from that direction. Another force, under General Gibbon, was to make a flanking movement around from the northwest, while General Crook was to drive on what

was thought to be the location of Sitting Bull's camp by marching up the Powder River.

The Sioux defeated the troops wherever their forces met them. All other Indian chiefs had been tacticians, fighting and running away; but Sitting Bull, a strategist, moved slowly. However, when the American generals exposed their men to attack, Sitting Bull's warriors under Crazy Horse cut them to pieces. Crook himself was badly beaten in the Battle of the Rosebud on June 17, 1876.

As Crook marched toward that disaster Buffalo Bill, then playing in Wilmington, was asked to join the army on the frontier —the word he had somehow expected providence to provide. Rushing onto the stage, he waved the telegram from General Sheridan's headquarters at the audience. "I'm through playing at war!" he shouted. "I'm going West to take part in it!"

It is well documented that the unhappy Cody, whose wife, despite her tendency to scold her husband, was in those days his capable costume designer and wardrobe mistress, was clad in an ornate black velvet and gold Mexican-cowboy type of uniform, ornamented with silver lace and buttons, and slashed with crimson, when he walked off the Wilmington stage, and that he was wearing the same theatrical uniform when he reached Cheyenne, Wyoming, four days later. Without stopping to change from his resplendent stage costume, which Louisa had made for gala performances, he took the first train West. He thought he would be sent to guide General Crook. Better than that, however, his orders were to proceed to Cheyenne and rejoin his old Fifth Cavalry outfit under General Carr, who had been recalled from Arizona.

Lieutenant Charles King, later a general and, happily for historians, also a meticulous memoirist, met him. As they

Buffalo Bill as he looked in the Mexican suit he wore on stage and at the famous duel with Yellow Hand.

walked into the army post many of the soldiers of the Fifth Cavalry greeted Cody with pride and warm feeling. "There's Buffalo Bill!" they shouted. General Carr heard them and came out of his headquarters to shake hands.

"Hey, Bill, where did you get that Spanish costume?" he asked. Cody was conspicuous, but no more bizarre than some of the other civilian scouts.

With Buffalo Bill in his old situation as chief scout of the regiment, they set out on June 22 to study the trails leading northward from the Red Cloud and Spotted Tail reservations. Spotted Tail had received the word from the chief that the Sioux and the Cheyennes were determined on open warfare, and the braves were responding enthusiastically to the call. Many were leaving to join Sitting Bull's forces.

General Carr had orders to prevent the Indian reinforcements from reaching Sitting Bull's headquarters, which were thought to be somewhere between the Yellowstone and the Big Horn Rivers. When he began his march, however, he did not know that the fighting Sioux had already met General Crook and driven him back. No news came to them from the other columns.

On June 25 Buffalo Bill found the trail along the valley of Mini Pusa, which is the South Fork of the Cheyenne River, sometimes called the Dry Fork. The Fifth Cavalry was following this trail when General Carr was recalled and General Wesley Merritt arrived to take command. He had orders to join General Crook. At the same

111

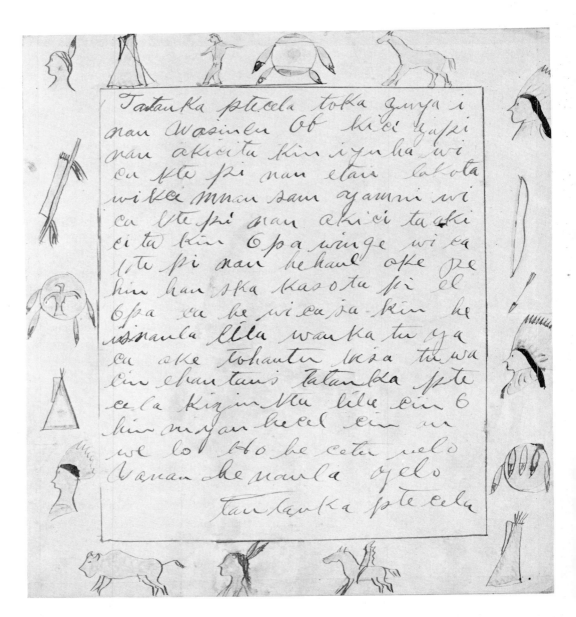

time, General Carr's orders stood. Apparently Merritt was expected to stop any Indians he found bound for Sitting Bull's forces, and simultaneously to go to the reinforcement of General Crook's troops.

Merritt sent out scouting parties in various directions. Some of them caught sight of Indians, but couldn't overtake them. This reconnaissance advertised the presence of the regiment to the Indians. They

112

Phonetic Sioux version of the Battle of the Little Big Horn.

camped at Sage Creek while Merritt sent couriers to Fort Laramie for further instructions.

On July 10 the word came to return to Fort Laramie, stock fully with field supplies, and then proceed by way of Fort Fettermen to join General Crook. At the same time Merritt learned from his scouts that the southern Cheyennes were about to go on the warpath to join Sitting Bull. His original orders, inherited from General Carr, were to stop any such movement. Should he go to the help of Crook or intercept the Cheyenne warriors?

Before he could move, the scouts brought him additional news. Eight hundred Cheyennes were leaving the reservation at Red Cloud the following morning. Merritt made his decision at once. Risking court-martial for disregarding orders, he told his fellow officers that General Crook could look after himself for the present. He must prevent the Cheyenne forces from joining the Sioux.

With the help of his staff he planned an ambush. Tracing their course on a map, he showed his officers where to cut the trail in advance of the Cheyennes. It would be necessary to march around two sides of a triangle, a long march of eighty-five miles.

Meanwhile word had reached them of the Custer massacre. The message read, "Custer and five troops, Seventh Cavalry, killed." They knew what it meant: Custer and all his men had been wiped out at the Battle of the Little Big Horn. The impetuous General Custer, in trouble with President Grant because he had helped expose

corruption in the War Department, ambitious to achieve quick fame for political purposes, had ignored all warnings and orders from his superior officers, and, eager for battle, had ridden into a trap prepared by Sitting Bull. Crazy Horse waited for Custer's regiment, slaughtered them to the last man. Only Custer's horse escaped.

When Merritt's men heard the news they vowed revenge on the Indians. Buffalo Bill rode ahead to catch the first sight of the enemy. A wagon train commanded by Lieutenant W. P. Hall performed the remarkable feat of keeping pace with the mounted troops. At 10 P.M. the regiment halted at Running Water after a march of thirty-five miles. Two hours later the wagon train rolled in. When the troops were aroused by the bugle at 3 A.M. they found a breakfast of fried mush, bacon, and coffee awaiting them before their start on the final fifty-mile dash. The column started at 1:30 P.M. on July 15 and its goal, the point at which the trail crossed War Bonnet Creek, was reached soon after 8 P.M. the next evening. This was the first of Merritt's celebrated lightning marches with the Fifth Cavalry.

Before daybreak on the morning of July 17, after the Fifth had bivouacked for the night at War Bonnet Creek (sometimes called Hat Creek), Lieutenant Charles King of Company K was detailed to establish an outpost toward the southeast, the direction from which the Cheyennes were expected. He took Buffalo Bill with him. As the first streaks of daylight began to appear they took their places on a little conical mound at the foot of a wave of prairie which descended gradually from the southeast. At the rear rose a line of bluffs which marked the tortuous course of the stream. King wrote later that from the southward not even an Indian eye could detect that close under those bluffs seven veteran companies of the Fifth Cavalry crouched, ready to spring. Corporal Wilkinson, who was also with King, was the first to sight the Indians along the ridge lying to the southeast at about 4:30 A.M. During the next half hour they saw half a dozen parties in that direction, at a distance of two or three miles. These Indians were apparently concentrating their attention upon something to the west, making no attempt to conceal themselves from the point at which the cavalry lay in ambush.

King immediately notified General Merritt, who arrived at 5:15 A.M. with a number of other officers. Cody had gone out to scout the Indian camp. Not far away, another eye-witness to the action, Chris

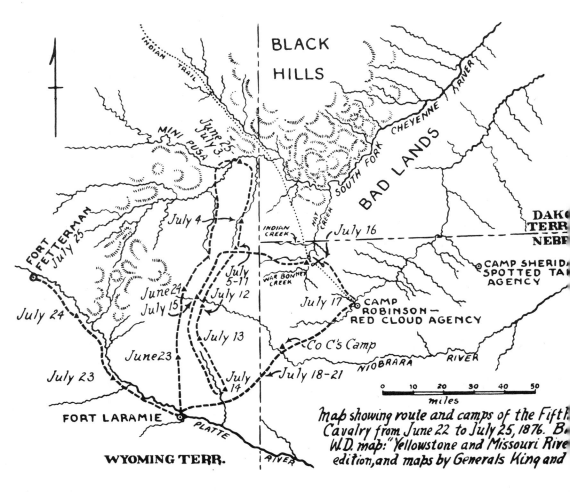

PLAN OF THE BATTLE AT WAR BONNET CREEK WHERE BUFFALO BILL MET YELLOW HAND.

114

The round hill from which Chief Scout Cody saw the Indians approaching, bluffs in foreground.

Madsen, a trooper from Company A assigned, in his capacity as signalman, to be a connecting link between the pickets and headquarters, had spent the night, with signal flag and torch ready, on the top of a neighboring butte. About daybreak, he declared later, Cody came directly to his post to notify the command that he had been close enough to the Indian camp to see them preparing to move. Buffalo Bill then hastened to Merritt to make his report personally.

Cody then returned to watch the Indians from King's outpost, and soon saw why they were preoccupied with some activity to the west. Coming into his range of vision were the top sheets of covered army wagons. Lieutenant Hall, by traveling all night, had, unknown to the regiment, nearly caught up with it. Moreover, Hall had two companies of infantry concealed in the wagons, which would give any attacking Indians an unpleasant surprise. General Merritt immediately ordered his

115

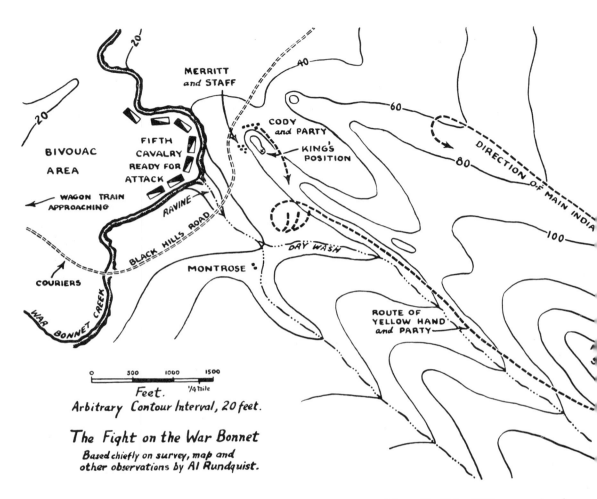

MERRITT and STAFF

CODY and PARTY

KING'S POSITION

DIRECTION OF MAIN INDIA

FIFTH CAVALRY READY FOR ATTACK

BIVOUAC AREA

WAGON TRAIN APPROACHING

RAVINE

BLACK HILLS ROAD

DRY WASH

MONTROSE

COURIERS

WAR BONNET CREEK

ROUTE OF YELLOW HAND and PARTY

20   40   60   80   100

| | | | |
0   500   1000   1500
Feet.   ¼ mile
Arbitrary Contour Interval, 20 feet.

The Fight on the War Bonnet
Based chiefly on survey, map and
other observations by Al Rundquist.

troops to saddle up. They finished their coffee and waited in a close mass under the bluffs.

Buffalo Bill was the first to note the unusual activity among the Cheyennes. Ahead of the wagon train rode two troopers, Anderson and Keith of Company C. A group of seven Indians advanced down the ravine, intent on cutting off these two couriers. In order to reach them, the Cheyennes had to pass close under the hill from which King was watching. Buffalo Bill recognized an opportunity.

"By Jove! General, now's our chance!" he exclaimed. "Let our party mount here and we can cut those fellows off!"

"Up with you then," ordered Merritt. "Stay where you are, King. Watch them until they are close under you; then give the word. Come down, every other man of you."

King was left alone on his hilltop to

give the signal for the rescue. Cody had the honor of leading the party, which consisted, besides himself, of two scouts, Tait and Buffalo Chips White, and five or six troopers. Other troopers crouched out of sight on the slope, ready to pass along the signal, while a sergeant and a corporal remained nearby.

The Cheyennes, resplendent in their war dress, approached with the sun flashing on their polished armlets and lance heads, with gaily painted rawhide shields, and with the wind streaming their long war bonnets out behind them. So intent were they on getting the scalps of the two couriers that they did not notice the head of Charles King peering over the hill crest, or the glint of his binoculars. All they noted was the still peaceful landscape and the approaching wagon train.

"All ready, General?" King asked Merritt.

"All ready, King. Give the word when you like."

King waited until he could hear the panting of the ponies. The Cheyennes were less than a hundred yards away.

"Now, lads," he said quietly, "in with you!"

With a cheer Buffalo Bill led his little band against the Indians' flank. Merritt, Wilkinson, and others watched the action from King's vantage point. For a moment both parties were out of sight. Suddenly Corporal Wilkinson pulled at the General's sleeve, pointing excitedly. A single Indian, following the original party, had halted. He was trying to make out what was happening.

"Shall I fire?" Wilkinson asked. Merritt nodded. At the shot the Indian swung down off his saddle, sending an answering shot whistling past the General's ear. He had fired, King believed, from under the horse's neck.

As these shots were exchanged two more shots were heard. King then saw the main body of the Indians rush down the ravine and appear by scores all along the ridge. He shouted a warning. Merritt at the same moment ordered his first company sent up. He then sprang into his saddle, and his staff officers followed suit.

The first company was K, King's company, commanded by Captain Julius W. Mason. As soon as King saw them he rushed back to mount his horse and join his comrades. The horse had broken away and King was perhaps forty-five seconds in running him down. Despite this, he mounted in time to join his company as it dashed by. Only a moment later he charged with them past Buffalo Bill, who was standing over the body of an Indian he had killed, waving the handsome war bonnet and shouting the famous line, "First scalp for Custer!"

The actions of the men on the hill seem clear enough from their reports. What happened on the prairie, in the swirling dust and tense excitement of the fight is not so easy to explain. There are many versions. The action can be reconstructed, however, on the basis of the accounts of King and of two soldiers who were with Buffalo Bill.

The scout and the Indian saw each other simultaneously. It is certain that they fired at the same instant. Buffalo Bill's shot pierced the Indian's leg and his pony's heart. The scout was not hit, but at the same moment his horse stepped into a gopher hole and threw him. He jumped to his feet, recovered his rifle, and fired again, killing the Indian, who was on the ground. They could not have been more than fifty feet apart. Cody then ran forward, saw that the Indian was probably dead, and for the benefit of the oncoming troopers, raised the Indian's war bonnet into the air with his famous cry, "First scalp for Custer!" The soldiers responded with cheers as they galloped past.

According to some accounts the duel ended with the Indian wielding a tomahawk and Buffalo Bill a Bowie knife, but these reports are unsupported.

Madsen, the signalman, still at his post on the butte, witnessed the whole action and said he saw the Indian's scalp being taken. Later, in passing the dead Cheyenne, he confirmed what he had seen. A sergeant who stopped to adjust his saddle also saw that the scalp was gone.

When Buffalo Bill saw the Indian on the ground he noticed two things: in one swift glance, he said, he saw that the Indian had an American flag wrapped around his groin, using it as a breechcloth, and that on the Indian's head, attached to his hair, was the scalp of a blonde woman which the Cheyenne was wearing as a kind of trophy headdress. These two sights so angered him that he forthwith scalped the Indian.

The Indian was identified as Hay-o-wai, a young Cheyenne chief. His name was translated at the time by "Little Bat," the half-breed scout, as meaning "Yellow Hand," and so the name has stuck. Others say it actually meant "Yellow Hair"; it might be that the scalp of the white woman he wore had earned him the name of "Yellow Hair."

Robert Lindneux, the painter who has lived in Denver for many years, is among those who insist the Cheyenne chief's name should be translated as "Yellow Hair." His painting of Buffalo Bill holding the scalp and the war bonnet aloft as the chief lies at his feet is now in the Buffalo Bill Museum in Cody, Wyoming. It has been reproduced many times, for it gives a sense of the melodrama of the occasion. Many have questioned the extraordinary size of the war bonnet, but Mr. Lindneux insists that all details are correct because he obtained them through an extensive correspondence with General King. But Mr. Lindneux apparently neglected to inquire about the magic costume, which was noted by the military men who observed the dramatic duel. His painting portrays Buffalo Bill in fringed buckskin, the usual habiliment of a scout, instead of in the black velvet vaquero ensemble, thereby, to a degree, weakening his claim to absolute accuracy.

As company K topped the ridge in the battle after the death of Yellow Hand, the Indians fired a scattering volley. When they saw the gray horse troop under Cap-

tain Robert H. Montgomery about sixty
yards to the right rear, and Brevet Lieutenant Colonel Sanford C. Kellogg's company galloping up from the left, the Indians wheeled and ran. The troops advanced
cautiously in open order to the ridge, but
after it was gained they beheld the Cheyennes fleeing in all directions. In their
flight they left a vast array of ammunition,
arms, and blankets which they abandoned
and flung to the ground as impedimenta in
their effort to outdistance their pursuers—
certain evidence of their intention to campaign with Sitting Bull. The regiment pursued them for thirty-five miles back to the
reservation, but were unable to kill or capture any of them.

Once there, it was impossible to tell
which were the Indians who had been on
the warpath, so nothing was done to pun-
ish the Cheyennes on the reservation. After
that brief duel no more southern Cheyennes
attempted to reinforce Sitting Bull. General Merritt, after this engagement, obeyed
the vexing orders which directed him to
Fort Fetterman. He had been delayed
about a week by the action at War Bonnet Creek. General Crook was displeased
at his delay, and if Merritt had not been
able to claim at least a partial victory,
Crook would probably have court-martialed him. As it was, he did not ask for
a report, so Merritt never made one for
army records.

When Buffalo Bill reached the Red
Cloud agency reservation he wrote to Louisa about the fight. "We have come in here
for rations," he said. "We have had a fight.

119

GENERAL WESLEY MERRITT, who commanded Fifth Cavalry when Cody killed Yellow Hand.

I killed Yellow Hand, a Cheyenne chief, in a single-handed fight. You will no doubt hear of it through the papers. I am going as soon as I reach Fort Laramie, the place we are heading for now, to send the war bonnet, bridle, whip, arms and his scalp to Kerngood [a Rochester neighbor who displayed it for weeks in his clothing-store window] to bring it up to the house so you can show it to the neighbors. . . . My health is not very good. I have worked myself to death. Although I have shot at lots of Indians I have only one scalp I can call my own; that fellow fought single-handed in sight of our command and the cheer that went up when he fell was deafening. . . ."

On his arrival at Fort Laramie on July 21 Cody found a wire from James Gordon

Bennett asking for an account of the fight. He asked King to write this for him, and King composed what he later referred to as a "brief telegraphic story, say one-eighth of a column." He read it over to Cody, who suggested no changes at the time, though King recalled the scout's remarking, "It's fine only—" and then saying no more.

The New York *Herald* account of the fight, published Sunday, July 28, 1876, follows:

THE INDIAN WAR

Details of General Merritt's Charge on the Cheyennes

A SHORT STRUGGLE

The Indians, Utterly Surprised, Rush Back in Disorder

The latest from General Crook's Camp

Ominous Absence of the Sioux

FORT LARAMIE, July 22nd, 1876—At War, Saturday, the 15th inst., the Fifth Cavalry under General Merritt were bivouacked on Rawhide Creek, eighteen miles from Fort Laramie to which point they were ordered on from the

Cheyenne River 100 miles to the north en route to join Crook. A courier suddenly appeared from the agency with despatches, stating that 800 Cheyennes were making preparations to leave at once for the Northwest to join Sitting Bull; that he had to throw himself across their lines of march in time to intercept them. Merritt had to make eighty miles before they could make thirty, but off he went and Sunday night found him hiding under the bluffs on War Bonnet or Hat Creek, upon their front.

THE INDIANS APPEAR

At daybreak Monday morning Lieutenant King, commanding the outposts to the southeast, sent word that the war parties were coming over the ridge from the direction of the reservation. Joining him at the advanced post, General Merritt found the report correct. The command noiselessly mounted and was massed under the bluffs, a quarter of a mile to the rear, out of sight of the Indians.

THE WAGON TRAIN

was some six miles off to the southwest, slowly approaching and the Indians were closely watching it, but keeping concealed from view of its guard. The two companies of infantry with it were riding in the wagons. At six o'clock the Indians were swarming all along the ridge to the southeast, some three miles away. Suddenly a party of eight or ten warriors came dashing down a ravine which led directly under the hill where Lieutenant King, with his six men, were watching.

WAITING FOR SCALPS

The object was suddenly apparent. Two horsemen, unconscious of the proximity of the foe, had ventured out ahead of the train and were making rapidly for the creek. They were couriers with despatches to the command. The Indians, utterly ignorant of the rapid movement of the Fifth, were simply bent on jumping on the couriers and getting their scalps. "Buffalo

GENERAL CHARLES KING, who as a lieutenant witnessed Cody's duel with Yellow Hand.

Bill," chief of the scouts, lay on the hill with King and instantly sprang to his horse down the hill.

"All of you keep out of sight," said the General. "Mount now, and when the word is given, off with you!"

Then, turning to the officer of the pickets, he said: "Watch them, King, give the word when you are ready."

Crouching behind the little butte, Bill and his party of scouts and six soldiers were breathlessly waiting; halfway up was the General with his staff. The Lieutenant lay at the crest watching the rapidly advancing foe. Down they came, nearer and nearer, the sun flashing from the brilliantly painted bodies and their polished ornaments. Then, just as they were dashing by the front of the hill, King shouts:

"Now, lads, up with you!"

With a rush and a yell the troopers are hurled upon the Indians' flank not fifty yards away.

121

THE FIRST REDSKIN SHOT

General Merritt springs up to see the attack just as a tall Indian reeled in his saddle, shot by Corporal Wilkinson of K Company. An answering bullet whistled by the General's head when King—still on the watch sung out:

"Here they come by the dozens."

The reserve Indians came swarming down from the ridge to the rescue, turning savagely on Buffalo Bill and the little party at the outpost.

CODY KILLS YELLOW HAND

The latter spring from their horses and met the daring charge with a volley. Yellow Hand, a young Cheyenne brave, came foremost, singling out Bill as a foeman worthy of his steel. Cody coolly knelt and, taking deliberate aim, sent his bullet into his horse's head. Down went the two, and before his friends could reach him, a second shot from Bill's rifle laid the redskin low.

A GRAND SURPRISE

On came the others, bent on annihilating the little band that opposed them, when, to their amazement, a long blue line popped up in their very front and K company, with Colonel Mason at its head, dashed at them. Leaving their dead, the Cheyennes scattered back helter-skelter, to the ridge, but their fire was wild and their stand a short one.

Notice the discrepancies, which are surprisingly few. The New York *Herald* story was written by "a correspondent at Fort Laramie." The previous narrative is based on further evidence after all the witnesses had reported.

The *Herald* story in its original form was probably written by King, who for some reason did not read the printed account until 1929. He then said the *Herald* had expanded his story to nearly a column and made a few alterations. Lieutenant King rose in the Army, became a general, and wrote a number of accounts of the Yellow Hand fight. The definitive and most accurate appeared in his book, *Campaigning with Crook,* published in 1890.

Meanwhile John M. Burke had been reading, of course, all the newspaper stories as they appeared, and he was led to realize more than ever what a legend could now be built around Buffalo Bill, a legend which could mean millions of dollars to them in the show business. He persuaded Cody to leave the Army six weeks after the duel and to return to the stage. Burke built the epic legend around the duel with Yellow Hand. He himself wrote semifictional accounts, and later hired press agents and dime-novel writers to write books purportedly written by Buffalo Bill. The extravagance of these yarns reached preposterous heights as they incorporated the invented details of the dime novelists. One of them, ostensibly written by Cody himself, illustrates the apocrypha that surrounded the saga of Buffalo Bill for the last forty years of his life:

"The chief was riding his horse back and forth in front of his men, as if to banter me, and I concluded to accept the challenge. I galloped toward him for fifty yards and he advanced toward me about the same distance, both of us riding at full speed, and then, when we were only thirty yards apart, I raised my rifle and fired; his horse fell to the ground, having been killed by my bullet. Almost at the same instant my own horse went down, he having stepped into a gopher hole. The fall did not hurt me much, and I instantly sprang to my feet. The Indian had also recovered himself, and we were now both on foot, and not more than twenty paces apart. We fired at each other simultaneously. My usual luck did not desert me on this occasion, for his bullet missed me, while mine struck him in the breast: he reeled and fell but before he had fairly touched the ground I was upon him, knife in hand, and had driven the keen-edged weapon to its hilt in his heart. Jerking his war bonnet off I scientifically scalped him in about five seconds."

In an even more fantastic account Yellow Hand is described as shouting a challenge to Buffalo Bill, yelling, "Come on! Come on! White Long Hair!" ("Cooa! cooa! Pe-He-Has-Ka" in Cheyenne).

The fight had some military, but considerable psychological, importance. It was one of the few instances in which a large war party of Indians was successfully ambushed by troops. That the trap was sprung too early, in order to save the lives of two couriers, limited the casualties to one Indian, but it did keep some eight hundred Cheyennes out of the camp of Sitting Bull.

In all, it took thirty years to subdue the Sioux. Indian agents finally swindled them out of their lands in the Black Hills. Sitting Bull escaped for several years into Canada. Later he toured one season (1885) with Buffalo Bill's Wild West Show, but

he continued his political struggle against the white men until the day of his death. Not until January 1891, after hundreds of Indian women and children had been slaughtered at the massacre of Wounded Knee, did the last of the Sioux surrender.

The accounts of Buffalo Bill's duel with Yellow Hand inspired much discussion of scalping. Most Americans have been horrified by stories of scalping, yet the white man was largely responsible for the practice. It undoubtedly was a projection of the colonial wolf-tail bounty to an Indian scalp bounty. Indians did little scalping in their ancient intertribal disputes. They counted "coup," which simply meant that the first warrior to touch an enemy in battle was honored for having achieved this "coup." That was a kind of game, and did not indicate scalping.

The tribes of the northeastern part of North America, particularly the Iroquois, did some scalping along the lower St. Lawrence in precolonial days. The practice spread because early colonial governments offered to pay bounties to friendly Indians for the scalps of enemies, especially during the French and British wars when both

123

sides employed Indian allies. The Indians frequently cheated both the French and the British when they discovered that the white man would pay for a small tuft of hair, even when more than one partial scalp was obtained from a single head.

The Indians gradually abandoned scalping as they obtained rifles and horses, because killing then reached wholesale proportions and it seemed futile to collect scalps. The white man on the frontier, from Daniel Boone's time onward, practiced scalping with gusto, became very adept at it, and looked on Indian scalps as souvenirs no more ghastly than the mounted heads, masks, or tails of wild animals shot in the wilderness for provender, protection, or sport.

Chapter 9

The Creation of the Wild West Show

BUFFALO BILL returned to the East as a hero. He did not immediately visit Louisa in Rochester, but met Burke in New York, and, after brief reunions and celebrations with his wealthy friends, went back on the road as the star of *Scouts of the Prairie.* The show reopened in Rochester.

He was now obsessed with an idea—a new conception of himself in the world of showmanship—that took several years to mature, and that completely obliterated all

his previous aversion to the theater as a temporary spurt of money-making make-believe. His new notion, which he discussed daily with Burke, was to introduce a panorama that would be more meaningful than a mere stage show. He wanted to bring to the public all the life he had known in all its sound, color, and action.

Additional impetus for the new show and for his assuming the role of its impresario came from the daily adulation of

125

the vast audiences at the *Scouts of the Prairie* in that autumn of 1876. His public now demanded him. Imitators were presenting melodramas of the West manufactured according to his formula, which was also finding increasing popularity in the dime novels of the 1870s. Buffalo Bill had shown them the way, with his *Scouts of the Prairie*. The show was copied by enterprising producers in the stock companies of all the large cities. All these shows involved Indians, cowboys, scouts, frontiersmen, a lost maiden to be rescued, and some kind of comic relief. The more violent and absurd, the more shooting, the more coincidences and predicaments, the better the audiences liked them. The pattern of latter-day western movies was emerging. But Buffalo Bill's show was the most conspicuous and successful, for no one could compete with Buffalo Bill in person. Overnight heroes usually enjoy a short reign, but Buffalo Bill was winning a lasting audience. He was the original; his imitators were stereotypes. John M. Burke, with the skill of a king-maker, fixed the image of Buffalo Bill in the public mind, with a stream of articles, interviews, reviews, and books.

The Wild West Show, as envisaged by Buffalo Bill, demanded new dimensions of showmanship. P. T. Barnum, the circus organizer, later said that he had thought of the idea, vaguely. It was inevitable that he should—but he did not think of it as a vehicle with a tremendous message as Cody did. With all his genius, Barnum could not master the subtle elements of

Only photo ever taken of Buffalo Bill in Indian dress.

western lore. He confined himself to the shocking effect of wild animals, acrobats, and freaks. Ned Buntline had the germ of the idea when he talked of using horses in the *Scouts of the Prairie*. Because Wild Bill Hickok attempted an outdoor show without preparation, he met disaster when his buffaloes ran away in the streets of Niagara Falls.

Cody was not satisfied with the tour of the theaters even though his melodramas made money. He needed to earn a lot of money to get a big show launched, and

126

he was too proud to seek to raise funds through his wealthy friends. He would also need larger audiences; and, he decided, he was building future audiences on his tours, and at the same time identifying his name in thousands of minds with the Wild West as the background for whatever spectacular shows might follow *Scouts of the Prairie.* What especially pleased him was that he was capturing the imagination of young people. Moreover, he was stimulating their anticipations through the dime novels based on his adventures, which were now selling by the millions; for between theatrical engagements during these few years Buffalo Bill, personally, became a professional writer. Books of which he was the hero or the author, and sometimes both, poured from the presses. In 1875 three of his tales had been published: "Pearl of the Prairies, or The Scout and the Renegade," in the *New York Weekly* of August 9, 1875; a month later, on September 11, 1875, "Deadly Eye," in the same paper; and finally, "Prairie Prince, the Boy Outlaw, or Trailed to his Doom," in *The Saturday Evening Post* for October 16, 1875. All three of these stories were signed William F. Cody.

Buntline had a hand in some of these stories, although he was no longer Buffalo Bill's partner. John M. Burke more frequently collaborated. This was also the period in which Cody's sister Helen, who later wrote *Last of the Great Scouts,* was helping Buffalo Bill on what she called his "literary work." She declared that she put in all the punctuation and the capitals.

Publishers such as Beadle, later Beadle and Adams, demanded short novels, to publish in paper-bound form, by the dozens. An audience of millions devoured them.

Buffalo Bill wrote naturally about border life; he made no apologies for his Davy Crockett sort of homespun style. Each story added a bit to the legend. To one publisher he wrote, "I am sorry to have to lie so outrageously in this yarn. My hero has killed more Indians on one war trail than I have killed in all my life. But I understand this is what is expected of border tales. If you think the revolver and Bowie knife are used too freely, you may cut out a fatal shot or stab wherever you think wise."

In 1876 Buffalo Bill's new autumn show was called *Life on the Border,* which he sometimes alternated with *Scouts of the Prairie.* He learned not to rely on himself alone to be the drawing card, but invariably tried to obtain other big names as box-office attractions. *Life on the Border* starred his teetotaling friend Captain Jack Crawford, a colorful adventurer experienced in border warfare. Born in Ireland, County Donegal, Crawford was brought as a child to Pennsylvania, where he went to work in the coal mines. When his father left for the Civil War, Jack followed him, and managed to enlist at the age of fifteen. Badly wounded at the Battle of Spottsylvania Court House, he spent some time in a hospital, where he learned to read and write.

Crawford's mother, on her deathbed, had made him promise never to touch liquor; and though he spent most of his life among heavy drinkers, he kept his promise. He went out to the border as a newspaper reporter, became a scout, and briefly succeeded Buffalo Bill as chief scout for General Merritt. When he went on the stage he also turned to writing poems, and succeeded in getting most of them published. He enjoyed reciting them, especially one of his most popular, entitled, "Mother's Prayers":

Mother, who in days of childhood
Prayed as only mothers pray;
Keep him in the narrow pathway,
Let him not be led astray.

And when danger hovered o'er me
And when life was full of cares,
Then a sweet form passed before me,
And I thought of Mother's prayers.

Later Captain Jack wrote three successful plays, and published more than a hundred short stories.

Buffalo Bill called the vehicle in which Captain Jack Crawford starred "a noisy, rattling, gunpowder entertainment." He opened in Rochester, then took the show to New York, where he played at the Grand Opera House on West Twenty-third Street at the corner of Eighth Avenue. The five acts of this carnival, he admitted, could be played in any kind of order. The story would have made just as much sense if he had started with the last act, but there is no record that he ever tried that experiment.

Buffalo Bill and Crawford also played

CAPTAIN JACK CRAWFORD, poet, scout, friend of Buffalo Bill.

at the Bowery Theater that season and at Hooley's Theater in Brooklyn. Then he took his drama to the Pacific Coast against the advice of theatrical men who told him such entertainment would fail in California. West Coast audiences, however, packed the houses; he played two weeks at the Bush Street Theater in San Francisco, and closed his season at Virginia City, Nevada.

During the summer of 1877, Buffalo Bill bought a Nebraska ranch in partnership with Major Frank North, who was then living in North Platte. They expected to make a lot of money in the cattle business, but the profits never materialized.

128

His biggest stage success came in the season of 1877–78 with *May Cody, or Lost and Won.* Gordon W. Lillie, later known as Pawnee Bill, then an interpreter at an Indian reservation in Oklahoma, borrowed a number of Sioux Indians for the show. The story, written by dime novelist Major A. S. Burt, was based on the Mountain Meadow Massacre which involved Mormons as well as Indians. The heroine's name was borrowed from Buffalo Bill's younger sister, although the story bore no relation to her or to any of her experiences. An actress named Constance Hamblin played the part. It opened at the Bowery Theater in New York on September 3, 1877. Included in the cast, in addition to the six Sioux braves, were some prairie ponies and a Mexican burro. After its run at the Bowery, *May Cody* played at the Eagle Theater in Brooklyn.

Cody also successfully tried out another show: *Red Right Hand, or Buffalo Bill's First Scalp for Custer,* which capitalized on the duel with Yellow Hand as well as the massacre of Custer. Into this drama he inserted a character named Dennis O'Gaff, a comic Irishman, and an Indian whose fictional name was Land-Wha-Hoo. One critic wasn't sure whether he was supposed to be an Indian or a Chinese.

Buffalo Bill, of course, took the leading role in all these plays. During the next two seasons he produced and performed in *Boy Chief of the Plains,* from time to time adding similar dramas with parallel titles to the repertoire. All the plots followed a tried-and-true formula. In 1880 the new

MAJOR FRANK NORTH, famous scout who was in cattle business with Buffalo Bill and later in the Wild West Show.

titles were *Knight of the Plains* and *Buffalo Bill at Bay, or The Pearl of the Prairie.* In the first of these a band of genuine Indians did a war dance and a scalp dance, led by "the boy chief of the Pawnees." The New York *Herald* commented, "The parts were simple and they sustained them well." It was followed on the boards by *East Lynne,* which was considered more sophisticated, but was no more popular.

The western melodramas bored Buffalo Bill; but he continued to hope they would lead to the big outdoor show of which he dreamed. His sister Helen saw him on the stage at Leavenworth, Kansas, where he was playing the part of a loving western

129

swain courting a charming prairie lassie. When Helen went backstage to see him, he seemed embarrassed. "Oh, Nellie," he cried, "don't say anything about it. If heaven will forgive me for this foolishness I promise to quit it forever as soon as this season is over."

The idea for the outdoor show now dominated Cody. He repeated, over and over to Burke, Buntline's advice: "Take the prairies and the Injuns and everything else right to 'em" (the people in the East). "That's the idea. There ain't room on a stage to do anything worth while. But there would be on a big lot where we could have horses and buffalo and the old Deadwood coach and everything! That'd be something they'd never seen before! That'd be showing them the West!"

In 1879, Buffalo Bill, assisted by John M. Burke, wrote the least fictional of all his autobiographies. It has since been rewritten many times by many hands over the years, and it has been relied upon as the most comprehensive story of his many adventures.

In 1880–81 his melodrama was called *White Beaver,* and featured Dr. Frank Powell and a number of Arapaho Indians. He then revived the *Prairie Waif* with the Pawnee Indians, touring the country. Loie Fuller, who later became a famous dancer, was the waif.

Early in 1882, when Cody was playing at the Grand Opera House in Brooklyn, a well-known showman, Nate Salsbury, got in touch with him. Salsbury was at that time at the Park Theater in Brooklyn with

130   "WELCOME WIGWAM," home built by Buffalo Bill at North Platte, Nebraska.

a stock company which he called Salsbury Troubadours, playing an early Bronson Howard opus called *Fawn of the Glen, or the Civilized Indian*. Born in Freeport, Illinois, and the same age as Cody, Salsbury had enlisted in the Union Army, in which he became a popular impromptu entertainer with a flair for comic songs. After the war he went on the stage, and his theatrical successes made him one of the outstanding actor-managers of his day. He loved horses, admired western cowboys and Mexican riders, and, like Cody, dreamed of an outdoor show in which there would be feats of horsemanship and portrayals of Indian warfare.

Having studied Buffalo Bill's career on the plains as well as his stage career, Salsbury decided that Cody was the man to head a Wild West Show which would be distinguished for its equestrian features. Cody met Salsbury at a Brooklyn restaurant, where the two men compared ideas and found that they had been thinking along almost identical lines. They agreed that such a show would be a tremendous success, not only in the United States, but abroad. Salsbury said he would gladly go to Europe, and look into the possibilities there. It would obviously require a great deal of money to finance such a spectacle, but the prospects fired their imagination.

Although Cody earned more than a hundred thousand dollars in the five years after the Yellow Hand duel, he saved practically none of it. He built a comfortable house in North Platte, and persuaded Louisa to move into it. He called it "Welcome Wig-

wam." When he was home he usually invited his cronies from the plains to visit them. Louisa was not pleased by their language, their hours, or their drinking habits.

At the end of the theatrical season of 1881 Louisa met him at Omaha. When she arrived at the hotel she found her husband bidding farewell to the actresses with more than perfunctory kisses. This so annoyed her that she did not speak to him throughout the entire summer. Soon afterward he asked her to sign some routine

ARTA CODY, who resembled her mother.

131

ARTA CODY at the age of nine with her famous father and mother.

legal papers, and, through an intermediary, she refused to sign anything. In a burst of generosity calculated to regain her good graces, he had the North Platte property placed in her name. Thereafter he could not borrow anything on it. During this grim domestic crisis, in his search for capital to start his Wild West Show, he instituted a law suit in Cleveland for some property which his grandfather had once owned. He claimed the papers and deed were forged, including his father's signature. He had high hopes of winning millions of dollars in this law suit, but he never was awarded a cent.

There seems, again, to have been a guardian angel hovering over the career of the intrepid scout encamped in the spacious Welcome Wigwam. In June of 1882, just as the future looked most foreboding, his fellow citizens of North Platte decided to put on what they called an "Old Glory Blow-Out" on the Fourth of July, and they asked Buffalo Bill to take charge of its presentation. From their original plan to put on a kind of rodeo and bronco-busting contest, Cody switched to the kind of Wild West Show of which he had been dreaming. He hired a number of Indians, and bought the old Deadwood stagecoach. With these, plus local cowboys, he enacted a famous stagecoach holdup. He put on horse races and a sharp-shooting contest. For good measure, he also included a drive on a small herd of buffalo. It was the first tryout for the Wild West Show which he and Burke had been planning for more than five years.

Dr. Carver, Nebraska dentist and crack shot, before he met Buffalo Bill.

The Old Glory Blow-Out was a sensational success. "I tried it on my neighbors," Buffalo Bill said, "and they lived through it and liked it, so I made up my mind right then I'd take the show East."

In a burst of typical rhetoric, John M. Burke said of the show, "Cody not only scored a howling success, if possible adding to his popularity, but the casualties were few and the result a revelation, even to those familiar with the possibilities of excitement, reckless daring, skill, and devil-may-care fun, represented in a program

133

where all were untrammeled and unconventional stars."

One of Cody's neighbors who participated in the show was Dr. A. W. Carver, a dentist who claimed to be Indian-born, and who often appeared in contests at carnivals and county fairs. Dr. Carver saw in this extravaganza an opportunity to get into the show business with Cody. He had been calling himself "The Evil Spirit of the Plains" and longed to match Cody's nation-wide fame. Carver was phenomenal as a trick marksman, shooting at nickels thrown in the air, which suggested to Buffalo Bill his famous later stunt of shooting glass balls tossed aloft by Johnny Baker. Carver was enthusiastic, and Cody impatient to get started, so they formed a partnership. They hired Captain A. H. Bogardus, a champion clay-pigeon shot, as a special feature. Gordon W. Lillie procured some Pawnees for them

from Oklahoma. Major Frank North, Cody's ranch partner, agreed to be billed as "The White Chief of the Pawnees." All during the summer they worked on plans. They hired cowboys from Nebraska ranches who could do lariat tricks and rope steers. They sketched the outlines for a pony-express act in the drama, showing how the riders changed horses. Cody kept the old Concord coach from Deadwood that he had used in the Fourth of July show. Burke worked on the advance publicity and promotion. At this time Cody wrote to Nate Salsbury, and invited him to come into the deal, but when that showman heard that Carver was a partner, he would have nothing to do with it.

After a winter of rehearsing and organizing they were ready for the road in the spring. Calling their spectacle "The Wild West, Rocky Mountain and Prairie Exhibition," Cody and Carver opened it at the

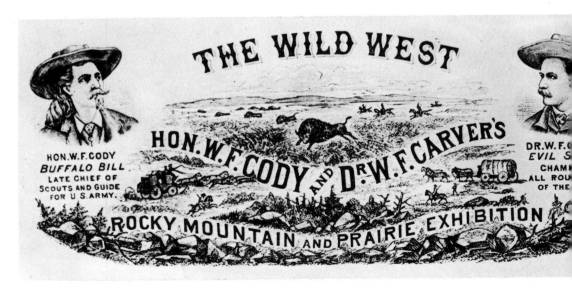

"Arizona John" Burke, Buffalo Bill's great press agent.

Fair Grounds in Omaha on May 17, 1883. The pattern of the Old Glory Blow-Out was now augmented by additional acts. Dr. Carver demonstrated more complicated trick shooting. Buffalo Bill attempted for the first time his later famous performance of shooting at tossed blue glass balls while on the gallop, and hit eighty-seven out of a hundred. Some spectators called the show a circus. But it certainly was not a conventional circus such as had ever been seen before.

Burke prepared the billboards and the program. His posters declaimed, "The Green Sward Our Carpet, Azure Canopy Our Canvas, No Tinsel, No Gilding, No Humbug! No Side Shows or Freaks."

The show displayed many of the elements of the later Wild West Shows, but it was badly organized, crudely put together, and far from smooth in its production.

Without a fully scheduled tour, they started out, intending to put on their show at fair grounds or vacant lots. They had no facilities for lighting their spectacle, so they gave only one show a day, in the afternoon. Neither Cody nor Carver had had any experience in handling such a variegated troupe. Many of the cowboys spent most of their time in saloons, and could not be found when due to perform their riding and roping stunts. The problems of transportation were almost too much for Carver and Cody.

The whole outfit lacked discipline, and Buffalo Bill had not yet acquired the easy ability to assert his authority. He often made the mistake of being "one of the boys." However, the crowds liked the show and the newspapers gave it excellent notices.

"Thunder of hoofs, clank of spurs, rattle of pistols," reported the Hartford *Courant,* in Connecticut, "glint of shattered glass balls, odor of gunpowder and cattle made it authentic. It began with a pony bareback riding race between Indians and went on to a climax with a grand realistic battle scene depicting the capture, torture and

135

death of a scout by savages; the revenge, recapture of the dead body, and victory of the government scouts. Cowboys rode bucking broncos, roped and tied Texas steers, lassoed and rode wild bison. A fleet-footed Indian ran a race with a mounted rival. The pony express rider dashed in, changed his *mochilla* to a fresh mount and dashed off again. The startling, soul-stirring attack on the Deadwood mail coach ended in a rescue by Buffalo Bill and Dr. Carver. Bogardus shot clay pigeons."

The temperamental dentist proved to be an uncongenial and unreliable partner, who usually exploded into violent rages when things went badly. In July they appeared at the Prospect Park Fair Grounds in Brooklyn and in August at Brighton Beach, where they found a spot between the Iron Pier and the Brighton Hotel. The place was brilliantly lighted, so they put on their first night performances. Salsbury saw the show there, and predicted disaster. P. T. Barnum, who graciously concealed with faint praise whatever flicker of jealousy he may have felt, commented, "The virtue of the show was that it did not need spangles, being of itself all life and movement, the effect of which was easily grasped by everybody."

As time ran on, the homesick cowboys and Indians became an unruly mob, and constantly quarreled among themselves. By the end of the season Buffalo Bill was scarcely speaking to the temperamental Carver. When they reached Chicago, Nate Salsbury, by good chance, was appearing there with his troubadours. Cody went to see him, implored him to join him as a partner. Buffalo Bill said he could not and would not be able to continue without him. Dr. Carver then announced that he was ready to leave the show, that no amount of financial success could compensate him for the strain of trying to manage such a combination of cowboys, Indians, horses, cattle, and bison. They flipped a coin for the property. Buffalo Bill won the toss, but they divided the equipment evenly and split their partnership. Salsbury then happily joined as partner and took charge of the business management. John P. Altgeld, a prominent lawyer, later governor of Illinois, drew up the historic contract between them.

Nate Salsbury and Buffalo Bill immediately began to make plans for the following year. Meanwhile, Salsbury was to go on with his Troubadours, which were fully booked a year ahead; but after that they would be in business together. The Wild West Show, in all its glorious extravagance, was soon to be seen by millions.

136

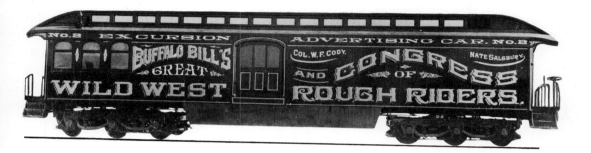

Chapter 10

The Show of Shows Tours the U. S.

THROUGHOUT their first year as equal partners Cody and Salsbury labored day and night to build up their show of shows. And through the next decade they added, improved, expanded, a little at first, and then, as the profits poured in, put money back into the show in substantial amounts for new acts, new equipment, making it a bigger and better show each year.

The Cody and Carver Prairie Exhibition had not actually been a big financial success. It suggested what could be done with a Wild West Show, an extravaganza on wheels, every act illustrating the great saga of the West. At the end of the first year of the Cody-Salsbury partnership the enterprise showed a $60,000 loss; but soon they were grossing millions a year, and in 1901 their net profits reached a million dollars apiece.

"The Only Real Novelty of the Century" Arizona John, who now called himself "Major" Burke, could honestly write. "The Amusement Triumph of the Age," his poster said, "The Romantic West Brought East in Reality. Everything Genuine... A Year's Visit West in Three Hours. Actual Scenes in the Nation's Progress to Delight, Please, Gratify, Chain and Interest

SPECIAL TRAIN carried all equipment for show as well as performers and animals.   **137**

JOHN NELSON, who drove the Deadwood Coach in Wild West Show.

driving park in St. Louis. Then they went on by easy stages to New York, where they showed at the Polo Grounds. Everybody who saw it said it was the greatest show in the world. A new spirit animated it; everything clicked. Small details revealed the zest with which the partners worked together: the Deadwood coach was lit with red fire so that it looked as if the occupants were, at the climax, being burned alive.

Then all of a sudden bad luck hit the first year's tour. First the weather turned wet and cold for weeks on end; then at Hartford Frank North fell from his horse, and although the horses following his swerved away, one trampled him. They carried him to the hospital badly injured. It was his last appearance as a performer.

Deficits began to mount. Salsbury had to leave the show to join his traveling Troubadours. He arranged to have the Exhibition continue on tour, and head South in the fall. The partners decided to take the show to New Orleans, where a Centennial Exhibition opened in December celebrating the anniversary of the exporting of cotton from that port, then tour the balmy South.

To organize the escape from northern weather, Buffalo Bill, who was forever hiring old pards, hired Bob Haslam, an old comrade of his pony-express days, to go ahead as advance agent. Haslam didn't know the first thing about the job. He foolishly rented a large lot for the Wild West Show. Worried about what Bob was doing, Buffalo Bill went South by train while the

the Visitor." And Buffalo Bill added, "A true rescript of life on the frontier as I know it to be, and which no fictitious pen can describe."

The show, now tightly organized under Nate Salsbury's direction, opened at the

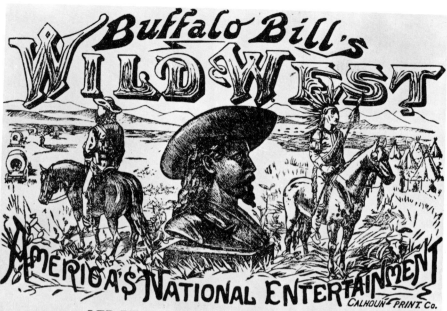

LED BY THE FAMED SCOUT AND GUIDE.

BUFFALO BILL

(HON. W. F. CODY).

Capt. A. H. BOGARDUS,
CHAMPION WING SHOT OF THE WORLD.

Major FRANK NORTH,
THE PILOT OF THE PRAIRIE.

"OKLAHOMA" PAYNE,
THE PROGRESSIVE PIONEER.

"BUCK" TAYLOR,
KING OF THE COW-BOYS.

"CON" GRONER,
THE COW-BOY SHERIFF OF THE PLATTE.

A Host of Western Celebrities; A Camp of Cheyenne, Arappahoe, Sioux, and Pawnee Indians; A Group of Mexican Vaqueros; Round-up of Western Cow-Boys; Company of Prairie Scouts; A Herd of Wild Buffalos; A Corral of Indian Ponies; A Band of Mountain Elk; A Drove of Texas Steers; Pack-Train of Mexican Burros; Mountain Lions, Coyottes, Deer, Antelope, Mountain Sheep, etc.

ARTISTICALLY BLENDING, LIFE-LIKE, VIVID, AND THRILLING

Pictures of Western Life.

W. F. CODY, NATE SALSBURY, & A. H. BOGARDUS, Proprietors.

JOHN M. BURKE, General Manager.

For Particulars, Date, and Description, see Posters, Small Bills, and Newspapers.

The Calhoun Printing Company, Hartford, Conn.

POSTER OF BUFFALO BILL'S FIRST TOUR with Nate Salsbury and Captain Bogardus his partners.

show was put aboard a Mississippi river-boat. It was raining when Cody arrived; he found the lot Haslam had selected flooded to a depth of several feet, so he arranged to lease the race track. Returning to his hotel, he received word that the riverboat with the show on it had met with a collision and had sunk. Wagons, arms, ammunition, steers, mules, buffaloes were lost. The horses, the Deadwood coach, and the band wagon had been saved.

Salsbury was playing in Denver. Buffalo Bill wired him: OUTFIT AT BOTTOM OF RIVER WHAT DO YOU ADVISE. A few hours later Salsbury replied: OPEN ON YOUR DATE HAVE WIRED YOU FUNDS.

Cody did the best he could to replace the equipment at New Orleans. He wired Frank North, who was home in Nebraska trying to recuperate, to get him some more Indians and buffaloes. North managed to get them. A week later he died.

In New Orleans, the distraught Cody was almost ready to give up.

John M. Burke, a difficult man to discourage, sat gloomily at the race track one afternoon watching the incessant rain. Bogardus, the crack shot, had quit. As he pondered this blow, two visitors, looking like a couple of midwestern farm folks, the woman small and shy, the man a little more self-assured, came to see the Major. They said they had just left Sells Brothers Circus because they didn't like the circus life. They were Butler and Oakley, Mr. and Mrs. Frank Butler, the best marksmanship team in America. Buffalo Bill's show was the kind of troupe they would like to join.

LITTLE MISSIE demonstrating that she can hit a target seen in a hand mirror.

Burke looked at Annie, thought of the stories he could write about her. He took her to the target range. No doubt about it—Annie Oakley was just what the show needed. But Burke knew how broke the show was. Moreover, a young lad, Johnny Baker, who was traveling with the show without salary, had been practicing; maybe he could fill in for a while.

140

ten. He had begged to go with the show; he'd do anything, he said, and he did practically everything he could to make himself useful. Cody encouraged him when he wanted to learn to be a marksman. Later he put him in the show as a crack shot; although he never made it legal, he practically adopted Johnny, and often called him "son."

When they started the new spring season in Louisville, Kentucky, in April the partners changed the show's name to "Buffalo Bill's Wild West." Salsbury had raised more capital from friends and family—and the show was bigger and better. Buffalo Bill was leading the parade in downtown Louisville when Mr. and Mrs. Frank Butler called on Major Burke for the second time.

"America's Greatest Entertainment" camped at Louisville's baseball park, where the Butlers found the wigwams, the corral, and the mess tent. They got out their guns and Annie practiced while waiting to see Buffalo Bill. She sighted with a hand mirror and shot backward as Frank threw glass balls in the air. She hit them all. Just at that moment a tall bearded man in a bowler hat stepped quickly across the grass toward them.

"I am Nate Salsbury," he said, taking off his hat and bowing. "Major Burke told me about you."

Annie continued to demonstrate what she could do when simply practicing. Yes, she said, she could shoot from a galloping pony. When the parade returned, Salsbury took the Butlers to the mess tent, where

Sadly Arizona John told the Butlers that Buffalo Bill was downtown; that Nate Salsbury was trying to raise some more money to keep the show alive; and that he couldn't hire them just then. "Come see us in Louisville in the spring," he said. "Then we can talk business."

The Johnny Baker to whom Burke referred was a North Platte boy who had worshipped Buffalo Bill ever since he was

Annie Oakley as she appeared in Wild West Show.

A Sioux family outside their wigwam. Wild West Show always had an "Indian Village."

they talked business. Buffalo Bill joined the group, looking his best in his buckskin jacket, the silk handkerchief around his neck held by the diamond pin which Grand Duke Alexis had presented to him. He swept his sombrero off his flowing locks with a courtly flourish. "They told me about you, Missy. We're glad to have you."

For the rest of her life Annie Oakley was Little Missy. A sweet little farm girl from Ohio, originally named Annie Moses, she might have been happy if she had spent her life in a small town. She possessed a remarkable gift, second to none in the world: she was a phenomenal shot. Her uncanny ability drove her to seek her fortune, to a career full of hazards, worries, tensions, but she never lost the shy sweetness of a little country girl. From the time she joined the Wild West she and her husband were "Butler and Oakley." She was billed as Annie Oakley; Frank Butler was her manager and constant attendant.

Annie started in the show that very afternoon—the first act on the program after the grand entry. Major Burke explained to newspapermen why she always afterward opened the show: "It was our first thought, when we planned the show, that so much shooting would cause difficulty, that horses would be frightened and women and children terrified. It was when Annie Oakley joined us that Colonel Cody devised the idea of graduating the excitement. Miss Oakley comes on very early in the performance. She starts very gently, shooting with a pistol. Women and children see a harm-

less woman out there and do not get worried.

"Gradually she increases the charge in her rifles until at last she shoots with a full charge. Thus, by the time the attack on the stagecoach comes, the audience is accustomed to the sound of shooting. In all our history of Wild West there has never been a horse frightened sufficiently to run away at any of our outdoor performances."

For seventeen years, as long as Annie Oakley was with the show, she was the opening act. With her magic presence, Buffalo Bill's big show swung into its stride and enjoyed its first triumphantly successful season.

ANNIE OAKLEY'S DRESSING-ROOM TRUNK used by her on tour for seventeen years.

143

In May they went to Chicago, where the crowds packed the West Side Driving Park. The first Sunday forty thousand people tried to get in; from noon until four o'clock they kept coming. The crowd laughed at the Pawnee war dance. "Rats," the West Siders shouted. "Whoop her up there, Jim! Dosey do!"

The Chicago *Tribune* reported on May 28, 1885 that "Buffalo Bill was the object of admiration, especially among the youthful romancers who saw in him the incarnation of their young ideals." The following Sunday twenty thousand people packed the driving park. The *Tribune* said, "Many of them were the kid type who hope someday to rival the famous scout."

Cody and Salsbury treated the reporters to a roast-beef barbecue dinner, which they ate without forks. As a special attraction Bronco Bill Irving rode a steer brought from the stockyards. Major Burke explained to the newsmen that "Buffalo Bill's Wild West" was now a fully copyrighted name. The full description was: "The Wild West, or Life Among the Red Men and the Road Agents of the Plains and Prairies. An Equine Dramatic Exposition on grass or under canvas of the Advantages of Fron-

tiersmen and Cowboys." That year four other Wild West Shows toured the country: Adam Forepaugh had one, Dr. A. W. Carver another; there was one called "Fargo's Wild West" and one known as "Hennessey's Wild West."

Buffalo Bill was the lion of Chicago society. General Phil Sheridan took him to Hooley's Theater, where they sat in a box. The audience recognized them and applauded. The Chicago Reform Alliance protested against the Sunday performances. A delegation waited upon Mayor Carter Harrison to ask him to prevent what they called the desecration of the Sabbath. He told the group that he could not refuse the Wild West a license, for if he did, he would also have to stop all theater performances on Sunday.

During this season of 1885, Major Burke hired Prentiss Ingraham to write publicity for the show. If there ever was a soldier of fortune, Prentiss Ingraham led the regiment. Born in Adams County, Mississippi, he fought in the Confederate Army. While in the light artillery he was once captured, twice wounded. After the Civil War, he joined Juarez's troops in Mexico; then he went to Europe to fight with Austria

144   SOME OF THE 200 DIME NOVELS written by Prentiss Ingraham with Buffalo Bill as hero.

against Prussia. Later he fought in Crete, Africa, and joined in the Cuban war for independence. He wrote, in all, six hundred novels, many plays, short stories, and poems. His literary career began in London in 1870. He turned out thrillers wholesale for Beadle and Adams, then for Street and Smith. Once he wrote thirty-five thousand words in a day and a night on a rush order, with a boy standing by to keep his fountain pens filled. His *Montezuma* had a long run on Broadway. Altogether Ingraham wrote over two hundred dime novels with Buffalo Bill as the chief character. His outstanding Buffalo Bill volume was *The Pony Express Rider, or Buffalo Bill's Frontier Feats,* the basis for many of the popular legends concerning that period of Cody's life.

In June of 1885 Buffalo Bill sent Major Burke to the Standing Rock Indian Reservation to talk with Sitting Bull. The great Sioux chief and medicine man would be a wonderful attraction for the Wild West's Indian Village, Cody thought. Already Sitting Bull had made a number of public appearances. He had gone to Bismarck, North Dakota, to meet General Grant, where he headed a parade celebrating the opening of the Northern Pacific Railroad main transcontinental line. On this occasion he discovered that he could make money selling his autograph.

Colonel Alvaren Allen in 1884 persuaded the Secretary of the Interior, Henry M. Teller, to give him permission to exhibit the famous Indian chief in the East. Sitting Bull agreed, on the condition that he could have an interview with the President in order to present his case on behalf of the Indians. The dignified and aging chief never saw the White House. Instead, Colonel Allen showed him off at the Eden Musee in New York among the waxworks.

Buffalo Bill had taught Major Burke how to get along with Indians. During the first season with the Wild West Show the press agent once gave an Indian a cigar, promised him "heap big cigars," told him he would bring him a whole box from town. Buffalo Bill quickly took Burke aside. "Don't forget those cigars. Maybe you didn't mean it. But don't ever promise an Indian anything without giving it to him. If you break a promise to an Indian you'll be no good to me or the show. Get a box

146   <small>Sitting Bull in Wild West Show with Buffalo Bill.</small>

of cigars in town and charge it to me. Don't forget."

Sitting Bull listened amicably to Burke's proposition, and agreed to tour with the Wild West for four months for fifty dollars a week and expenses. When Burke wrote out the contract the old chief added another clause: he was to have the sole right to sell photographs of himself, or to have visitors photographed with him by the tintype concessionaire.

Sitting Bull joined the show at Buffalo, and immediately became the chief attraction. During the show he sat with impassive dignity on his horse. Some of the spectators thought it was patriotic to boo and yell at him, because he had vanquished Custer. But the philosophical Indian chief had expected this; he endured it without complaint. Moreover, he sold his photographs by the hundreds.

The Sioux chief had great affection for Buffalo Bill. The two men understood each other. He called Cody by an Indian name, Pahaska—"Long Hair"—and said that the great scout was sincere and genuine. Sitting Bull took a fatherly interest in Annie Oakley, admired her shooting, called her "Little Sure Shot," and in a formal ceremony adopted her as his daughter. This all made wonderful newspaper copy. Major Burke never worked harder or to better effect.

Even the usually restrained city of Boston raved in superlatives about the rejuvenated Wild West Show. The papers called Little Missy "the demure sharpshooter of the Plains," and Sitting Bull was, for this center of culture, "Sedentary Taurus." One reporter commented that the chief reminded him of Daniel Webster.

Canada turned out even more enthusiastic crowds than the United States, for the Canadians had no sentimental feelings about General Custer. They greeted Sitting Bull as "the illustrious Indian general and statesman." Canadian newspapers filled pages with stories of Sitting Bull; he achieved more space than Buffalo Bill, who finally made the headlines when he told the press at Toronto, "In nine cases out of ten when there is trouble between white men and Indians, it will be found that the white man is responsible. Indians expect a man to keep his word. They can't understand how a man can lie. Most of them would as soon cut off a leg as tell a lie." Thousands of souvenir photographs were sold of Buffalo Bill with Sitting Bull, captioned, "Enemies in '76, Friends in '85."

On another occasion in Canada Buffalo Bill said:

"The defeat of Custer was not a massacre. The Indians were being pursued by skilled fighters with orders to kill. For centuries they had ben hounded from the Atlantic to the Pacific and back again. They had their wives and little ones to protect and they were fighting for their existence. With the end of Custer they considered that their greatest enemy had passed away. Sitting Bull was not the leader of the Sioux in that battle. He was a medicine man who played on their superstitions—their politician, their diplomat—who controlled their emotions through the power of his argument and the vehemence of his speech."

The 1885 tour ended at St. Louis. There Sitting Bull met his old antagonist of the plains, General E. V. Carr, in a hotel lobby. The General smiled cordially and greeted the Sioux chief, but Sitting Bull remained impassive and refused to shake hands, remembering too much of the campaigns of the Fifth Cavalry. Arizona John, of course, was in the lobby and witnessed the little drama. Everything, it seemed, was grist for his wonderful stories.

The show had grossed over a million dollars that season, and made a profit of more than a hundred thousand dollars, after all salaries and expenses. That fall Buffalo Bill completed his Scout's Rest Ranch, three miles from North Platte, which he stocked with 125 of the best Herefords, shorthorns, and polled Angus. He imported a great Hereford bull, Earl Horace. The Omaha *Herald* described Scout's Rest as follows: "The waters of the great Platte flow through no prettier or more natural stock ranch. Nature in all her bounteous gifts never designed a place more fitting. The river skirts along the northwestern portion for four miles; in the southern portion a small, overflowing creek, fed by a cool living spring, flows nearly through the center from west to east, dividing it into two parts, and while on the south side the rich nutritious buffalo grass grows and furnishes food on which the cattle grow fat in summer, on the north side a long, juicy wild prairie grass is found which when cut and cured furnishes a provender unequaled for cattle in the winter. He has a tract of nearly four thousand acres here, the eastern portion adjoining the city's limits which the rapid growth of North Platte is making valuable."

Now that Cody and Salsbury had money to spend on the show, they stinted nothing. By the spring of 1886, Buffalo Bill's Wild West had its own railroad train of white cars with the name in gold along the side of each car. It carried not only the personnel, 240 people in all that season, but seats and a canvas canopy, a lighting system, a vast painted canvas background mural representing the Wyoming mountains. The personnel was organized into crews, each with a boss; they were trained and disciplined, and each had his job and did it. One new feature was "Custer's Massacre," re-created in detail. Salsbury insisted on long rehearsals until everything was perfect. Sitting Bull never toured again, although Buffalo Bill wanted to take him to Europe in 1887. For the 1886 tour the partners added cowgirls to ride with the cowboys.

This tour was one long triumph from beginning to end. From St. Louis they headed East through Terre Haute, Dayton, Wheeling, to Washington. The weather was perfect, and the cowboy band played "Marching through Georgia" all the way up Pennsylvania Avenue. When they passed the White House the Indians cheered, although President Cleveland wasn't there—he was away on his honeymoon (married June 2, 1886).

Even more extraordinary was the parade

SHORT MAN, one of famous Indians in show.

150   Two FAMOUS INDIANS in the show: High Heron and Has-No-Horse.

in New York, carefully staged by Cody and Salsbury on June 27, 1886. They marched off the Twenty-third Street ferry to Eighth Avenue, where the cowboy band struck up "Oh Susannah, don't you cry for me!" and headed up to Forty-second Street, across to Fifth Avenue, and then down Fifth Avenue to Broadway and the Battery. The whole city turned out to cheer them.

All summer the show played to ever increasing crowds at their own grounds at Erastina on Staten Island. Everybody in the city, and visitors from the whole country, wanted to see it and to talk about it. Buffalo Bill's Wild West was fashionable that summer. Distinguished visitors set the style: Governor David B. Hill, Mark Twain, Henry Irving (the great English actor), Prince Dom Augusta of Brazil, whose battleship anchored in the harbor. Old P. T. Barnum limped around the grounds. "When Salsbury takes this show to Europe," he said, "it will astonish the Old World." One trip to Erastina was not enough for most families, the children had to go again and again, happily munching Cracker Jack as they looked with wonder at the Indians and the cowboys. The ferries were jammed from Manhattan, Brooklyn, Jersey City. The partners chartered special boats to handle the throngs.

"Down to its smallest details the Show is genuine," wrote Mark Twain to Buffalo Bill, who now was on a first-name basis with most of the eminent men of his time. "It brought back vividly the breezy wild life of the Plains and the Rocky Mountains. It is wholly free from sham and insincerity and the effects it produced upon me by its spectacles were identical with those wrought upon me a long time ago on the frontier. Your pony expressman was as tremendous an interest to me as he was twenty-three years ago when he used to come whizzing by from over the desert with his war news; and your bucking horses were even painfully real to me as I rode one of those outrages for nearly a quarter of a minute. It is often said on the other side of the water that none of the exhibitions which we send to England are purely and distinctly American. If you will take the Wild West Show over there you can remove that reproach."

The New York *World* reporter declared that Buffalo Bill "could ride with a cup of water on his head and not spill a drop." This feature writer, who signed his stories "Nym Crinkle," spent the night at Erastina and described his bivouac "within half an hour of City Hall." He particularly admired Buck Taylor, "who can stand in the path of any Mexican steer and turn it over by the horns"; Con Groner, "the Sheriff of North Platte, who took Jesse James and his gang off a train"; Bronco Bill, "full of bullets." "You can't help fancying that the toot of the absurd Staten Island railroad is the yelping of the coyotes."

Burke put on special western exhibitions for the press, and pointed out to the newspapermen that Cody and Salsbury had spent eight thousand dollars on four miles of railroad to serve their show-ground establishment. The Wild West had come

151

to New York like a cyclone to a Kansas town," one reported. Samson carried off the gates of Gaza, but Buffalo Bill brought the great West to New York. Even though there were no shows on Sunday, the crowds still came; children to see the Indians, fraternal Elks to see the twin elk calves born on the lot, old soldiers to visit Sergeant Bates and relive the battles of the Civil War, which he was wont to describe in copious detail. During the last weeks on Staten Island in September the partners planned the Drama of Civilization which they would put on at Madison Square

Garden beginning November 24. Steele MacKaye saw the possibilities in such a pageant, designed a wind machine that would blow the stagecoach across the arena, new lighting effects, new ways to tell the great historical story.

The old Madison Square Garden, demolished soon after the unhappy Democratic National Convention of 1924, filled the block between Madison and Fourth Avenues, from Twenty-sixth to Twenty-seventh Street, a huge brown mass of brick, masonry, and marble, with colonnades covering the sidewalks. It housed circuses,

152

POPULAR WILLIE-SPOTTED-HORSE traveled in Wild West Show.

153

band concerts, horse shows. Here Steele
MacKaye bossed a crew of artists and technicians in September and October for the
fashionable horse show, working all night
nearly every night. Madison Square was
the center of fashion in those days. The
best department stores were nearby on
West Twenty-third Street. The old Fifth
Avenue Hotel stood at Twenty-third and
Fifth. Other popular and fashionable hotels
were a few blocks north on Fifth: the Bruns-
wick, Hoffman House, Holland House. On
the opposite side was Delmonico's.

It was a busy, exciting autumn in New
York. The Statue of Liberty was being
mounted on its pedestal and was finally
dedicated with appropriate ceremonies,
with President Cleveland speaking and
later reviewing a naval display. Stanley,
the explorer, returned, having met Livingston, the missionary, in darkest Africa.
Theodore Roosevelt ran third in a tempestuous political campaign for mayor; Abram
S. Hewitt won, with Henry George a close
second.

Nate Salsbury decided that the financial
risks of putting the Wild West Show on at
the Garden were too great for him to swing
alone. Adam Forepaugh, who sold or
loaned animals to circuses and then some-

CHIEF RED CLOUD, BUFFALO BILL, AND CHIEF AMERICAN HORSE at Madison Square Garden.

times took over the circuses in payment, came in as an additional partner, so the advertisements read: "Adam Forepaugh sole lessee . . . W. F. Cody and Nate Salsbury Proprietors and Managers . . ."

The show opened the night of November 24, 1886. The next day was Thanksgiving, and the newspaper advertisement on the front page of the New York *Herald* announced:

The Greatest Triumph Ever Known in the History of the City

Thousands Turned Away

BUFFALO BILL'S WILD WEST

Grand Thanksgiving Matinee Today, Tonight and Every Night with regular matinees Thursdays and Saturdays. Buffalo Bill Has Grand Army of Scouts, Cowboys, Indians, United States Troops, Mexican Vaqueros and Women and Children in a mighty Drama of Civilization.

The Grandest Stage Pictures, the Most Thrilling Tableaus, the Most Amazing Episodes. An Aggregation of Marvelous and Entrancing Scenes and Occurrences. Never before placed before any public. Admission 50¢ Children 25¢ Reserved Seats 75¢, $1., $1.50. Boxes $8., $10., $15. Doors open at 1 and 7 P.M.

The headline on the news story was "The Wild West Parades and Appears at Madison Square Garden . . . History of Civilization." The reporter began with a novel lead for those days: "Here they come! Here they come!

"The 'they' were a vicious, disgusting looking lot of redskins mounted on wiry little ponies, and the speaker, or rather crier, was a youngster with a wonderful pair of lungs who loved real, live Indians better than his supper. He stood on the curb facing the Madison Avenue entrance of Madison Square Garden.

" 'Golly what a Lulu' " the youngster cried as Chief Rocky Bear hove in sight.

" 'Dems de Cossacks!' 'And the Deadwood coach!' "

The reporter continued: "At Madison Square Garden, where Moody and Sankey sang their hymns, where Terpsichore and Bacchus have made such a night of it, Buffalo Bill appeared last night with his company of long haired cowboys.

"In one of the boxes were General William Tecumseh Sherman, in another Henry Ward Beecher. In other boxes were: Congressman Perry Belmont, Mrs. August Belmont, Oliver Belmont.

"The vast interior was cut in half with a partition on the east side of it, with a proscenium arch. On this stage Steele MacKaye presented as Dream First: 'The Primeval Forest of America before Its Discovery by the White Man!.' No one present could deny it being quite accurate. Frank Richmond, the silver tongued orator, appeared in a sort of pigeon loft to the left of the stage and recited words from MacKaye's golden tinged vocabulary."

The explanations of the "dreams" as the show proceeded the *Herald* reporter declared were tiresome, but the animals were interesting, especially an elk which was pursued stealthily by an Indian. "The elk sniffed the air, and paused before Mrs. Belmont. She raised her opera glasses. The elk turned his head toward Congressman Belmont. The wily red man then approached. The elk turned on him, the redskin ran and the crowd roared."

There was much more, especially the wind machine built by Nelse Waldron which blew down an Indian village and drove the stagecoach by its gale force halfway across the arena. Annie Oakley was in the show. Other acts were the coming of the settlers, the emigrant train, the attack by Indians, and, most thrilling of all, a prairie fire. Johnny Baker had an act all to himself, for he was now a crack shot.

Finally the audience beheld the Battle of the Little Big Horn with Buck Taylor as General Custer. When Custer's whole army was slaughtered, Buffalo Bill rode in, the spotlight on his majestic figure. He saw the carnage and on a screen appeared the simple words, "Too late!" The great scout reverently took off his Stetson and bowed his head. The lights dimmed, all was darkness for the change to the next scene. After the Deadwood coach attack the whole company came out as all the lights went on and the nine thousand spectators roared their ovation.

The great pageant played until February, while the preparations went on for the transportation of the company to England. A million people saw the show that season in New York.

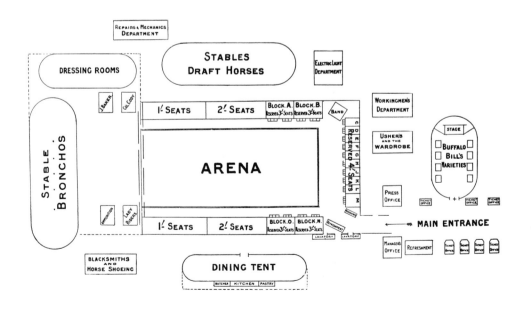

PLAN FOR LAYOUT OF THE SHOW when it was playing in England.

Chapter 11

London Sees the Wild West

BUFFALO BILL'S superb sense of the thrilling and dramatic entrance was never better displayed or more beautifully timed than in his appearance in London in the spring of 1887.

The British Empire was devotedly and merrily celebrating the Golden Jubilee of Queen Victoria. Her Majesty's fifty triumphant years on the throne reached a climax of good feeling and empire sentiment that made the June social season the most memorable one of the century for the Court of St. James.

Buffalo Bill and the Wild West Show arrived in May. It never occurred to Cody that he might have been considered an American intruder amid the carefully planned royal festivities. With wily frontier innocence he simply assumed that he would be welcome. And, as it turned out, the itinerant 41-year-old scout of the plains met the crowned royalty of Britain and Europe on the basis of American equality and dramatized a new understanding among the peoples of the English-speaking world.

THE QUEEN AND RED SHIRT.

157

BUFFALO BILL AND STAFF in London, in the front row (in silk hat) Nate Salsbury, Supt. Fisher, Jules Keene, Supt. Foinett, John M. Burke, Red Shirt.

The people of Britain were prosperous, contented, pleased with themselves and their place in the universe. The atmosphere was one of rejoicing, in a cozy sense of security at the heart of a vast empire. Yet, despite the surge of healthy imperial-patriotism at this historic moment, the people, and the Queen and her court, took Buffalo Bill and the Wild West Show to their hearts.

With the arrival of the Wild West Show the 68-year-old Queen seemed to fling off the melancholy mood of mourning which had dampened her spirits for a quarter century after the death of her consort, Prince Albert. Obviously, Buffalo Bill was only a contributory factor; yet it could not have been entirely a coincidence that after her first visit to the Wild West Show, and her exposure to Cody's glamorous natural artistry, her spirits noticeably brightened and she began to rediscover the joy of being a spectator at other unofficial events. With conspicuous energy the Queen entered into the plans for the regal ceremonies after she had seen, as she wrote in her journal, "a very extraordinary and interesting sight—a performance of Buffalo Bill's Wild West."

Earlier, in March of that year, Governor John M. Thayer of Nebraska had honored his state's most famous citizen by commissioning William F. Cody a colonel in the National Guard. It is likely that Major

158

Burke suggested the colonelcy as a potential asset for Cody in titled English society. Cody, who had earlier turned down a commission in the regular Army, now appreciated rank and used his honorary military title of colonel even after Governor Thayer elevated him to brigadier general in 1891. To this day Buffalo Bill is known in the Wyoming town of Cody as "The Colonel."

Major Burke and Nate Salsbury hit upon the happy choice of the S. S. *Nebraska* as the chartered vessel to transport the show directly to London. On Thursday, March 31, 1887, the company marched aboard: a cast of two hundred including cowboys, Indians, Mexican vaqueros, rifle shots, Annie Oakley, and the staff for the mess, the stables, and the supervision of the box office and seating arrangements. There were also buffaloes, Texas steers, burros, broncos, racing horses, elk, bear; and tents, wagons, the Deadwood stagecoach, band instruments, arms, ammunition; not to mention brand-new costumes for the invasion of England.

Everyone except the entrepreneurs was nervous about this undertaking. Many of the cast feared the tempestuous waves of the wild Atlantic and dreaded the two weeks of confinement aboard ship. The Indians recalled the old tribal superstitions which held that disaster would befall them if they crossed the ocean. Even Red Shirt, the Sioux chief, believed that a malady would consume their flesh, and that they would become skeletons which would never find burial. Every morning during the voyage he examined his body for signs of fatal decay.

Major John M. Burke had gone ahead to Britain. Nate Salsbury had made all the arrangements in careful detail. An enterprising Yorkshire businessman, John Robinson Whitley, had conceived the idea of an American trade exhibition; but the plan nearly failed for lack of a drawing card. As it happened, the exhibition of American-manufactured products—the first such American exhibit outside the United States —was almost eclipsed by Buffalo Bill's Wild West. Salsbury, through Whitley, had managed to include the Wild West Show under the semi-official sponsorship of the trade fair.

The Wild West company felt more fear than rejoicing in anticipation. However, as the S. S. *Nebraska* sailed down the North River, the cowboy band bravely struck up "The Girl I Left Behind Me." By the time the ship passed Sandy Hook nearly everybody was seasick. The whole aggregation was so depressed that on the first Sunday out Buffalo Bill called the personnel together and preached them a cheerful sermon. Nate Salsbury followed with the old song and comedy routines which had earned such success with his Salsbury Troubadours. The cowboys, Indians, and staff felt a little better, but their homesick spirits did not rally until the ship reached Gravesend, at the mouth of the Thames. There a tug, flying the stars and stripes, steamed out to meet them, and to their amazement a small band appeared on the tug's deck and played "The Star-Spangled

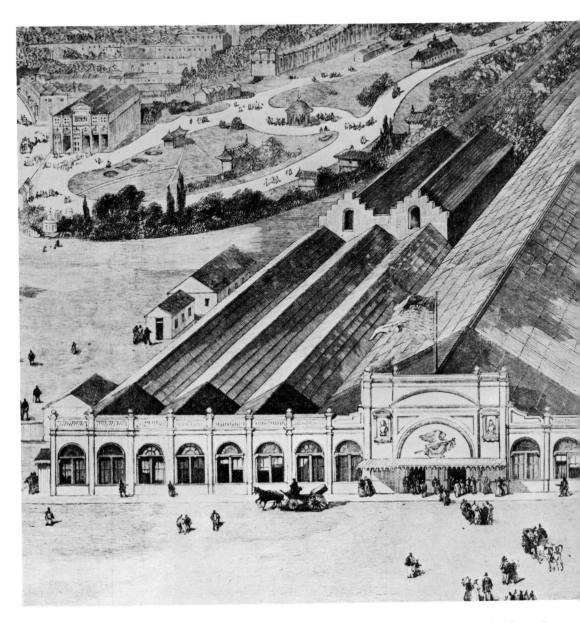

Banner." Hastily the cowboys assembled their band instruments and responded with "Yankee Doodle."

Led by John M. Burke, and followed by Lord Ronald Gower and the directors of the American Exhibition in London, the welcoming party climbed the ladder to the deck of the *Nebraska*. Her Majesty's government, they announced, were extending every courtesy to the Wild West Show and

THE AMERICAN EXHIBITION, EARL'S COURT, WEST BROMPTON, AND WEST KENSINGTON.

had granted special permits for the animals to be landed. A boat train was provided to take all passengers and cargo from the Royal Albert docks in the East End of London to the Earl's Court grounds in Kensington, where already $130,000 had been invested in the arena, grandstand, stables, and equipment for the show. The open grandstand held twenty thousand persons, sheltered stands held ten thousand more; and there was standing room for ten thousand. Salsbury had planned meticulously for the landing and the order of disembarkment. There was no confusion when the large troupe docked early in the morning. Each performer looked

161

after his own horse. The Midland Railway had the train waiting; it proceeded directly to Earl's Court. By four in the afternoon the horses and animals had been stabled and watered, all had been fed, and the camp equipment and bedding had been distributed.

A vast crowd watched the arrival with mounting excitement and admiration. When everything seemed to be organized and settled, Colonel Cody ordered the band to play "God Save the Queen." Then the entire company sat down to supper, eating in full view of the gaping crowd. By nine o'clock in the evening the assembly was ready for bed. Many people in the crowd expressed astonishment at the enterprise of these pioneering Americans, the London newspapers reported, and a number were heard to say, "These Yankees mean business."

One of the first of many distinguished visitors to the encampment was the actor Henry Irving, who was soon to be knighted. He was then playing in *Much Ado About Nothing* with Ellen Terry. Already he had welcomed the Wild West Show in an article in the London *Era:* "I saw an entertainment in New York which impressed me immensely," he wrote. "It is coming to London. It is an entertainment in which the whole of the most interesting episodes of life on the extreme frontier of civilization in America are represented with the most graphic vividness and scrupulous detail. You have real cowboys with bucking horses, real buffaloes, and great hordes of steers, which are lassoed and stampeded in the most realistic fashion imaginable. Then there are real Indians who execute attacks upon coaches driven at full speed. No one can exaggerate the extreme excitement and 'go' of the whole performance. It is simply immense, and I venture to predict that when it comes to London it will take the town by storm."

The show's impending arrival had been announced on April 12 by the *Morning Post:* "The famous huntsman, Buffalo Bill, the idol of the *petit peuple* of America, arrives next week and ere long the Aborigines of the Great Republic will be as familiar in London streets as need be."

The actual arrival was reported by the London *Daily News* on April 16: "One could not help recalling the delightful sensations of youth, the first acquaintance with the Last of the Mohicans, the Great Spirit, Firewater, Laughing Water, and the dark Huron warrior." The reporter glimpsed a squaw "whose teeth" he said, "should make her a treasure for any honest dentist."

This and similar newspaper stories started a boom at the bookstores for the works of Fenimore Cooper. Prentiss Ingraham's *Border Romances of Buffalo Bill* also had a tremendous sale, selling edition after edition at the bookstalls, and the British public seemed to accept every word of it. Once the show opened it set the whole population reading, thinking, and talking about the American West.

Among the callers during the first days after the show's arrival were Ellen Terry, Justin McCarthy, U. S. Minister Phelps, Consul General Thomas Waller, Deputy

Consul Moffat, Henry Labouchere (Member of Parliament), and Charles Wyndham, the famous actor. Lord Gower, who was honorary chairman of the American Exhibition—the trade fair of American products adjacent to the arena—came almost daily. Other visitors to the encampment were Sir Cunliffe Owen, Lord Paget, Lord Charles Beresford, Grank Duke Michael of Russia, Lady Monckton, Sir Francis Knollys (secretary to the Prince of Wales), Colonels Clarke and Montague, Lady Alice Beckie (whom the Indians called "Sunshine of the Camp" after she had made repeated visits), Lord Strathmore, Lord Windsor, Lady Randolph Churchill, and Mrs. John W. Mackay. Society led the way, the nobility set the example, and all of London followed en masse.

The press seemed delighted to publish pages of copy about the show even though the Jubilee demanded precedence in space. "It is certainly a novel idea," said the London *Illustrated News,* "for one nation to give an exhibition devoted exclusively to its own frontier history, a story enacted by genuine characters, of the dangers and hardships of its settlement, on the soil of another country, 3,000 miles away. Yet this is exactly what the Americans will do this year in London and it is an idea worthy of that thorough-going and enterprising people.

"We frankly and gladly allow that there

163

is a natural and sentimental view of the design which will go far to obtain for it a hearty welcome in England. The progress of the United States, now the largest community of the English race on the face of the earth, is a proper subject for congratulation, for the popular mind in the United Kingdom does not regard, and will never be taught to regard what are styled "imperial interests"—those of mere political dominion—as equally valuable with the habits and ideas and domestic life of the aggregate of human families belonging to our race. The greater the numerical proportion of these, already exceeding sixty millions, are inhabitants of the great American republic.

Buck Taylor (King of the Cowboys) and his horse, Chieftain

"This is his scalplock"

"It would be unnatural to deny ourselves the indulgence of a just gratification in seeing what men of our own blood, men of our own mind and disposition in all essential respects, though tempered and sharpened by more stimulating conditions, with some wider opportunities for exertion, have achieved in raising a wonderful fabric of modern civilization and bringing it to the highest prosperity across the whole breadth of the Western continent. We feel sure this sentiment will prevail in the hearts of hundreds of thousands of visitors to Buffalo Bill's American camp, about to be opened at the West End of London; and we take it kindly of the great kindred people of the United States that they now send such a magnificent representation to the motherland, determined to take some part in celebrating the jubilee of Her Majesty the Queen."

On April 25 the Right Honorable William Ewart Gladstone, until a few months previously the Prime Minister—then seventy-eight—called at one o'clock with Mrs.

Gladstone and the Marquis of Lorne, husband of Princess Louise, attended by Lord
Gower and Mr. Waller. Nate Salsbury welcomed them with the cowboy band, which
swung into "Yankee Doodle" as the visitors met Colonel Cody who was looking
his immaculate best in white buckskin and
sombrero.

The party were introduced to Chief Red
Shirt. "The manly frankness of this splendid specimen of American backwoods-
man," noted the London *Evening News*
on April 28, "highly interested Mr. Gladstone, and he remained in conversation
with him for some time. The former Sioux
Chief Red Shirt's bright appearance and
intelligent face won much admiration from
the distinguished party and Mr. Gladstone

we sketch each other

The "Pop-gun Puzzle"

was amused by some of his replies." The
"roving correspondent" of the London
Daily Telegraph fortunately overheard part
of the conversation. "Mr. Gladstone asked
Red Shirt what he thought of the English
climate. The chief said he had not much to
complain about so far. Mr. Gladstone asked
if he thought the Englishmen looked
enough like the Americans to be kinsmen
and brothers. Red Shirt wasn't sure about
that." After this little discussion, Buffalo
Bill put himself at the head of the whole
body of horsemen and wheeled them into
line for a salute to the former prime minister. Major Burke, witnessing the affair, said
that Mr. Gladstone appeared to enjoy himself like a schoolboy.

Red Shirt gave a special interview to the
Sheffield *Leader* on the treatment of the In-

dians in the United States. It was published in that paper on May 5, 1887. "The red man is changing every season," the chief said. "The Indian of the next generation will not be the Indian of the last. Our buffaloes are nearly all gone, the deer have entirely vanished, and the white man takes more and more of our land. But the United States government is good. True, it has taken away our land, and the white men have eaten up our deer and our buffalo, but the government now gives us food that we may not starve. They are educating our children and teaching them to farm and to use farming implements. Our children will learn the white man's civilization and to live like him."

Punch used the Wild West Show as a subject for political cartoons, drawing British faces on the cowboys, captioning the pictures with topical references. On May 4, London *Sporting Life's* humorous writer published his reminiscences of the American West: "The first bronco I ever saw reached out his right-hand foot and expostulated with his would-be rider, so that he died. . . . I once saw a clever down-east equestrian get on a bronco with much pomp and a derrick."

Soon after his arrival Buffalo Bill was made an honorary member of a number of the best London clubs. At the Reform Club he was formally presented to the Prince of Wales and the Duke of Cambridge. He dined at the Beaufort Club with the Duke of Beaufort. At the Savage Club he met Wilson Barrett, the actor, and Henry Irving again. At the United Arts he

was entertained by the Duke of Teck; at St. George's by Lord Bruce, Lord Woolmer, Lord Lymington, Christopher Sykes, and Herbert Gladstone. He dined at Lord and Lady Randolph Churchill's, where he met their son Winston Spencer Churchill, then thirteen years of age. Lord Charles Beresford took him frequently to the Coaching Club. He was also honored by a lunch at the Mansion House with the Lord Mayor and Lady Mayoress of the City of London.

If Nate Salsbury, Cody's equal partner, preoccupied with the details of organizing the show, felt abandoned by the star during Buffalo Bill's immediate social success, he gave no evidence of jealousy or resentment. He had successfully coped with every last-minute problem except the noise of occasional railway trains on the nearby main line, and even on this minor annoyance he had persuaded the railway officials to curb the hoot of the locomotive whistles as they passed by.

The Prince and Princess of Wales visited the Wild West camp on May 6. Colonel Cody entertained the Prince (later Edward VII) with the first complete performance of the show on English soil, a grand dress rehearsal for the public opening which was scheduled for May 9. The performance went on even though the day was unpleasant and the field muddy. The Royal Box was decorated with American and British flags, the first time in history that they were displayed in such combination. The Prince was accompanied by the Princesses Victoria, Louise, and Maude,

THE PRINCE AND PRINCESS OF WALES visit Wild West Show at Earl's Court

the Marquis of Lorne, the Duke of Cambridge, the Duke of Teck, his son Francis, the Comtesse de Paris, the Crown Prince of Denmark. Lady Suffield and Miss Knollys were in attendance on the Princess of Wales. Others in the royal party were Lady Cole, Colonel Clarke, and Lord Edward Somerset. The London *Chronicle* reported that the Prince of Wales was so excited he remained standing throughout the show. Later the Prince presented Colonel Cody with a diamond copy of his crest—three ostrich feathers mounted in gems and gold —as a scarf pin.

After the show Annie Oakley was presented to the royal guests. The Princess of Wales astonished her countrymen by shaking hands with Little Missy. Custom dictated that royalty offer the left hand, which the person presented kissed lightly. The Princess then offered Chief Red Shirt a welcome to England, and he replied, "Tell the great chief's wife that it gladdens my heart to hear words of welcome." Then the royal ladies visited the Indian village, and noting John Nelson's half-breed papoose, patted it on the head.

Before he left the grounds the Prince of Wales inspected the stables. He was particularly interested in Buffalo Bill's famous horse Old Charlie, then twenty-one years of age. Buffalo Bill told the Prince the story of Charlie, a half-breed Kentucky horse, probably the most publicized horse of his time. "Charlie is an animal of almost human intelligence. When he was quite young I rode him on a hunt for wild horses, which he ran down after a chase of fifteen miles. At another time on a wager of five hundred dollars that I could ride him over the prairies a hundred miles in ten hours, he went the distance in nine hours and forty-five minutes." In spite of his age, Charlie was still the star horse of the show. Grand Duke Michael also took a fancy to him and rode him in the show on one occasion during the chase after buffalo. Incidentally, the Grand Duke had come to London, it was officially rumored, in search of a wife, but took more interest in the Wild West than in titled ladies.

A London newspaperman also met Charlie: "I saw Buffalo Bill's horse, Charlie, twenty years old (a tame old gee-gee who licked my hand). Mr. Cody had ridden him upwards of fourteen years in his campaigns and western exploits." Colonel Cody rode Charlie at full gallop when he shot the glass balls tossed by Johnny Baker. When Buffalo Bill rode him at the command performance at Windsor Castle, the horse seemed to realize the importance of the occasion and was at his best, spectators declared.

The London press outdid itself with unaccustomed superlatives to describe the first public performance. *The Illustrated Sporting and Dramatic News* said on May 14, 1887, "Saddling and mounting these 'outrages' (as Mark Twain calls them) by the cowboys, Buck Taylor, Jim Mitchell, Billy Bullock, and other celebrities, is perhaps the most interesting part of the performance. Some six or eight skinfuls of iniquity are successfully dealt with, amongst them the well known mare, Dynamite. This is a fiend. Born a buck-jumper, and encouraged in her wickedness from a foal, she humps her back like an angry tomcat, rises from the ground with her head between her hoofs, her legs stiff as area railings, and comes down with that diabolical jerk, and at that uncomfortable angle which implies to the ordinary good rider, not only a peremptory notice to quit, but an injunction to emigrate to the adjoining parish. Her squeal is of itself sinful; it approaches bad language as near as a horse ever got. . . . Happy creature! Appreciated only on account of her perversity; valuable in direct proportion to her viciousness. What a delightful world it would be, and

COL. W. F. CODY and his old war horse "Charlie"

to what high office might we not aspire in it, if a similarly inverted code of human morality prevailed amongst us.

"The horseman's feat of picking up a handkerchief from the ground (a small coin is more difficult) is admirably executed by Buffalo Bill himself. The trick is common with *vaqueros* and *arrieros* generally, but then it is usually a mere trick. The left spur, firmly embedded in the folds of the saddle, forms a fulcrum upon which the rider can swing back easily into his seat, for it is this swinging back to the saddle that constitutes the difficulty of the performance. Colonel Cody's gigantic proportions enable him to dispense with all such extraneous aid. He can afford to ride comparatively slowly, not at a full gallop. A foot or so of extra reach makes little difference to him. He trusts to an accurate eye, a supple waist, a firm grip of the left knee, and the strength of his right stirrup-leather. He swoops, and picks up his property without any apparent effort or appearance of scooping it.

"The Indian pony races remind one forcibly of Olympia, and the snap shooting at glass balls of the Aquarium and the music halls; but the races are well ridden, and Miss Oakley and Miss Smith, and the Great Buffalo Bill himself could probably give points to Colonel Carver and Bogardus.

"The show will be popular, and well deserves the popularity it will enjoy. It is genuine, and it is a healthy sign of the times that the great British public will appreciate and applaud it solely for that reason."

The Golden Jubilee was a busy year for the Queen, and every minute was carefully planned. However, to the astonishment of her subjects, she journeyed to Earl's Court three days after the première. On May 12 she visited the show intending to stay for an hour. She remained for the whole performance, even though she had to return to Windsor by carriage afterward. Her enthusiasm was unprecedented, for she never went to the theater. If she wanted to see a play, which was seldom, it was performed for her at Windsor Castle. The Queen arrived at the grounds at five in the afternoon. She drove around the arena in her carriage-and-four, escorted by scarlet-coated outriders, and then entered the Royal Box. With her were the Prince and Princess of Battenberg, the Marquis of Lorne, the Dowager Duchess of Athole, the Honorable Ethel Cadogan, Sir Henry and Lady Ponsonby, Colonel Sir Henry Ewart, and Lord Ronald Gower.

When they were seated, Buffalo Bill rode into the arena carrying a large American flag on a staff. The Queen rose and bowed

Buffalo Bill before the Queen—The American flag, carried by Sergeant Bates.

169

1. The scene in the arena.

impressively as he waved the flag above his head, then handed it to Sergeant Bates to dip to Her Majesty. Thereupon the whole Court party rose, ladies bowed, the military men saluted, and English noblemen took off their hats. "Then there arose," relates Major Burke, "such a genuine heart-stirring American yell as seemed to shake the sky. For the first time in history since the Declaration of Independence a sovereign of Great Britain saluted the Star-Spangled Banner."

After the performance Buffalo Bill was presented to the Queen and they enjoyed a long conversation together. Nate Salsbury and Red Shirt followed. The Indian chief told the Queen "he had come a long way to see Her Majesty and felt glad."

2. Miss Smith showing the Queen her rifle.

3. The Sioux Chief "Red Shirt" presented to the Queen.

4. The Queen and the Indian squaws.

Queen Victoria enjoyed the show so much that she insisted upon seeing it again, and she particularly wanted her royal guests who were then arriving for the Jubilee ceremonies to see it. She thereupon arranged for a command performance at Windsor Castle the day before the great Jubilee ceremonies at Westminster Abbey. The command performance was given on the morning of June 20. The Queen's special guests were the King of Greece, the King of Saxony, the King and Queen of the Belgians, the King of Denmark, the Crown Prince of Austria, the Prince and Princess of Saxe-Meininger, the Crown Prince of Sweden and Norway, Princess Victoria of Prussia, the Duke of Sparta, Grand Duke Michael of Russia, Prince George of Greece, Prince Louis of Baden, and the Prince and Princess of Wales.

It was on this occasion that four kings rode in the Deadwood Coach while the Prince of Wales rode on the seat high up front beside Buffalo Bill, who drove. The often repeated story, told in various versions, is that the Prince of Wales remarked to Colonel Cody, during the collation afterward, "You held a pretty good poker hand there, with four kings." Whereupon Buffalo Bill replied, "Not only four kings, but a prince as well made it a royal flush such as no man ever held before." Later, when he returned to the United States Colonel Cody varied the story to say, "Not only that, I had the royal joker!"

Inevitably, with this genuinely warmhearted royal reception the show was not only a sellout for every performance but Buffalo Bill became the social rage of London. He took rooms in Regent Street, in the heart of the fashionable West End, over Hope Brothers' haberdashery, next to Ralph D. Blumenfeld, then the London correspondent for the New York *Herald,* who wrote, "Cody can now wear evening dress and adjust a white tie as easily as he could skin a buffalo calf. He has a fine sense of humor and laughs at himself when he sees his mantel covered with invitations." Buffalo Bill was embarrassed, however, by the overwhelming mass of flowers received daily from female admirers. He told Blumenfeld, "I've been reading about Bret Harte and Tom Thumb. They were lionized here for a while, too, but only while there was excitement about them."

Blumenfeld in his diary wrote that he had two heroes as a boy, "Robin Hood and Buffalo Bill, and delighted in Cody's stories of the Pony Express and Yellow Hand. Everything was done," he wrote, "to make Cody conceited and unbearable, but he remained the simple, unassuming child of the plains who thought lords and ladies belonged in the picture books and that the story of Little Red Riding Hood was true. I rode in the Deadwood coach. It was a great evening in which I realized a good many of my boyhood dreams, for there was Buffalo Bill on his white rocking horse charger, and Annie Oakley rode behind him."

Colonel Cody was never too busy to listen to stories of old veterans of the Crimea or the Franco-Prussian war, Blumen-

H.R.H. Princess of Wales

H.M. the Queen

H.R.H. Princess Beatrice, Battenberg

Countess of Dudley

Grand Duchess Serge of Russia

H.R.H. Princess of Saxe-Meiningen

H.R.H. Princess Mary Adelaide

Duchess of Leinster

Princess Louise

Queen of the Belgians

Distinguished Visitors to Buffalo Bill's Wild West, London, 1887.

173

feld relates, and he also loved fairy tales. One evening a man known as Miguel, an educated Chilean castaway, told Buffalo Bill many stories borrowed from Greek mythology. After he had heard some of these classic tales the Colonel asked Blumenfeld, "That fellow Hercules must have been a pretty good cuss, but there aren't any centaurs left now, are there?" The newspaperman shook his head sadly. "No," he said to Colonel Cody, "they are all dead."

Lord Ronald Sutherland Gower persuaded the Gladstone family to visit the show grounds soon after Buffalo Bill arrived. Lord Gower described some of these moments in his diaries, referring to what the Londoners called the "Yankeries," or the "Buffalo Billeries" as *Punch* christened the exhibition. Lord Gower described the Queen's visit: "The Queen seemed delighted with the performance; she looked radiant. At the close of the performance Buffalo Bill, at Her Majesty's desire, was presented, as well as the Indian chief, two of the squaws with their papooses, whose little painted faces the Queen stroked. I hope that Melton Prior [the artist] who was there will make a drawing of the scene as it would make quite a pretty picture."

Years later after another command performance Queen Victoria noted in her diary . . . At 5, . . . we went on to the East Terrace, and watched from a tent, open in front, a sort of "Buffalo Bill" performance, on the Lawn below. It was extremely well arranged, and an excellent representation of what we had also seen 5 years ago at Earl's Court. There were Cow Boys, Red Indians, Mexicans, Argentinos taking part and then a wonderful riding display by Cossacks, accompanied by curious singing, and a war dance by the Indians. There were extraordinary buck jumping horses, shooting at glass balls, by Col. Cody (Buffalo Bill) and display of cracking huge long whips. The whole, was a very pretty, wild sight, which lasted an hour. At the conclusion of the performance, all advanced in line at a gallop and stopped suddenly. Col. Cody was brought up for me to speak to him. He is still a very handsome man, but has now got a grey beard."

A number of distinguished Americans visited London for the Jubilee, and Buffalo Bill invited them to the Wild West camp for an Indian breakfast. James G. Blaine headed the list of guests, which included Joseph Pulitzer, the proprietor of the New York *World,* Chauncey M. Depew, Lawrence Jerome (Cody's old hunting companion), Murat Halstead, and General Simon Cameron. The Indians dug a big hole in the ground in front of the mess tent, and cooked a rib roast at nine o'clock in the morning, and afterward the Indians put on a war dance for the guests.

Buffalo Bill was such a social success that the prima donnas of the day in the world of fashion and the arts, particularly Oscar Wilde, showed some jealousy of the attentions accorded the famous scout. However, Wilde attended the opening, and *Vanity Fair,* the society gossip magazine, reported facetiously that during the attack on the Deadwood coach Mr. Wilde

174

"was greatly alarmed for the safety of his scalp." Miss Ellen Terry, this paper reported, was "wrapped in a dust-veil and dust coat, evidently under the impression she was at the Derby." During the Deadwood coach attack Lord Ronald, beside the driver, was observed "blowing his nose calmly at the most critical moment, when his scalp was presumably in such imminent danger, which lent considerable realism to the proceedings." Others present were Cardinal Manning, T. P. O'Conner, and Count Karolyi.

The Wild West played to packed audiences all summer and on into the autumn before moving on to Manchester and other cities in England. *The Times* of London gave it a dignified farewell tribute:

"The American Exhibition which has attracted all the town to West Brompton for the last few months, was brought yesterday to an appropriate and dignified close. A meeting of representative Englishmen and Americans was held in the presidency of Lord Lorne, in support of the movement for the establishing a Court of Arbitration for the settlement of disputes between this country and the United States. At first it might seem a far cry from the Wild West to an International Court.

THE WILD WEST SHOW, the company forming in line.

"Yet the connection is not really remote. Exhibitions of American products and scenes from the wilder phases of American life certainly tend, in some degree at least, to bring America nearer to England. They are partly cause and partly effect of increased and increasing intercourse between the two countries, and they tend to promote a still more intimate understanding. Those who went to be amused often stayed to be instructed. The Wild West was irresistible. Colonel Cody suddenly found himself the hero of the London season. Notwithstanding his daily engagements and his punctual fulfillment of them, he found time to go everywhere, to see everything, and to be seen by the world.

"All London contributed to his triumph and now the close of his show is selected as the occasion for promoting a great international movement, with Mr. Bright, Lord Granville, Lord Wolseley and Lord Lorne for its sponsors. Civilization itself consents to march in the train of Buffalo Bill. Colonel Cody can achieve no greater triumph than this, even if someday he realizes the design attributed to him of running the Wild West Show at Rome. . . . It is true that Red Shirt would be as unusual a phenomenon on Broadway as in Cheapside. But the Wild West, for all that, is racy of the American soil. We can easily imagine Wall Street for ourselves; we need to be shown the cowboys of Colorado. Hence it is no paradox to say that Colonel Cody has done his part in bringing America and England nearer together."

Buffalo Bill, assisted by Burke, acknowl-edged all the auspicious press comments, and answered all his mail and invitations personally—yet still found time to write letters home to Louisa and his small daughters, and to his sister Julia. The pomp and ceremony of formal society had not affected his natural simplicity or diverted him from playing the arduous role of super-scout. He was scarcely aware of his enormous earnings, which Salsbury carefully stewarded—over half a million dollars, without income tax, and with a purchasing power at least four times that of a similar amount today.

The triumphant Wild West company returned to New York in the spring of 1888 on the chartered ship *Persian Monarch,* the voyage saddened by the death of Old Charlie. Colonel Cody's first impulse was to take the carcass of the horse home and bury him at North Platte, but he finally decided to give his old pard a handsome burial at sea. Wrapped in canvas and covered with the American flag, Old Charlie was brought on deck while Colonel Cody delivered his final farewell:

"Old fellow, your journeys are over. . . . Obedient to my call, gladly you bore your burden on, little knowing, little reckoning what the day might bring, shared sorrows and pleasures alike. Willing speed, tireless courage . . . you have never failed me. Ah, Charlie, old fellow, I have had many friends, but few of whom I could say that . . . I loved you as you loved me. Men tell me you have no soul; but if there is a heaven and scouts can enter there, I'll wait at the gate for you, old friend."

Chapter 12

Europe Sees Buffalo Bill

AFTER the next spectacularly successful season at the old site on Staten
Island, during which Buffalo Bill lived at
the Waldorf-Astoria Hotel in New York
and held open house every night for the
rank and fashion of New York, the Wild
West Show was ready to invade the continent of Europe. For a brief period, while
Cody rested with his family at North Platte
—dividing his time between his wife and
daughters at the Welcome Wigwam house
and the nearby Scout's Rest Ranch where
his sister Julia was living with her husband

—Salsbury made the final preparations for
the tour.

Salsbury applied his proven formula to
the schedule: go where the crowd is already gathering. He insured the financial
success of the first Continental tour by
planning to be in Paris during the Exposition of 1889. Great numbers of people
would be there with money to spend, and
a desire to see everything that was novel
and well publicized.

Annie Oakley, who had been on a tour
with Pawnee Bill's show while the Wild

BUFFALO BILL IN VENICE WITH SOME OF HIS INDIAN BRAVES.

177

West was organizing for Europe, rejoined Buffalo Bill. Everyone, including Salsbury, knew that the Continent presented difficulties because of the variety of languages they would encounter; but no one except the Indians in the cast was frightened by the prospect of another ocean voyage.

The advance publicity had been so well planned that by the time the Wild West Show was encamped in the Bois de Boulogne, in Paris, the small shops of the French capital were full of American souvenirs—pottery, tiny molded sculptures, and toys representing Indians, bucking horses, bison, cowboys, saddles, and Buffalo Bill. The Wild West motif became high style, as well. For the grand opening Burke, now skilled in diplomacy, had managed to produce royalty, nobility, practically everyone who was fashionable or celebrated. President Carnot of the Republic of France occupied a box with his wife. With them came members of the cabinet, important officials, and generals, with their families. All the prominent Americans then in Paris appeared, including Whitelaw Reid, then the American ambassador in London, Louis MacLean, the American ambassador to France, and Thomas Edison, who was touring France with his wife.

Leaders of the *haut ton* of French society gave elaborate breakfasts for Buffalo Bill, and smart salons lured him into the most sophisticated intellectual circles. Prince Roland Bonaparte interviewed the Indians, and when it became known that the Vicomtesse Chardon de Briailes had

Rosa Bonheur painting Buffalo Bill in Paris.

entertained Cody, he became the social lion of the season.

Buffalo Bill had come to realize, chiefly through his experience in London, what tremendous publicity value a ride in the Deadwood stagecoach could have. He established a new status for European nobility: if they didn't ride in the Deadwood coach during the attack by Indians they were not up to the standards set by the British. Isabella, ex-queen of Spain, rode in the coach, as did the Shah of Persia, who declared it was the greatest emotional experience of his European tour.

French artists, led by the example of Rosa Bonheur, flocked to the show with drawing boards and easels. Rosa Bonheur was enchanted by the horses and Indians,

178

Rosa Bonheur's portrait of Buffalo Bill. (See frontispiece for color reproduction.)

180

and spent many days on the grounds. She painted a famous portrait of Buffalo Bill, which is now owned by the estate of Cody's late friend W. R. Coe and frequently exhibited in the United States.

After the summer exhibition in the Bois de Boulogne the Wild West toured the South of France, and then went to Barcelona. But in Spain the weather was cold and wet, and the company was often reduced to half strength by severe colds. In spite of all Major Burke's publicity, Spanish audiences did not turn out. Since the show included no bull fights, the people of Barcelona were not interested. Burke had a band of Indians photographed in front of a statue of Columbus, but no paper published it. Frank Richmond, who announced the acts, died of influenza. Everybody was depressed, and eventually happy to get out of Spain alive.

Italy was next. Naples proved as much of a new experience for the Americans as their Wild West Show did for the Neapolitans. An imaginative Neapolitan had counterfeited two thousand or more reserved-seat tickets, which produced fantastic confusion at the opening. Instead of the painted canvas depicting the Wyoming buttes, Vesuvius provided the mountainous background. It was springtime in Italy. The crowds were enormous and the Spanish losses were soon recouped.

American tourists in Italy that year were amazed by and proud of the reception given to Buffalo Bill and his Wild West. The first sensation was the riding of wild horses by the American cowboys. The Duke of Sermoneta saw the show in Rome and challenged the cowboys to tame his ferocious horses, of which the Italians were terrified. It was rumored that the beasts were so fierce that they ate people, and that they were brought to the arena in chains. The crowds shuddered at the thought of what would happen if the wild horses got loose and charged into the crowd, so special barricades were set up. The Duke said no cowboy in the world could conquer his animals.

Twenty thousand people demanded to see the historic performance. Two of the Duke's horses were released within the improvised and reinforced corral. Buffalo Bill announced that they would be tamed in full view of the audience. A New York *Herald* reporter wrote, "The brutes made springs into the air, darted hither and thither in all directions, and bent themselves into all sorts of shapes, but all in vain. In five minutes the cowboys had caught the wild horses, saddled, subdued, and bestrode them. Then the cowboys rode them around the arena while the dense crowds applauded with delight."

As one of the cowboys explained later, the job was easy. They simply lassoed the wild horses, tied them, and kept them under control with ropes. Cowboys on horseback rode up to the animals as they got to their feet, one on each side of them. The horses quickly discovered that there was no way they could escape, and were subdued within five minutes. Thinking there must be a trick, the crowd was indignant at first. They had expected a ferocious struggle, and were betting that these beasts would outwit the Americans. But the whole thing was over so quickly that it seemed anticlimactic. The Italian pride was hurt, and the American cowboys were booed by some of the audience.

Then Buffalo Bill challenged the Italians who had come from the South of Italy with the wild horses to tame the western broncos. Every would-be Italian rider was tossed into the air and onto the ground in less than a minute. The Colonel allowed the Italians to try their methods: using irons and chains; but after they had worked for half an hour, Cody called it off because the Italian methods were too brutal.

The Wild West didn't show in the Coliseum as Buffalo Bill had announced. He had not known that the historic arena was cluttered with too much rubble and stone work for showing horses or driving the Deadwood coach. However, the whole company was photographed there—and the legend persists that the Coliseum was the scene of Cody's Roman triumph.

Buffalo Bill and the cast were received by Pope Leo XIII. Beforehand, Major Burke lectured the Indians on how to behave. Deeply impressed and obedient, they lined the corridor while the Pope was carried out on his *sedia gestatoria*, wearing the tiara or triple crown, and accompanied by Cardinal Rampolla. The visit had been arranged by Monsignor O'Connell of the American College in Rome, supported by Archbishop Corrigan of New York. One of the Indian squaws fainted, and another squaw died at camp that night, which greatly upset the superstitious Indians.

The show then visited Florence, where there was a troublesome delay because the local customs officials tried to place entrance duties on the animals in accordance with their weight. After that difficulty was cleared up the show went on, then visited Milan, Venice, where the Indians rode in gondolas, and Verona, where the show played in an amphitheater built by Diocletian.

Everywhere in Europe—except in apathetic Spain—Buffalo Bill was the center of attention, and sometimes of controversy as well. American newspaper reporters in Europe delighted in describing for their home press the quick taming of the wildest horses of the Continent by Cody's plain western cowboys. These performances, and the dramatic reports of them, stirred up endless discussions in Europe, England, and the United States. Theodore Roosevelt contributed to the discussion in his role as sportsman, hunter, and writer. In one of the books, *The Wilderness Hunter*, about his hunting exploits in the early 1890s, he wrote:

"When Buffalo Bill took his cowboys to Europe they made a practice in England, France, Germany, and Italy of offering to break and ride, in their own fashion, any horse given them. They were frequently given spoiled horses from the cavalry services in the different countries through which they passed, animals with which the trained horse-breakers of the European

COLONEL CODY AT HEIGHT OF HIS SHOW CAREER TOURING EUROPE. **183**

armies could do nothing; and yet in almost all cases the cow-punchers and broncobusters with Buffalo Bill mastered these beasts as readily as they did their own western horses. At their own work of mastering and riding rough horses they could not be matched by their more civilized rivals; but I have great doubts whether they in turn would not have been beaten if they had essayed kinds of horsemanship utterly alien to their past experience, such as riding mettled thoroughbreds in a steeplechase, or the like. Other things being equal (which, however, they generally are not)

a bad, big horse fed on oats offers a rather more difficult problem than a bad little horse fed on grass.

"After Buffalo Bill's men had returned," Roosevelt continued, "I occasionally heard it said that they had tried cross-country riding in England, and had shown themselves pre-eminently skillful thereat, doing better than the English fox-hunters, but I take this liberty to disbelieve. I was in England at the time, hunted occasionally myself, and was with many of the men who were all the time riding in the famous hunts; men, too, who were greatly im-

BUFFALO BILL SHOOTING THE BLUE GLASS BALLS.

pressed with the exhibitions of rough riding then being given by Buffalo Bill and his men, and who talked of them much; and yet I never, at the time, heard of an instance in which one of the cowboys rode to hounds with any marked success." Then in a footnote Teddy remarked, "It is, however, quite possible, now that Buffalo Bill's company has crossed the water several times, that a number of the cowboys have by practice become proficient in riding to hounds, and in steeple-chasing."

One of the biggest questions in the minds of the European audiences was: How many Indians did Buffalo Bill kill in his lifetime? The number had been multiplied to legendary proportions by the dime novelists. Colonel Cody did not want to diminish the legends about himself, so he usually answered this question by telling a story. When asked in Italy he answered with a

story about an old German who had been with the show at Madison Square Garden. The old fellow, Cody said, had a habit of loafing around saloons and telling about the great numbers of Indians Buffalo Bill had killed. One day the saloonkeeper asked, "Fritz, just how many Indians has he killed? Did he kill as many as a hundred?" Fritz stalled for a while, then said, "One hundred Indians look like a lot of Indians when you see them on the warpath." Finally he blurted out, "Py kolly, I don't know for sure if he ever killed any." "If you want a definite answer," Buffalo Bill said archly, "you can say simply that I never killed an Indian except when my life was in danger."

The Wild West Show continued north from Italy into Germany, where it was a sensational success. The Germans particularly admired the shooting and the horse-

Race between Indian, Cowboy and Vaquero. *Drawing by Carl Henckel*

185

manship. The show opened in Berlin in the Kurfurstendam on July 23, 1890, and played for a month—until August 22. The *Zeitung* gave it two columns, beginning, "The show is simply incomparable and unrivaled."

After this first European tour (and after the American tours of the show which are the subject of the next chapter of this book), Buffalo Bill in 1902 took the Wild West to Europe for a four-year itinerary which opened at Olympia in London. Salsbury, in that year, was too ill to accompany the show. Edward, who had been Prince of Wales in 1887, was on the throne. He saw the show twice with Queen Alexandra. Buffalo Bill toured Britain and Ireland for a year and stayed through the winter. The Wild West competed with George Sanger's famous circus, with no harm to either entrainment, although there was, of course, some apparent jealousy. Then the whole company went on to the Continent, staying for a year in France, with winter quarters near Marseilles.

The later European tours were managed by James A. Bailey, the circus man, whom Salsbury brought into the business as a partner. Baily had already had a brilliant career with Barnum, working out the detailed plans for touring with a big, complicated organization. It was Bailey who persuaded Buffalo Bill that he could play one-night stands successfully in America. Colonel Cody didn't believe it could be done with such a conglomeration of people and equipment, but Bailey showed him how a specially equipped circus train could operate—loading, unloading, putting up the show and tearing it down, and moving on to another town overnight. He adapted the same methods to European conditions, and his triumph over the French railroads was as spectacular in its way as that of the cowboys over the French public.

New scenes, based on the sure-fire principle of catering to immediate topical interests, were introduced. When there was fighting in China, the extras impersonated Chinese and Japanese; the Fall of Tientsin was enacted. For variation there was also a train holdup. Another scene was called "Holiday at TE Ranch" and depicted an Indian attack successfully repulsed by Buffalo Bill and his cowboys.

When the tour reached Vienna in 1906, Buffalo Bill met his old London companion Grand Duke Michael of Russia. "How old are you, Bill?" the Grand Duke inquired.

"Sixty," the Colonel replied.

"Is that all?" exclaimed the Duke. "Why, you are quite a boy yet!"

Tragedy hit the show in France at the end of the 1905 season when the horses contracted glanders, a serious and highly infectious disease. Two hundred horses had to be shot, forty-two of the finest horses in one day. The news could not be suppressed, although Major Burke did the best he could. He simply told newsmen, "The least said the better."

On a second visit to Italy the King and Queen attended the show, and Cody gave a dinner for George Ade, Booth Tarkington, and a number of other Americans who were touring Italy at the time. The irrepressible Ade, a practical joker, gave the snake charmer, who was in the side show, a mechanical snake which leaped out of

GERMAN "DIME NOVEL" ABOUT BUFFALO BILL.

187

what looked like a big box of candy. It nearly scared the wits out of her.

In Austria, Grand Duke Frederick expressed skepticism about the bucking broncos. He didn't think they were as wild as they appeared to be. So the cowboys put on a special exhibition for him in the morning. The Duke was nearly killed when a bronco leaped at him, but a cowboy saved him by lassoing the animal in the nick of time.

The German Crown Prince—later Kaiser Wilhelm II—had seen Annie Oakley shoot a cigarette out of a man's mouth at the show in London. The following year she went to Berlin on a special tour, independent of Buffalo Bill's Wild West. Crown Prince Wilhelm visited the show. In the middle of Annie Oakley's performance he walked out into the arena and asked her to do the trick he had seen her do in London. He would smoke the cigarette. He put it to his lips, lighted it, and Little Missy obligingly fired. The cigarette spark and ash were neatly detached from the portion which remained in the cool Crown Prince's mouth. During World War I, when he was Kaiser, Annie told newsmen she would like to have another shot; she said she would gladly spoil her act for the good of her country.

The Indians with the Wild West Show never enjoyed Europe. They were homesick and frightened by strange lands. They kept remembering old superstitions and warnings not to cross the great water. Troublemakers, possibly rivals in the show business, spread rumors that the Indians

188   ATTACK ON EMIGRANT TRAIN as imagined by German artist after seeing Wild West Show.

were not well treated; and although Buffalo Bill denounced the rumors as false, they persisted.

At the same time there was trouble again on the Indian reservations. An obscure Indian fanatic, claiming to be a prophet, started ghost dances—religious dances which the Indians continued until they dropped with exhaustion, in the belief that the ceremony would summon a messiah who would lead them in a victorious uprising against the whites. Sitting Bull had nothing to do with this hysteria, but there were rumors that he did. The whole movement was complicated by politics, greedy Indian agents, and speculators who wanted to get control of the Indian land.

General Miles thought perhaps the business could be settled by a visit from Buffalo Bill. If Cody could talk with Sitting Bull and other Indian chiefs, the rebellious Indians could perhaps be calmed down and trouble averted.

Colonel Cody responded with alacrity to the appeal of General Miles. He took temporary leave from his show and returned to America. He went out to the Standing Rock reservation. The Indian agent in charge, James McLaughlin, angered at what he considered unwarranted interference, wired President Benjamin Harrison and protested against Colonel Cody's plans to visit Sitting Bull, saying it would be very dangerous.

BUFFALO CHASE as visualized by German artist, Carl Henckel.

189

A gift to Buffalo Bill from Russian Czar: a standard to hold the flag, placed over a saddle and carried by horse in parade.

Buffalo Bill declared he needed no protection from the Indians. He would go out alone, with a wagon bearing presents for Sitting Bull. The night before he was to start, the Indian agents tried to prevent his expedition by drinking with him all night, taking turns. The experienced Colonel drank them all under the table, and was up early and started out with his wagon.

Halfway to Sitting Bull's tepee, he was stopped by mounted troopers, who forced him to return. McLaughlin had managed to get orders from Washington countermanding those of General Miles. Disappointed and disgruntled, Buffalo Bill returned East and announced that he was going back to Europe to rejoin his show. He believed that a great opportunity had been missed, not for a grandstand publicity play as his critics declared, but to bring peace to the troubled Indian territory.

He might have saved Sitting Bull's life. Soon afterward special police employed by McLaughlin arrested Sitting Bull. The old Indian chief peacefully surrendered, but he was shot in the back by the police who said he had tried to escape.

Indians were then arrested by the Army and held as hostages. Buffalo Bill wanted to take them with him to Europe when he resumed his tour, and General Miles agreed. The final outcome—after peace had been achieved with the recalcitrant Indian ghost dancers—was that Buffalo Bill acquired a hundred Indians for his Wild West Show.

Chapter 13

Bigger and Better Shows

FOR more than a decade after the first Continental tour the Wild West Show grew bigger and more spectacular every year with new acts, and a greater variety of professional headline features, attracting ever larger crowds. Finally, in 1901, Salsbury broke down under the strain, his death in the following year attributed by some members of his family to the crushing burden of dealing with the generous impulsiveness and egotism of Col. Cody. Meanwhile, so far as the world knew, and indeed so far as the troupers, now a body of over five hundred, ever knew, Cody and Salsbury complemented each other perfectly. Whenever one of them had an idea, the other would find a way to make it work. Even though Salsbury began to express his brooding conviction that the Colonel was unreliable, the worst feared disasters never occurred. Buffalo Bill, despite his lively social life, and occasional brief, passing romances with attractive young ladies, missed very few performances. The show always went on as scheduled, and as advertised.

A SPECIAL PASS SIGNED BY THE COLONEL HIMSELF.

The most conspicuous success of the show in America was during the summer of 1893 at the Columbian Exposition and World's Fair in Chicago. Buffalo Bill hit the bull's eye of mass popularity at that moment. The year 1893 opened an era of railroad travel for restless America. The transcontinental passenger trains had become comfortable and attractive, and it was an exciting experience to ride on them, whether to visit distant relatives or just to see the country.

The Chicago World's Fair gave easterners a special opportunity to see what life was like on the other side of the Alleghenies. Scores of thousands of people from the Atlantic seaboard discovered, with mingled pride and patriotism, the rich and varied cities and towns of the Middle West. Those who did not venture beyond Chicago could do so vicariously at the Wild West Show. Buffalo Bill gave millions a historic vision which they could remember and talk about for the rest of their lives.

From the rapidly growing midwestern communities, too, the farmers and small-town folks felt an urge that summer to go to Chicago, their metropolis, for the great Exposition, and it was considered a social disgrace not to see Buffalo Bill's big show. Six million people paid to see it between the end of April and the end of September.

Since there was not sufficient space inside the fair grounds for the Wild West,

Buffalo Bill, General Nelson Miles, Captain Baldwin, and Captain Miller at Pine Ridge Indian Reservation, 1891.

PEACE MEETING, PINE RIDGE 1891. GEN. MILES & STAFF.

Salsbury leased land at Sixty-third Street, between Madison and Stony Island Avenues, opposite the Exposition. The managers of the World's Fair indirectly stimulated attendance at the Wild West by closing the Fair on Sundays. Throngs went to the site, and when they found the Fair closed, saw Buffalo Bill instead. No one was disappointed. The Exhibition was easy to reach by trolley, by the Illinois Central, or by the newly built "el"—which is still using the equipment built to handle the crowds of 1893. There were also lake steamer excursions from the Loop.

The entertainers were at their best, and Major John M. Burke was at the peak of his talents as a press agent. He carefully timed the arrival of each new attraction so that each would get the maximum publicity and no group would overshadow an-

PEACE MEETING idealized into poster for show.

other. First to arrive in Chicago, and well announced on the front pages of the newspapers, were the Ogallala Sioux Indians, few of them less than six feet in height. They were followed by Chief Rain-in-the-Face, who arrived on crutches. When he was seventeen he had fought alongside Crazy Horse at the Battle of the Little Big Horn, and he proudly boasted that he had killed Tom Custer, at the feet of his father. He was only the first of many who were ideal subjects for interviews. Then came Hank Monk, the famous stagecoach driver, who told the reporters how he had driven Horace Greeley on a hair-raising ride in Colorado which had thoroughly scared the New York newspaper publisher. Noticing the fright of the man who had coined the phrase, "Go West, young man, go West!" and thinking he looked ready to jump for his life, Hank said he shouted the memorable words, "Keep your seat, Horace, I'll get you there on time!"

The homely touch had sure-fire appeal to midwesterners, and this was provided by Mama Whitaker, wardrobe mistress and general housekeeper for the show, who kept a well-publicized maternal eye on the younger personnel. It was provided too, of course, by Little Missy, whose tent was surrounded by a neat little garden of bright flowers.

Colonel Cody brought his youngest daughter, Irma, to stay with him while he was in Chicago, spoiling her with his proud affection. A newspaper poet, "inspired by witnessing the Prairie Chief Caressing His Baby Daughter Little Irma Cody" (she was then eleven), wrote lines which were widely quoted:

Only a baby's finger, patting a brawny cheek
Only a laughing dimple in a chin so soft and
*   sleek*
*   Only a crooning babble, only a frightened*
*   tear*
But it makes a man both brave and kind
*   To have them ever near.*
The hand that seemed so harsh and cruel
*   Nerved by a righteous hate*
As it cleft the heart of Yellow Hand
*   In revenge for Custer's fate*
Has the tender touch of a woman
*   As, rifle and knife hard by,*
He coos and tosses the baby
*   Darling "apple of his eye."*

That was the kind of sentimental note that never wearied Major Burke; and no cynic could deny its effectiveness as an advertising theme.

On the Sunday before the World's Fair opened, the wife of General Nelson A. Miles visited the show grounds, as did Francis Wilson, a popular American actor. The newspapers published an amusing story about Rudolph Maxstein, a nearby grocer from Sixty-third Street, who brought all the little Maxsteins, six in number, to meet the famous scout.

For the benefit of reporters, Nate Salsbury introduced the native Bedouin horsemen who were in the show and talked with the head sheik in Arabic, which the Chicago *Times* stated authoritatively he spoke with a "slight accent." Major Burke per-

suaded the Chicago *Humane Journal* to retell the touching story of the death of the horse Old Charlie at sea. The account concluded, typically, with Burke's style of rhetoric: "Many a rough hand dashed a tear from a sunburned cheek." Then more Indians arrived: Red Cloud, Kicking Bear, Two Strike, Short Bull, Young Man Afraid-of-Horses—(reporters asked where was Young Man Afraid-of-His-Mother-in-law?) —Rocky Bear, and finally little No Neck, a Sioux waif found as a tiny baby beside the body of his father after the slaughter of the Indians at Wounded Knee.

For the program Major Burke wrote a tribute to Buffalo Bill: "Besides mere personal bravery a scout must possess the moral qualities associated with a good captain of a ship—full of self-reliance, a thor-

ough student of nature, a self-taught weather prophet and geologist, by experience an astronomer, by necessity a naturalist." So the image grew in the public mind, an image that could be seen in the flesh for the price of admission. It was not only Buffalo Bill's Wild West, it was also described as the "Congress of the Rough Riders of the World." The phrase "rough riders" was coined by Cody five years before Theodore Roosevelt used it for his cavalry in the Cuban war.

After the Cowboy Band overture, the show opened with a Grand Review introducing the Rough Riders of the World and the Fully Equipped Regular Soldiers of the Armies of America, England, France, Germany, and Russia. Colonel Cody had assembled detachments of about a dozen

men from each country, a chore requiring great care and considerable diplomacy. They looked formidable in their cavalry uniforms, mounted on spirited chargers. When the arena was clear and the dust had settled over the stillness, Annie Oakley came in alone, looking exquisitely small and demure, to "illustrate the dexterity of firearms." She was followed by a horse race between a cowboy, a Russian Cossack, a Mexican vaquero, and an Arab, each riding a horse of his native country.

The Fourth Scene was the pony-express demonstration of "how letters and telegrams were distributed across the immense continent previous to the railways and the telegraph." After the dashing riders had performed their duty, an emigrant wagon train slowly emerged from the painted backdrop of Wyoming mountains and crossed the plains before the spectators' eyes. It was attacked by marauding Indians, then was saved by Buffalo Bill and his scouts and cowboys. The wagons used in this drama were the same old Conestoga wagons which had crossed the plains thirty-five years before.

Next a group of Syrian and Arabian horsemen appeared illustrating "their style of Horsemanship with Native Sports and Pastimes." Behind them galloped the "Cossacks of the Caucasus in Feats of Horsemanship and Native Dances." A moment

of quiet followed and then Johnny Baker marched in, alone and very self-assured, to demonstrate his "feats of marksmanship."

Additional acts continued the pageantry. A group of "Mexicans from Old Mexico demonstrated the use of the lasso" and performed various feats of horsemanship. A race followed between prairie, Spanish, and Indian girls. Act Eleven illustrated "Cowboy Fun" in picking objects from the ground, lassoing wild horses, and riding the bucking broncos.

Then came the representatives of four armies. The program advertised "A Company of the Sixth Cavalry of the United States Army; a Company of the First

196

197

198   COLONEL CODY WITH ARTA AND ORA. Note the Stetson on the shelf of the table.

Guard of the Uhlan Regiment of His Majesty King William II, German Emperor, popularly known as the Potsdamer Reds; a Company of the French Chasseurs (Chasseurs à Cheval de la Grande Republique Française); a Company of the Twelfth Lancers (Prince of Wales' Regiment) of the British Army. The Potsdamer Reds were the most spectacular: twelve men wearing red helmets with plumes of horsetails, blazing red jackets, and blue trousers, and carrying fourteen-foot lances. The twelve soldiers from France who came next wore brass helmets, sky-blue coats, scarlet trousers, patent-leather boots, swords rapier-style, lances, and revolvers. The British Hussars wore full parade dress.

When Mayor Carter Harrison requested the Fair officials to admit poor children of the city free on a special day, and was refused, Buffalo Bill sprang forward with the announcement that the Wild West Show would not only admit them free but provide free transportation, free candy, and free ice cream. Fifteen thousand screaming, happy youngsters stormed the entrance for the most exciting afternoon of their lives.

The most widely discussed publicity stunt, which filled yards of newspaper space for two weeks, was the 500-mile cowboy race to Chicago from Chadron, Nebraska. The editor of the Chadron paper suggested the feat, but Major Burke made it a Wild West production by announcing that Buffalo Bill would meet the winner at the entrance to the show with $500 and a Colt revolver as first prize.

The race began on June 13 despite ardent efforts by the Humane Society to stop it. Buffalo Bill declared that five hundred miles were nothing at all for a western horse or a cowboy, and Burke, ever mindful of public relations, invited agents of the Society to travel along the route. The first entrant to take the lead, and the headlines, was Rattlesnake Pete, the favorite, riding a horse he called General Grant. But no sooner was the race under way than other contestants got into fights along the way. Rules were made and then broken immediately. The lagging cowboys accused those ahead of such infractions as hitching rides in hacks or farm wagons and guzzling beer while their horses were hooked behind the wagons. One, it was charged, had shipped fresh steeds ahead by rail. Several declared they would have won had they not become lost in the suburbs of Chicago. Some of the horses that finished the race, it was alleged, had never been west of the Mississippi. Several cowboys discovered they could not drink whiskey and ride at the same time. Most of those who finished had two horses —one on a lead rope, so that horses could be ridden alternately.

The publicity was sustained as every day brought another, unexpected story; every contestant seemed good for a yarn. John Berry, who won, said his victory was due to knowledge of the route and the short cuts. He was challenged, and finally the prize money was divided, Buffalo Bill making the presentation in a special ceremony in the middle of a Wild West performance.

COL. W. F. CODY, President

COL. CODY'S ONLY CARD
TO THE PUBLIC.

Now for all, and at once, to end reports to the contrary, not ephemeralizing, I beg to state positively, notice for comrades, friends, patrons and the press, that wherever and whenever

"Wild West and Congress of Rough Riders of the World"

is billed to appear, there will I be with it also. That I not only always personally direct it as a whole and every production connected therewith, but invariably appear at each and every afternoon and evening performance, conscientiously fulfilling every advertised promise made in my name. My place has ever been at the front. I have not been gazetted to the father of the rest.

Yours very truly,
W. F. CODY,
"BUFFALO BILL"

An Absolutely Original and He

The Only One which Kings, Chief Rulers, Famous Generals, Nobles and the Most Illustrious and Enlightened Men
Theme of Artistic, Poetic and Historic Inspiration. Which of All the Millions it has Entertained, Taught and Tr

COPYRIGHT 1896 BY BIEN & CO. NEW YORK

If Any Seek to Imitate It, They Defraud
If Any Claim to Rival It, They Falsify
If Any Copy Its Announcements, It Is Forgery

It Controls All the Genuine Material of Its
It Alone Commands the Confidence of Potentates
It Is the Only Exhibition With Which Governments Co-

THE ONLY EXHIBITION IN ALL THE WORLD THAT

READ THESE MEMORABLE WORD

"BILLY; FOR MY CHILDREN AND GRANDCHILDREN, WHO C.

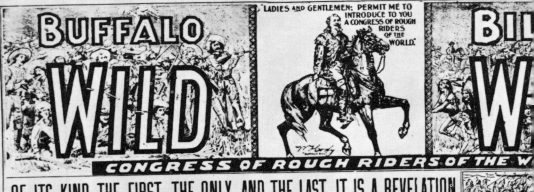

"LADIES AND GENTLEMEN: PERMIT ME TO INTRODUCE TO YOU A CONGRESS OF ROUGH RIDERS OF THE WORLD."

BUFFALO WILD

BIL W

CONGRESS OF ROUGH RIDERS OF THE W

OF ITS KIND THE FIRST, THE ONLY, AND THE LAST, IT IS A REVELATION

THE MOST COLOSSAL AND THE STRANGEST ENTERTAINMENT EVER ORGANIZED OR DREAMED OF.

The Only Object Teacher History has Ever Had, or Recreation Furnished. Whatever Others May Say or Claim, the Whole World Pronounces it Supremely and Originally Great. The Mirror of American Manhood. The Camp of the Makers of a Nation's History.

Promoted by Kings, Honored by Nations. A Paragon at Home, a Triumph Abroad. Rough Riders Schooled to Hardship, and to Whom the Saddle is an Heirloom. An Equine and Equestrian Study, with Horse and Man a Sculptor's Beau Ideal.

Hazardous Pastimes of which the Great Plains and Deserts are the Natural Playground.

A HOLIDAY REFLECTING YEARS OF ROMANCE
AND THE REALITY OF IMPERISHABLE DEEDS.
FEATS OF FEARLESS SKILL, FASHIONED BY NECESSITY,
PERFECTED IN DANGER, AND CROWNED BY VICTORY.
THE ONE PRESENTMENT OF GRIM-VISAGED WAR BEFORE THE STARTLED FACE OF SMILING PEACE.
MAKING THE NEW WORLD AND THE OLD APPEAR IN
BRAVEST AND MOST BRILLIANT RIVALRIES
ITSELF A NOBLE PART OF WHAT IT SHOWS, WHICH OFTEN SEEN THE MORE ATTRACTIVE GROWS.

Enterprise of Inimitable Lustre.

...ght to Honor. The Only One which has its Country's Army as its Sponsor. The Only One which is the Splendid
...er Deceived, Harmed or Disappointed a Single One. The Like of Which You and Your Children Will Never Look Upon Again.

NATE SALSBURY, Vice-President.

To America and Americans

After months of industrious preparation, continuous effort and most elegant
and thorough research, to present to this
greatly enlarged and perfected exhibition
to the approval of my countrymen for
the season of 1896 I beg to direct their
special consideration to the fact

That it was absolutely original crea-
tion, without precedent, or parallel and
which can have no successor.

That it is just as genuine as original
in every presentation and in regards
every particular.

[remainder of column text illegible]

NATE SALSBURY.

...than Historic: It Is History Itself in Living Lessons | NOT AN EMPTY CHEATING ECHO, BUT DARING DEEDS INCARNATE
...Imitations of Fancy, but the Stupendous Realism of Facts | TELLING ITS THRILLING TALES WITH RIFLE, SWORD and SPEAR
...Speculation of Apes, but an Institution of Heroes | USING in PLACE of HALTING WORDS INSPIRING, SPLENDID, ACTION

COUNTERPART.   EXCLUSIVELY ITS OWN CREATION.

...ERAL SHERMAN TO COL. CODY:

...R SEE THESE THINGS AS WE SAW THEM, I THANK YOU."

ITS GREAT ORIGINATOR NOW RIDES ALONE UPON FAME'S WARPATH
THE LAST IN SERVICE OF THE GREATER SCOUTS TO WHOM OUR ARMY'S SAFETY WAS ENTRUSTED.

The Master Horseman, More Picturesque and Perfect than Alexander on Bucephalus. | No Hundred Theatres Combined Inclose Its Proud Reviews and Battle Spectacles.
Commanding the Grand Host of All the World's Most Noted Riders. | The Plains, the Steppes, the Pampas, Are its Platform.
No Toppling Tents Could Cover Such An Equestrian Gathering of Nations | The Free Range of the Open Air, the Coliseum Nature Builds for It.

Among Its Features, Martial Pageants, Dazzling Reviews, Savage Displays of Fearful War and Foray.

Wild & Most Wondrous Riders on Naked Steeds
STRANGE AND EXCITING NOMADIC RACES.
THE REGULAR CAVALRY OF MANY FLAGS.   DESERT-BORN BEDOUINS IN AMAZING FEATS
THE THRILLING EPISODES, STRUGGLES, ESCAPES, ADVENTURES, MARKSMANSHIP AND UNIQUE PASTIMES OF BORDER LIFE.

REGULAR ARTILLERY JUST AS IN ACTION
THE WARLIKE ACTS AND ARMS OF MANY LANDS.
NOT ONE OF WHICH CAN EVER ELSEWHERE BE PRODUCED OR DUPLICATED

THE ROUTE BOOK OF THE SHOW FOR YEAR 1899.

From the moment that President Cleveland opened the Wild West Show until it closed at the end of the season, the reserved boxes were filled with distinguished visitors. They included the Duke of Veragua and the Princess Infanta of Spain, James Cardinal Gibbons, the Duke of Seramonte and the royal Italian commissioners, and every notable personality of Chicago and the Middle West. From all over the world journalists, artists, statesmen, scientists, flocked to the arena to thrill to the Old Frontier. It was the peak of Buffalo Bill's career as a showman. The season's profits exceeded a million dollars, and Buffalo Bill looked forward to spending his share on ranches and cattle in Wyoming.

202

ROUTE-BOOK

ɪffalo Bill's Wild West

1899.

AINING ALSO THE OFFICIAL ROUTES
SEASONS OF

1895, 1896, 1897, 1898.

COMPILED BY

GEORGE H. GOOCH.

BUFFALO, N. Y.
THE MATTHEWS-NORTHRUP CO.

The side show, a great hit although Nate Salsbury
disapproved of it.

Buffalo Bill's Wild W

COL. W. F. CODY, *President.*
NATE SALSBURY, *Vice-Presiden*
MAJOR J. M. BURKE, *Gen'l Man*

DIRECTORS OF TOUR.

JAS. A. BAILEY,   W. W. C
     LOUIS E. COOKE, *General Agent.*

BUSINESS MANAGERS.

For Cody & Salsbury,   For Bailey &
     JULE KEEN.   ERNEST CO

SECRETARIES.

For Cody & Salsbury,   For Bailey &
     L. E. DECKER,   JOS. F. QU

TREASURERS.

For Cody & Salsbury,   For Bailey & Co
     JULE KEEN.   FRED B. HUTCHA

DIRECTOR OF ENTERTAINMEN
          JOHN BAKER.

SUPERINTENDENT OF GROUND
          HENRY BARNUM.

MANAGERS OF PRIVILEGES.
     Messrs. DREW AND CAMPBELL.

2

During that summer, a few miles from the Buffalo Bill Wild West show grounds a young scholar read a learned paper before a select group at the Chicago Art Institute. The thesis contained no reference to Colonel Cody—but its author was to share some of the fame of the men of action that Cody portrayed in his noisy, dusty arena. The scholar was Professor Frederick Jackson Turner, and his monograph bore a title which was to become internationally known as a classic: *The Significance of the Frontier in American History.*

204

GENERAL STAFF.

hn Baker, ... *Arenic Director.*
hn McLaughlin, *Master of Transportation.*
an Taylor, ... *Master Mechanic.*
. B. Bailey, . . *Sup't of Electric Lights.*
ke Platt, ... *Sup't of Canvas.*
as. Evans, . . *Sup't of Baggage Stock.*
. W. Reedy, . . *Sup't of Bronco Stock.*
. W. Ramsey, *Sup't of Confectionery Dep't.*
m. Sweeney, . . . *Leader of Band.*
m. McCune, . . . *Officer of the Day.*
rris Kern, . . *Principal Door Tender.*
. W. Rogers, ... *Detective.*
J. McCarthy, ... *Orator.*
u. Decker, ... *Mail Carrier.*
hn Noble, . . . *Head Car Porter.*
en & Langan, ... *Caterers.*
Martin, ... *Head Waiter.*
hn Stacks, . . . *Parade Wardrobe.*
as. Wichelhausen, . . . *Properties.*
m. Smith, ... *Ammunition.*

EPARTMENT OF PUBLICITY.

uis E. Cooke, *General Advance Manager.*
Coyle, ... *Railway Contractor.*
ward Arlington, . . *Excursion Agent.*
ajor John M. Burke, *General Press Agent.*
ank J. O'Donnell, *Contracting Press Agent.*
ss Maymie Jester, . *Special Press Agent.*
xter E. Fellows, . . *Special Press Agent.*
H. Semon, . *General Contracting Agent.*
H. Woods, *Assistant Contracting Agent.*
Manton, ⎫ . . . . *Bill Inspectors.*
as. Curtis, ⎭

ADVERTISING CAR No. 1.
P. S. Mattox, *Manager.*
H. Alberts, ... *Boss Bill Poster.*
m Lyons, ... *Boss Lithographer.*
as. Hayes, ... *Secretary.*
an Lewis, ... *Programmer.*

BILL POSTERS.

w Curry,   Richard Le Fever,
ver Lester,   Chas. Welsh,
. Baldwin,   Martin Slivers,
rry Campbell,   John Alvather,
e Dunn,   Sam Sanders,
R. L. Bean, *Car Porter.*

3

Top going up when the show hits town, 1901.

205

LITHOGRAPHERS.

Fred Seyboth,   John Gray,
          Chas. R. Coleman.

**ADVERTISING CAR No. 2. — EXCURSIC
DEPARTMENT.**
Al. Riel, *Manager.*

Geo. Frazier, ... *Boss Bill Post*
Kurt Eisfeldt, ... *Lithograph*
Chas. Venable, ... *Banner Me*
Al. Boshell, ... *Board Me*
Victor Cooke, ... *Card Me*

EXCURSION BILL POSTERS.

Thos. Deansfield,   H. Sayers,
Wm. Shea,   Chas. Dering,
A. J. Choffin,   Wm. Fannon,
Geo. Houghtaling,   Geo. Nelson,
Dan Pheney,   H. Robinson,
H. Leschinsky,   Chas. Loughridge
          Geo. Hurst, *Car Porter.*

OPPOSITION BRIGADE.
Fred Beckman, *Manager.*

Dan Pheney, ... *Boss Bill Pos*
Kurt Eisfeldt, ... *Lithograp*
Herman Leschinsky,)
Frank Raymond,   ) . . . *Bill Pos*

LAYERS-OUT.
Harry G. Barnum,   Thos. Clear.

———

TICKET SELLERS.
MAIN TICKET WAGON.
Fred B. Hutchison,   John Flandreau.

OUTSIDE TICKETS.
John Tippetts,   Lou. Decker,
          Frank Cloud.

DOWN-TOWN OFFICE.
Harry Gray.

DOWN-TOWN ORATOR.
S. H. Davis.

4

After Chicago the show was a national institution and in constant demand. In 1894 the Wild West played at Ambrose Park in Brooklyn from May 12 to October 6. Sunday shows were omitted. It had a run of 126 days. After that, life for Buffalo Bill was a series of one-night stands in America and Europe for nearly twenty years.

The year 1895 was like many that followed: 321 performances; Colonel Cody did not miss a single one. The show, resplendent in a train that often ran in three sections, traveled 8,980 miles during a season of 195 days. This record was topped in 1899, the biggest and most profitable in the show's history, even greater than Chicago's memorable summer, for it covered 11,111 miles during a 200-day season, making 132 stands and giving 341 performances.

RESERVED-SEAT TICKETS.

Jule Keen *in charge.*

r Pixley,   Geo. Dittmar,
Sam. T. Bitmead.

MAIN DOOR TENDERS.

. Brogan,   Dan. Taylor,
ris Kern,   John McLaughlin.

RESERVED-SEAT TENDERS.

ter H. Cleary,   Arthur Waterman.

USHERS.

Wm. McCune, *Head Usher.*
Dave Jarrett, *Assistant.*
Eddie Walton, *Assistant.*

RESERVED-SEAT USHERS.

Barry,   Wm. Hunter,
Quinlan,   Ed. Howard,
Davis,   Wm. Hutton,
Gallagher,   Sam. Maitland,
Wm. King.

BLUE SEATS.

Arnold,   Lee Fuller,
e Burns,   Wm. Murphy,
y Eagan,   T. McBurney,
Gibson,   G. Pratt,
Smith,   J. White.

John Condon, *Director.*
Jos. Collins, *Wardrobe.*

COWBOY BAND.

Wm. Sweeney, *Leader.*

Sweeney, ... Solo Cornet.
rt Ziehm, ... Solo Cornet.
d O'Hara, ... Solo Cornet.
Allen, ... First Cornet.
N. Tinkham,   .   .   . Second Cornet.
er Parlett, ... E♭ Cornet.
y Nelson,   .   .   . Solo B♭ Clarionet.
stian Schetting, .   . Solo B♭ Clarionet.
k Genter,   .   .   . First Clarionet.
ey Benham,   .   . Second Clarionet.

5

THE COWBOY BAND LEADS THE STREET PARADE, 1901.

207

When the war with Spain began, Colonel Cody wanted to join the forces of his old friend General Miles, but the show could not go on without him. Then, when Cuba got into the news as a result of the war, Cody and Salsbury employed a group of wounded Cuban veterans. Known as Garcia's Scouts, they were cheered by the crowds as martyrs for Cuban independence.

The year after the Spanish American War Buffalo Bill re-enacted the Battle of San Juan Hill. It was not quite as dramatic a spectacle as his rendition of Custer's Last Stand—but gradually even General Custer was being forgotten as a new, very lively national hero, a personal friend of Colonel Cody's, rode into prominence. Buffalo Bill, of course, played the role of his friend, Theodore Roosevelt. He had hired some of Roosevelt's Rough Riders, whom he had called "Teddy Roosevelt's Rough Riders." These were led by Sergeant G. A. Webb, with William McGinty as color bearer. Into the epic battle the Colonel threw nearly all his troops: groups from the Ninth and Tenth Cavalry, the Twenty-fourth Infantry, Grimes's Battery, Garcia's Cuban Scouts, as well as the old pack train. The first scene showed a halt on the road to San Juan; the second dramatized the storming of the hill. Teddy Roosevelt was triumphant at every performance.

208

COWBOY BAND.—Continued.

Frank Carothers, ... E*b* Clari
Chester C. Larned, ... Picc
Ed. Weber, ... First *A*
John C. Howard, ... Second *A*
W. H. Dickin, ... Third *A*
John Galligan, . . . First Tromb
Lon Williams, . . . Second Tromb
Chas. Baas, ... Third Tromb
Thos. V. Murphy, . . . First Bari
John Schilling, . . . Second Bari
W. A. Frank, ...
M. A. McAdams, ...
Geo. C. Foehlinger, ... Small D
Geo. W. Turner, ... Bass D

Johnnie Baker, *Expert Marksman.*
Miss Annie Oakley, *Lady Rifle Shot.*
Frank Butler, *Manager for Miss Oakl*

DRIVER OF STAGE COACH
John F. Burke.

U. S. CAVALRY.
Jas. G. Warren, *Sergeant.*
Chas. Rieth, *Color Bearer.*

Wm. Baker,	Frank Stryker,
J. Wortman,	W. J. Taylor,
Dennis Langan,	Chas. Humbers
Peter Fay,	Ed. Gallagher,
Harry Jackson,	Jas. Brown,
Granville Corr,	Andy Milen,
Frank McCormack.	

U. S. ARTILLERY.
Herman Kanstein, *Sergeant.*

PIECE NO. 1.		PIECE NO.
J. R. Myerly,	)	Harry Wilkes,
Thos. Gibney,	*Drivers*	R. I. Clapham,
Chas. Wolff,	)	Jas. Ryan,
Jack Langan, *Corp.*		Victor Hudson,
L. Wagner, No. 1.		C. Triangel, N
R. Hegeman, No. 2.		Pony Moore, N
C. Hobart, No. 3.		A. Miller, No.
Jas. Degnen, No. 4.		Geo. Davis, N

6

OSEVELT'S ROUGH RIDERS.

G. A. Webb, *Sergeant*.
Wm. McGinty, *Color Bearer*.

.. Newcomb,	J. Kline,
Beal,	Ed. Loughmiller,
Holmes,	F. Byrne,
Cook,	Ben Miller,
Isbell,	H. Meagher,
). Miller,	J. H. Tait,
Langdon,	L. Muxlow.

AMERICAN COWBOYS.

Joe Esquivel, *Chief*.
John Franz, *Assistant*.

Compton,	Jesse Nelson,
Schenck,	Tom Hunter,
Gabriel,	Bob Singletree,
Jennings,	Lem Hunter,
er Scott,	Carl Sorrensen,
Joyce,	A. McCann.

ENGLISH LANCERS.

Thos. Cook, *Sergeant*.
W. House, *Color Bearer*.

Rapley,	E. Plummer,
arke,	W. Ridgwell,
Ryan,	W. Barrett,
Wandland,	T. Dennis,
aingler,	A. Brown,
agott,	W. Pocock.

GERMAN CUIRASSIERS.

Julius von Natzmer, *Captain*.
Heinrich Sprittule, *Sergeant*.
O. Weinrich, *Color Bearer*.

Vittmann,	T. Schwark,
ultz,	H. Damm,
aempfer,	A. Zippliss,
	A. Rother.

7

KIDS LOVED THE SHOW, WOULD SEE IT, HOOK OR CROOK.

Buffalo Bill enjoyed another great hour of triumph, also in 1898, when Omaha held its Trans-Mississippi Exposition and on August 31 celebrated Cody Day. Twenty-four thousand people came to pay him tribute. The Wild West played on the same grounds from which it had started on its career of world-wide fame.

An old comrade declaimed:

You bet I knew him, pardner, he ain't no circus freak. / He's western born and western bred, if has been late abroad; / I knew him in the days way back, beyond Missouri's flow, / When the country round was nothing but a huge Wild Western show / When Injuns were as thick as fleas, and the man who ventured through / The sand hills of Nebraska had to fight the hostile Sioux. / Those were hot times, I can tell you, and we all remember still / The days when Cody was a scout and admit his name was Bill . . .

They tell me that the womenfolk now take his word as laws / In them days laws were mighty skerce, and hardly passed with squaws. / But many a hardy settler's wife and daughter used to rest / Because they felt from Laramie and down to old Fort Sill / Bill Cody was a trusted scout, and all their men knew Bill.

210

MEXICANS.

Vicente Orapeza, *Chief.*

Manuel Pena,	Pedro Aleman,
Epifania Martinez,	Yrineo Munoz,
Luio Alba,	Manuel Castillo,
Santiago Munoz,	Agapita Alba.

COSSACKS.

David Cadjaia, *Chief.*

Dimetri Mgaloblichvily,
Toma Baramidzi,
Miron Tschonia,
Ivan Baramidzi, Ermile Antadz,
Loucas Tschartishvily,
Michael Antadzi,
Vladimir Jacutahvi

ARABS.

Sheik Hadji Tahar, *Chief.*
Hadji Cheriff, *Whirling Dervish.*

Moly Ambark,	Oshan,
Ameen Abou Hamed,	Masand,
M. Muzie,	Nagim Abdullah,
H. Abachi,	Nageeb Ballish,
Mohammed Agram,	Willie Masand,
Hadji Hamid,	Brodie ben Hadji,

Togler ben Hadji.

CUBANS.

Col. Mariano Aymerich, *Chief.*
Lieut. Evaristo M. Alonso.
Lieut. Andres Fontanilla.

Antonio Marti,	Manuel Portuond
Rafael Rodriguez,	Ramon Ferreno,

Benito Carreras.

HAWAIIANS.

David Kipi,	K. Natsia,
J. Kulia,	W. Hopili,
G. Makalina,	Isabella Pary,

Ribaka Natsia.

8

FILIPINOS.

x Alcantara,   Geronimo Momo,
    Isidora Alcantara.

INDIANS.

CHIEFS.

Tail,   Growler,
k Fox,   Iron Cloud,
    Has No Horse.

BRAVES.

ted Weasel,   Sam Stabber,
Horse,   White Belly,
es Out Holy,   Eagle Fox,
g Horse,   Pluck Porcupine,
Kills Brave,   Red Calf,
ling Soldier,   Jacob Iron Eagle,
e Bird,   Charging Thunder,
Bull,   Dreamer,
es Last,   Wounded,
es Out Bear,   Loud Thunder,
rd Lip,   Frank Meat,
ed Horse Fight, Albert Thunder Hawk,
e Bonnet,   Ed. Porcupine Knee,
in Loge,   Sam Lone Bear,
s Killing,   Mounted Sheep,
Bear,   Whirlwind Horse,
    Kills Enemy.

SQUAWS.

Kills Enemy, Jennie Spotted Horse,
  White Cow.

PAPOOSE.

Willie White Bird.

INTERPRETER.

David Bull Bear.

ATCHMAN OF INDIAN CAMP.

J. J. Ryan.

9

HAS-NO-HORSE.

Colonel Cody responded to this and other acclamations with a speech: "The whistle of the locomotive has drowned the howl of the coyote; the barbed-wire fence has barrowed the range of the cowpuncher; but no material evidence of prosperity can obliterate our contribution to Nebraska's imperial progress.

"How little I dreamed in the long ago that the lonely path of the scout and the pony-express rider would lead me to the place you have assigned me today. Here, near the banks of the mighty Missouri, which flows unvexed to the sea, my thoughts revert to the early days of my manhood. . . . Time goes on and brings with it new duties and responsibilities, but we who are called old-timers cannot forget the trials and tribulations which we had to encounter while paving the path for civilization."

212

"BRONCHO" STABLE.

W. W. Reedy *in Charge.*

J. F. Meade,	}		Cowboy Stri
Hugh Harkins,	}		
Jas. Bass,			English Lanc
M. T. McKenzie,			Rough Rid
Naber E. Smith,			U. S. Cava
Geo. Bare,			Mexic
Dan White,		Hawaiians and Filipi	
Al Hook,			Coss
Wm. Jones,			A
Chris Peterson,			Gern
Chas. Judd,	}		Artill
Sam. Harkins,	}		
Marshall Ochoa,	}		
W. Dyer,	}		Ind
Dewitt Genung,	}		
Chas. Kelly,	}		
J. W. Porter,			M
Russell Churchill,			Bucking Hou
Giess Stine,			Col. Cody's St
Jas. Murphy,		Col. Cody's Coachm	
J. R. Ziegler,	Driver of "Buffalo" Wa		
Harry Murphy,		In Charge of Buffa	

"WILD WEST" BLACKSMIT

Fred Kurz,   Joseph Ferren.

WARDROBE AND PROPERTI

Chas. Wichelhausen.

Chas. J. Ansert,   Wm. Monday,
Jas. Fish,   Martin Dillon.

AMMUNITION.

Wm. Smith *in Charge.*

Tom Edwards,   Roy Myers,
            Jas. Berger.

BAGGAGE STOCK.

Chas. Evans, *Superintendent.*
Wm. McNaul, *Assistant.*

10

EIGHT-HORSE DRIVERS.

Driver.	Helper.
Thomas,	Henry White,
y Camp,	Andy Johnson,
. Elliott,	Chas. Miller,
d Denio,	Chas. Foley.

SIX-HORSE DRIVERS.

Miller,	Jas. Robinson,
Montgomery,	Grant Hulvey,
. Mitchell,	Jas. McGovern,
Harry E. Mills.	

FOUR-HORSE DRIVERS.

Afford,	Jas. Williams,
Woodman,	Wm. Donohue,
Gallagher,	J. F. Tewell,
Eastman,	Rob't Burns.

PULL-UP TEAMS.

Laird,	Chas. Cook,
Thos. Lee.	

BUGGY STOCK.

Jack Lewis.

D BARS AND BODY POLES.

Frank Emery.

FEED.

John Puget.

ACKSMITH AND REPAIR DEPARTMENT.

Dan Taylor, *Master Mechanic.*

Keller, ...	Carpenter.
Collins, ...	Harness Maker.
orbury, ...	Blacksmith.
Young, ...	Blacksmith.

II

JOHNNY BAKER THROWS THE GLASS BALLS WHILE BUFFALO BILL SHOOTS THEM.

RAILROAD DEPARTMENT

John McLaughlin, *Master of Transporta*
R. P. Murphy, *Assistant.*

John Rose, ... Car Inspe
A. H. Miller, . . Watchman 1st Sec
Joe Brown, . . Watchman 2d Sec
Wm. Remack, ... Chande
Paul Spearing, ⎱ . . . . P
Frank Arnett, ⎰

TRAINMEN.

Frank Coyle,   A. E. Meyer,
L. D. Bottarff,   John Bennett,
John Fallon,   Jere Murphy.

SPECIAL WATCHMEN.

John Stacks, . . . White Ticket W
Frank Quinn, ... Private C
M. Hogan, ... 2d Section S

CAR PORTERS.

John Noble, *Head Porter.*

Wm. Vogel, Car 51,   Pete Wallace, C
Geo. Long, Car 52,   Chas. Carroll, C
Harry Gears, Car 53,   F. C. Hawley, C
Wm. Reilly, Car 57.

COL. CODY'S PRIVATE CAR No.

Alfred Heimer, *Porter,*
W. L. Brown, *Cook.*

SIDE-SHOW.

Messrs. Drew & Campbell, *Manage*

PERFORMERS AND CURIOS.

Ashida and Koh, . . . Japanese
Olga, ... Snake Encha
Wm. Baker, ... Boy
Chemah and Pearl Robinson, . M
J. G. Sheidler, ... King of
Balbroma, ... Fire
Victorina, ... Sword-swa
Val Vino, ... J
Millie Owen, ... Long-haired
Prince Oskazuma, . . . Kaffir W
Ben Casper, ⎱ . Venetian Glass B
W. F. Greiner, ⎰
J. McClellan, ⎱ Electrograph and
Ben Powell, ⎰   Mind-r

12

At that moment he could easily have been elected governor of the state, but he belonged to the show. This was his life; and duties, responsibilities, troubles, and hard work lay ahead of him. The log book of the show for 1899 is typical of the routes traveled. The Wild West opened in Baltimore on Monday, April 17. The trains with the canvas, the seats, and all the equipment had arrived Saturday morning. The show opened auspiciously for four performances to crowded houses. Then a note: "Harry Skeen, for several seasons our car repairer, died suddenly in the hospital here. . . . Cowboy Nelson goes to the hospital with a bad case of blood poisoning."

214

LECTURER.
Burt Davis.

ORATORS.
J. Staunton,   Jos. F. Ferris,
Frank Cloud.

DOOR TENDER.
Frank Quinn.

SIDE-SHOW CANVASMEN.
H. E. Tudor, *Superintendent.*
m. Powers,   J. Martin,
m. Allen,   Geo. Fuller,
Jno. McLean.
arry Tudor, ... Inside.

SIDE-SHOW BAND.
L. Sacketts, *Leader.*
Rechhia, ... B♭ Clarionet.
Donato, ... E♭ Clarionet.
Grella, ... Solo B♭ Cornet.
Scerni, ... First B♭ Cornet.
Renzi, ... B♭ Baritone.
D. Paolo, ... B♭ Trombone.
Pellazzo, ... E♭ Alto.
Zuglielmo, ... Bass Drum.
Barbieri, ... Small Drum.

CONFECTIONERY DEP'T.
Chas. L. Ramsey, *Superintendent.*
S. H. Davis, *Assistant.*
C. W. Spadi *in Charge of Supplies.*

BUTCHERS.
E. Fearn,   C. E. Brooks,
rry Merrick,   Fred Roteman,
White,   Arthur W. Horton,
Burke,   Garrett Henry,
Watt,   Lou C. Cloud.

NEW ENGLAND POP-CORN FACTORY.
M. C. Bowers.

13

A TYPICAL INDIAN CHIEF.

WHIRLING-HAWK.

216

CONCERT COMPANY.

"The Ramseys," . . . . Comedy
Bessie Searles, ... Serio-Co
Schafer and Read, . . Musical Com
Cloud and Kershaw, . . Irish Comed
"The Brannigans," . . . . Jig Dar
Nellie Waters, ... Comedie

CONCERT ORCHESTRA.

J. Schilling, ... First V
Ed. Weber, ... Second V
Wm. A. Frank, ... V
M. A. McAdams, ...
F. Genter, ... Clari
A. Ziehm, ... Co
L. Williams, ... Trom

OFFICIAL PROGRAMMES

J. & H. Mayer, *Publishers.*
Tom Burke *in Charge.*
H. Mayer, *Solicitor.*

AGENTS.

Wm. Conroy,   Frank Clear,
Walter Miller,   Ed O'Connell.
Geo. Manchester,
    Agent for "Buffalo Bill's" Hi

ELECTRICAL DEPARTMEN

M. B. Bailey, *Superintendent.*
D. MacDonald, *Chief Electrician.*
Wm. J. Connor, *Chief Engineer.*

FIREMEN.

Archie Clements,   Wm. M. Penn.

ASSISTANTS.

Maurice Doody,   Joe McCann,
Geo. H. Gooch,   Bernie McBrid
Henry Reever,   Larry Murphy.

CALCIUM LIGHTS.

Maurice Doody,   Geo. H. Gooch

14

CHANDELIERS.
Jack Cullen *in Charge*.
Ed. A. Combs, *Assistant*.

CANVAS DEPARTMENT.
Jake Platt, *Superintendent*.
John Eberle, *First Assistant*.
David Jarrett, *Second Assistant*.
Jack Dawson, *Horse Tents*.
, Smithey, *Dressing Room and Backing*.

McCaffrey,	M. Mack,
Condon,	Larry Sullivan,
White,	Wm. Cronin,
allahan,	John Murphy,
Maitland,	Wm. Hunter,
ert Parkes,	Mike Jones,
arry,	John Weaver,
Hutton,	Ed Howard,
Halpin,	Pat Burke,
Burns,	Lee Fuller,
Wood,	Thos. Ryan,
Davis,	M. Quinlan,
McFrine,	Larry Eagan,
r King,	Wm. Murphy,
n Mayo,	Wm. Thomas,
McManus,	Jos. Collins,
Sampson,	Geo. Amos,
Lavesta,	Chas. Vanberg,
Smith,	Ernest Yelland,
Arnold,	Edward Bitting,
Cair,	Geo. Pratt,
rempley,	Mike Keating,
Foley,	John Walsh,
Buckner,	Jack Bryan,
D. Fulton,	John Morrow,
ergeman,	Jas. Harrison,
racy,	John Rassler,
Peterson,	Harry Hoskins,
obia,	John Bauersis,
	Geo. Hunt.

FRONT END.
John A. Eberle, *Superintendent*.

SEATS.
Jas. McCaffrey, *in Charge*.
John Condon, *Assistant*.
John White, *Leveler*.

15

At Washington, on April 19, an accident delayed the show train for two hours. There were four performances to crowded houses. At Richmond, Virginia: "arrived 7:30 A.M. Half mile haul to lot. Weather clear; big business at both performances." At Staunton, Virginia: "arrived at 8 A.M. One mile haul to the lot. Weather clear; big attendance in afternoon, light in the evening." At Lynchburg, two days later, "the show did not reach town until 11 A.M. Weather clear, business big." The show moved on to Roanoke the following day. It appeared in Bluefield, West Virginia, and then jumped to Bristol, Tennessee.

217

So the record runs through dusty weather, broken axles on flat cars, an occasional death, accident, sometimes rain; in Cincinnati the roof of an old pavilion collapsed under the weight of four hundred standees. At Pottsville, Pennsylvania, the large horse tent burned. By May 27 they had already played a hundred performances that season.

The pace was too strenuous for Nate Salsbury and he said so. Buffalo Bill talked of making his farewell. But they both went on. As a precaution Salsbury persuaded James A. Bailey, the circus man, to buy a share of the show, for Bailey had a genius for organization; he knew the amusement business thoroughly. From the time Bailey entered the enterprise, however, it became more and more of a circus, and less of a Wild West Show.

218

JACK SETTERS.

Bob Callahan,   Herbert Parke
Sam Maitland,   Wm. Hutton,
          Hugh Gallagher.

TOE-PIN DRIVERS.

John Halpin,   Andy Wood,
Ed Barry,   Geo. Davis,
Mike Burns,   Alex. McFrine

BLOCKS.

Lyman Mayo.

KIDS.

Walter King.

BACK END.

Dave Jarrett, *Superintendent.*

SEATS.

M. Mack *in Charge.*
Larry Sullivan, *Assistant.*
Wm. Hunter, *Leveler.*
Mike Jones, *Toe Leveler.*

JACK SETTERS.

John Weaver,   Pat. Burke,
Ed. Howard,   Lee Fuller,
          Thos. Ryan.

TOE-PIN DRIVERS.

Larry Eagan,   Mike McMar
Wm. Murphy,   Wm. Sampsc
Wm. Thomas,   Chas. Lavest

BLOCKS.

Geo. Smith.

KIDS.

Wm. Murphy.

16

RESERVED SEATS.

M. Quinlan *in Charge.*

STRINGER SETTERS.

Arnold,   Chris Cair.

JACK SETTERS.

Trempley,   Thos. Foley,
Murphy,   Harry Buckner.

TOE-PIN DRIVERS.

Hoskins,   John Rossler,
aily,   Wm. Ryan.

BLOCKS.

Chas. Vanberg.

KIDS.

Jos. Collins.

TOP STAKE AND CHAIN,
Nos. 6 and 11.

Murphy,   Wm. Cronin.

HORSE TENTS.

John Dawson, *Superintendent.*

Ryan,   Unix Robia,
Tracey,   Ed Dailey,
Amos,   Harry Peterson,
Rassler,   Harry Buckner,
Welsh,   Thos. Foley,
Harrison,   Thos. Murphy,
Carey,   Harry Hoskins.

STAKE WAGON No. 14.

John Walsh.

17

FLYING-HORSE.

219

In 1898 it included the beginnings of many side shows: Japanese magic, a snake enchantress, a boy giant, midgets, a king of cards, a fire king, a sword swallower, a juggler, a Kaffir warrior, some Venetian glass blowers, and a couple of mind readers. The organization of the Wild West had a large general staff, a crew of zealous billposters who sometimes covered the advertisements of competing shows with "Wait for Buffalo Bill next week." It carried a crew of ticket sellers, a blacksmith and repair department, a railroad department, a canvas department; and, helping Major Burke, a publicity department of ten, including Dexter E. Fellows, later the celebrated circus publicity man.

220

BACKING AND DRESSING RO●

Wm. Smithey, *Superintendent.*

RIGHT CURTAIN.
John Bauereis,   Geo. Hunt.

CENTER CURTAIN.
Edward Bitting,   John Bergeman,
Ernest Yelland,   John Morrow.

LEFT CURTAIN.
Jack Bryan,   John D. Fulton

FRONT-DOOR MEN.
Geo. Pratt,   Mike Keating.

SAIL MAKERS.
John Weaver,   Geo. Halpin,
John Walsh.

COOK HOUSE.
Messrs. Keen & Langan, *Caterers.*
Chas. W. Petty, *Advance.*
Fred Bowman, *Accountant for Wild We●*
Sam. T. Bitmead,
        Accountant for Keen &° Lar●

COOKS.
Wm. Myers, *Head Cook.*
Harry Holmes,   Henry Hiler,
John Hammond.

BUTCHER.
Chas. Felix.

CAMPFIRE.
Mike Connelly.

WAITERS.
M. Martin, *Head Waiter.*
Wm. Walsh, *Assistant Head Waiter*

18

TABLE No. 1—STAFF.
d. Adams,   Eddie Walton,
Thos. Rafferty, Coffee-boy.

ABLE No. 2—COWBOYS AND BAND.
Stewart,   Jos. McCaffrey,
Joe Gillin, Coffee-boy.

TABLE No. 3—PRIVILEGE.
Kelly,   W. Sproegal.

TABLE No. 4—ARABS, ETC.
Coleman,   H. Bird,
G. Packett.

BLE No. 5—AMERICAN SOLDIERS.
Hutchison,   J. Hobson,
B. Palmer, Coffee-boy.

**BLE No. 6—ENGLISH AND GERMAN
SOLDIERS.**
Nist,   Chas. Black,
J. Ruffells, Coffee-boy.

TABLE No. 7—INDIANS.
J. Furlong.

RKMEN'S TABLES Nos. 8, 9 AND 10.
Carson,   C. Whitney,
Binne,   Wm. Ives,
Wagstaffe,   Wm. Basman.
Jas. Knight, ⎫ Coffee-boys.
John Kehoe, ⎭

DESSERT BOYS.
Routledge,   Bert Cohn.

DISHWASHERS.
e Jackson,   Jos. Jackson.

LAUNDRYMAN.
D. McMillan.

NIGHT WATCHMEN.
s. Nicholson,   Thos. Devine.

NIGHT-LUNCH STAND.
Tom Austin.

19

SAMUEL LONE-BEAR.

221

TWO BULLS.

OFFICIAL PROGRAMME.

Overture, "Star Spangled Banner,"
Cowboy Band, Wm. Sweeney, Leader.

Grand Review, introducing the Rough
Riders of the World — Indians, Cowboys,
Mexicans, Cossacks, Gauchos, Arabs,
Scouts, Guides and detachments of fully-
equipped Regular Soldiers of the Armies
of America, England, Germany and Russia,
a Color Guard of Cuban Veterans, and a
squad of Hawaiian, Porto Rican and Fili-
pino Rough Riders.

Miss Annie Oakley, Celebrated Shot,
who will illustrate her dexterity in the use
of firearms.

Race of Races. Race between a Cowboy, a Cossack, a Mexican, an Arab, a
Gaucho, and an Indian, on Spanish-Mexi-
can, Bronco, Russian, Indian and Arabian
horses.

U. S. Artillery Drill, by veterans from
Capt. Thorpe's Battery D, Fifth Regiment.
U. S. Artillery.

**Illustrating a Prairie Emigrant
Train Crossing the Plains.** It is attacked by marauding Indians, who are in
turn repulsed by "Buffalo Bill" and a
number of Scouts and Cowboys.

Pony Express. A former Pony Post
rider will show how letters and telegrams
of the Republic were distributed across our
continent previous to the building of railways and telegraph.

A Group of Mexicans from Old Mexico will illustrate the use of the lasso and
perform various feats of horsemanship.

The Battle of San Juan Hill. Intro-
ducing detachments from Roosevelt's
Rough Riders, Twenty-fourth Infantry,
Ninth and Tenth Cavalry, Grimes' Battery,
Garcia's Cuban Scouts, Pack Train, etc.,

SCENE 1 — A halt on the Road to San
Juan.
(Several hours are supposed to elapse be-
fore the opening of the second scene.)
SCENE 2 — Storming of the Hill.

21

Fellows joined the show in 1895 and learned his articulate trade from Burke. Fellows declared that there was much good-natured ribbing between Cody and Burke, a lifelong argument whether Burke had ever killed an Indian. "You know darn well," the Colonel would say, "the only Indian you ever killed was a Delaware Indian you worked to death on your grandfather's farm."

In the days that Fellows first knew him Burke was clean shaven except for a thick moustache whose ends made a semicircle around his chin. He wore his hair long in imitation of Buffalo Bill, but he pinned it up under his Stetson hat with hairpins. He dressed to perfection, or so it appeared— but Fellows said he never wore a shirt, and that fastened around his neck was a "dickie," or false bosom of starched linen. Attached to the sleeves of his undershirt were white cuffs.

223

Burke showed Fellows how to open the doors of newspaper editors. Once, when Fellows was curt to an office boy, Burke told him, "Shouldn't have acted that way. Some day that boy may become a managing editor."

Burke told Fellows never to refer to the place where the Wild West played as the "show grounds"—it was always the "exhibition grounds"; nor was he to use the word "lot"—a vulgar circus term.

10—**A Group of Riffian Arab Ho** men will illustrate their style of horsen ship, together with native sports and times.

11—**Johnny Baker,** Celebrated Y American Marksman.

12—**Cossacks,** from the Caucasus of sia, in feats of horsemanship, n dances, etc.

13—**Gymkana Race.** Riders gallop, mount, turn coat inside out, remount, lop, dismount, light cigar, put up umbr mount and come in with umbrella up cigar lighted.

14—**Cowboy Fun.** Picking objects the ground, lassoing wild horses, riding buckers, etc.

15—**Indians** from the Sioux, Arapa Brulé and Cheyenne tribes will illus the Indian mode of fighting, war da and games.

16—**Military Musical Drill,** by a det ment from the 16th Lancers (Qu Own), British Army, and a detach from the Garde-Kürassiers of His Ma Kaiser Wilhelm II.

17—**Sixth United States Cavalry.** erans from Col. Sumner's celebrated ment at Ft. Meyer, Va., in military cises, and an exhibition of athletic s and horsemanship.

NOTE.—The men will wear the unif adopted by the United States Army o frontier. The horses are Western horses, used in this manner for the time in history. The Army and Nat Guard use the "American" horse.

18—**Attack on the Deadwood M Coach by Indians,** repulse of the Ind and rescue of the stage, passengers mail, by "Buffalo Bill" and his atter Cowboys.

19—**Racing by Indian Boys on B back Horses.**

22

—**Three Minutes With the Rough Riders of the World.**

—**Col. W. F. CODY** ("Buffalo Bill") n his unique feats of sharpshooting while iding at full speed.

—**Buffalo Hunt**, as it was in the Far West of North America, by "Buffalo Bill" nd Indians exhibiting the last of the only nown native herd of buffalo.

—**Attack on Settlers' Cabin** and rescue y "Buffalo Bill" and a band of Cowboys, couts and Frontiersmen.

—**Salute**, by the entire company.

E ANNUAL SPRING OPENING.

he show was moved from "Ambrose " to Madison Square Garden for the ning of the season on Sunday, March 26th. parade which was to have taken place Tuesday, 28th, had to be postponed until following day on account of inclement her.

he first performance was given on Wed- ay night, March 29th, before a crowded e. Several entirely new features were duced in the programme, the chief being e Battle of San Juan," which proved an ntaneous success.

Friday, April 7th, the afternoon perform- was given for the benefit of the orphans inmates of the different asylums and in- tions around New York. Altogether, -one performances were given during tay in the Garden, at each of which the en was well filled, while on several oc- ns the doors had to be closed for the performance. The season proved the successful ever given in New York.

KILLS-FIRST.

COLONEL CODY SHAKES HANDS WITH CHIEF JOSEPH, one of the last Indian chiefs to fight the white man. He visited the Wild West show at Brooklyn.

When Fellows first met him, Buffalo Bill, although only in his forty-sixth year, was beginning to show signs of wear. "He sometimes looked tired and harassed," Fellows wrote. "Perhaps he was worried by poor investments or by Salsbury's inability to take a more active part in the management."

Not long afterward Buffalo Bill told Fellows, "As a fellow gets old he doesn't feel like tearing about the country forever. I do not want to die a showman. I grow very tired of this sort of sham worship sometimes."

Fellows was excessively proud of the Rosa Bonheur painting of Cody. He wrote in his memoirs, "One of our posters that year showed two men on white chargers. One was Cody and the other Napoleon. In the center sat Rosa Bonheur painting Cody 'to perpetuate his fame'. The caption under one of the riders read, 'The Man on Horse of 1795' and the other 'The Man on Horse of 1895'. It was good advertising and contained a grain of truth, for certainly Cody was at the height of his fame and was as well known in America at least, thanks to the skillful exploitation of his managers, as 'The Man on Horse of 1795.'"

226

Chapter 14

Buffalo Bill Spends his Fortune

IT was like a fairy tale come true for Buffalo Bill, with lavish gifts for family and hands, to return from the road each year for the rest season at North Platte. Louisa remained at the Welcome Wigwam house in town, while his sister Julia—Mrs. Goodman—supervised the Scout's Rest Ranch. On her famous brother's instructions she replaced the small frame house with a sixteen-room mansion, and the whitewashed sheds with enormous barns. The big main barn held nearly a thousand tons of hay; and the ranch often carried three thousand head of cattle and fifteen hundred horses. It was at Scouts' Rest that Buffalo Bill enjoyed his holidays before he finally moved

to Wyoming, and that Fred Garlow met Colonel Cody's daughter Irma, whom he later married. At Scouts' Rest, Chief Red Shirt told visitors from all over the world that his was the first Indian papoose to be born in the Old Country. One of the cowboys, Walter Scott, later famous as Death Valley Scotty, was a horse trainer for the show.

It was from Scouts' Rest that a draft of horses was started for Sheridan, Wyoming, on the expedition that gave Cody's Wyoming ranch its TE brand and name. At Deadwood some horses were bought from Cody's friend Mike Russel, and a total string of five hundred horses were trailed

BRANDING IRON OF THE TE RANCH.

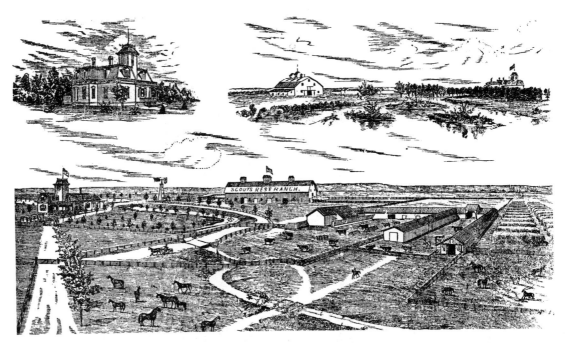

DRAWING OF SCOUT'S REST RANCH, Buffalo Bill's 4000-acre ranch near North Platte, Nebraska.

over the Big Horns. It was easier to buy the brand of Russel's horses than to re-brand several hundred horses, so the TE brand became attached to Cody.

When he was away from North Platte the Colonel wrote faithfully to Julia on fancy engraved personal notepaper—or on the stationery of the best hotels, usually that of the Waldorf-Astoria, for example, in New York. But except for his splendid wardrobe, and good notepaper, Buffalo Bill was not self-indulgent on private luxuries, although he enjoyed being a generous host to friends and open handed to all appeals for help.

Nobody, least of all Buffalo Bill, ever knew how much money passed through his hands. In the days when the Wild West was making big profits—up to a million yearly, often more—he spent it lavishly. Sometimes it seemed as if he were trying to give it away faster than he earned it.

If he was feeling fine—he usually was in the 'nineties—he would go to the box office after the show, draw out a fistful of greenbacks, and go to town with it. Along the way he met friends, cronies, spongers, most of whom had been watching and waiting for him, eager to enjoy his largesse. From the nearest bar to the final nightcap nobody could pay for anything except the Colonel.

His family were never neglected, financially. When his sister Helen was married, he bought her a $30,000 house in Duluth, which unfortunately later burned down.

228

The Colonel relaxes in front of his tent.

He also bought the Duluth *Press* for her and her husband, but it failed. How many people he put on an annual retainer basis nobody knows. It is believed that Major Alexander Majors, Buffalo Bill's first employer, was one of them.

He delighted in the large gesture. When he went to the Big Horn Basin he became so enthusiastic about the country while there that he bought forty thousand acres on Carter Mountain, near Cody. He built the Irma Hotel in Cody, starting it in 1901. It was finished in 1902 when the town boasted only a thousand inhabitants. He believed there was valuable oil in the region, but he never made any money out of it. Most of it was exploited later, and today the whole of the region is dotted with paying oil wells.

When he was heading his show at Madison Square Garden, beggars would wait for him at the door when he came out. If he didn't have money with him, he would borrow it from friends in order to pass out dollars to the down-and-outers. Any such sums that he borrowed, he always paid back promptly.

Although he supported Louisa in grand style, eventually, the more he was away, and as his success and fame increased, he moved farther and farther away from her in sympathy and understanding. She hated traveling with the big show and never had liked his theatrical or frontier companions. When he brought his cronies home, she worried about their manners, their language, and their drinking. She was fiercely jealous when women made a fuss over him.

Since Cody was a virile, romantic, handsome man, he inevitably attracted women to him. Some adored him, some enjoyed being seen with a celebrity, and some used him as a stepping stone to a theatrical career. When he was bored, worried, or lonely he naturally turned to women who could make life interesting. He hated to go home to a complaining wife, and wished that there was some way he could get away from her for good, for she nagged and made him feel that he had failed to grow up and settle down.

He once contemplated a permanent marital separation and for long periods they did not see each other. Louisa not only stayed at North Platte while he was traveling with the show, but frequently remained there when he went to his TE Ranch near Cody. Many of his friends said one reason he was so fond of this ranch was that it was one place he could get away from Louisa.

On his second appearance in London he fell in love, or thought he did, with a beautiful actress named Katherine Clemmons. After he met her he determined to get a divorce from Louisa. His friends told him that Louisa would never let him go, would never give him a divorce, that he had no legal grounds.

When he came back to North Platte after his second London appearance, Louisa served him a supper of cold salmon that had been in an opened can, and it made him so ill with food poisoning that he thought he was going to die. In the state of mind he was in it was easy for him

KATHERINE CLEMMONS, the English actress, with whom Buffalo Bill fell in love at height of his career.

to imagine that she was deliberately trying to poison him. To a man looking for grounds for divorce, this might prove a persuasive point.

When he saw Katherine Clemmons again, he began financing plays in which she was cast as the star. It is estimated that he spent somewhat more than eighty thousand dollars on Miss Clemmons's career. When he could not get a divorce, she be-

came impatient and married another man. Eventually, her husband heard about her friendship with Buffalo Bill, and tried to get Colonel Cody to admit that there had been a serious affair. But displaying his customary chivalry, Buffalo Bill would do no such thing. Against all advice from friends, however, he continued to urge his lawyers to get a divorce for him. The judge threw his case out of court, but nevertheless there was considerable publicity. An indication of the fantastic charges and countercharges was a suggestion from a friend of Louisa's that Buffalo Bill had had a romantic affair with Queen Victoria.

Wyoming provided an escape from the unpleasant domestic atmosphere of North Platte. When Cody was asked when he had first seen the Big Horn Basin, he replied, "In 1870 I was detailed by General Sheridan to act as guide for Professor Marsh, the noted geologist of Yale, who, with four or five professors and about twenty-five students, desired to make the trip into the Basin in search of fossils.

"We outfitted at Old Fort Laramie and came over the mountains by way of Powder River and the Paintrock. I was much interested in the conclusions of the professors, who stated that conditions throughout the centuries had served to make the soil of the Basin the richest and deepest to be found in America. There was first the inland sea, then the wash as the waters receded, step by step, after they had made their initial break through the mountains.

"The rich soil deposited on the beaches would, they believed, make this the most

231

THEODORE ROOSEVELT, a fellow rancher and cowboy of the west, as he looked at his first round-up, 1885.

fertile valley in America. They read the Basin like an open book. They said it would prove rich in oil and gas and all kinds of minerals.

"Their talk made a great impression on me and I found myself constantly recalling what they had said. I had picked out a beautiful ranch on the North Fork of the Shoshone. I wanted a railroad in the Basin, and I went to President Perkins of the Burlington with the hope that I might prevail upon him to build it. He said they could not do so at that time, as they had gone to the extent of their resources. Later, after I pointed to the wonderful resources of the Basin, he told me if I would come in and help in its settlement he could build the road at the earliest opportunity.

"I came in and was the first to operate under the Carey Act [establishing Reclamation Service]. Then the first deed under the act was given to Johnny Baker, one of my men. When President Perkins was about to resign he recalled his promise to me and said, 'I promised Colonel Cody to build that line, and I am going to do it before I quit,' and he did. If it had not been for me you would not have had your railroad." (From the Cody *Enterprise*, February 20, 1946, quoting an interview from the *Big Horn County Rustler* of January 21, 1910).

Buffalo Bill always claimed that the Big Horn Basin was a natural paradise, and when a friend complained of the high

232

winds in that part of the country, Colonel Cody replied, "You know where those winds come from? Well, this country up here is so close to paradise you can feel the breezes from heaven. That wind comes from the angels' wings. When they flap their wings the wind comes right down this valley."

Frequently, as time ran on, the Colonel would talk of nothing except the Big Horn Basin country. In 1901 he told a reporter, "If I thought I was to die a showman I would go out of business tomorrow. I don't want to die and have people say, 'Oh there goes another old showman.' I don't like to be remembered that way. When I die I want the people of Wyoming who are living on the land that has been made fertile by my work and expenditure to remember me. I would like people to say, 'This is the man who opened up Wyoming to the best of civilization.' Why, all I have been running this show for is to get money to put into that Wyoming land. I have 205,000 acres, watered by irrigation from the Shoshone River in the Rockies. I have 150 miles of sluices. The loam is 21 feet deep."

Early in the 1880s Buffalo Bill began dreaming what he would do, and by 1895 he had plans drawn for laying out a town. George T. Beck was one of the early promoters. He started work on a canal to irrigate the valley, and persuaded Colonel Cody to invest in the project. He also interested Nate Salsbury in the company which was being formed with six other men. They laid out a town site to be named for De Maris Springs, west of Cody,

which were discovered by John Colter in 1807. They were hot, boiling sulphur waters in which the Indians used to bathe, and it was thought that they might be developed into a successful health resort.

Beck laid out the streets of the town, which he made one hundred feet wide as a protection against fire. Buffalo Bill came out to see the site after he had toured with his show. While there he built a cabin on Carter Mountain. Beck built a camp in the town, a commissary building, a schoolhouse. Then they applied for a post office, asking for the name "Shoshone," which the Postmaster General refused to let them have because there was a post office on the Shoshone Indian reservation. Since Buffalo Bill was the most prominent of the promoters, they decided to name the place for him. Later Beck interested Mrs. Phoebe Apperson Hearst, wife of Senator George Hearst of California and mother of the late William Randolph Hearst, in the irrigation project and she invested in it.

Through Buffalo Bill's efforts the Burlington Railroad was finally persuaded to build a branch line to Cody in 1901. He showed representatives of the railroad the whole country between Cody and Yellowstone Park, pointing out that a road from Cody to the Park would attract thousands of tourists. They would take the Burlington to Cody and then go to the Park by horse-drawn stages. The Colonel later organized the stagecoach company. He then planned two small inns to be built along the road, Wapiti and Pahaska Tepee, as overnight stopping places.

The opening of the Irma Hotel was one of the most celebrated events that ever happened in Wyoming. That was in the middle of November 1902. All the Cody relatives participated. Finley Goodman, the Colonel's nephew, wrote his recollections of the event for the Cody *Enterprise* in 1939: "People came from every direction from many miles around. There were bands playing in the old dining room and on the porch. There were so many people in the barroom they stood six to eight deep." When somebody mentioned how good business was Colonel Cody agreed. "Yes, and this is once when I am on the right side of the bar."

Goodman also recalled some stories about how hard the wind blew. "A man named Joe Vogel lived at the end of the town. Joe said that when he wanted a new hat all he had to do was to go along his woven wire fence after a stiff wind and make his selection as to size and color of the assortment of Stetsons along the fence."

George T. Beck has written how the Episcopal church was founded in Cody. Beck, Tom Purcell, and Colonel Cody were playing poker in Purcell's saloon with two cattlemen. The jackpot grew to $500. At that point they decided that the man who won the jackpot would have to contribute it to building a church. Beck won the pot when it reached $550. He stipulated that the Episcopal church receive the donation. Later, for lack of a parson, Beck took over the job of reading the Sabbath lesson. He also started a choir, enlisting everybody who thought they could sing, with the result that there were more choir members than regular congregation.

Buffalo Bill spent much of his time hunting when he came to Cody. He had the happy ability to make everybody on a hunting party feel that they shared his fame and that of his prominent guests.

When the Burlington branch line to Cody was finished, a station was built on the far side of the Shoshone River. At the height of the season in the summer eighteen or twenty Pullmans arrived daily, many of them filled with Cody's guests. Spend-a-million Gates, the son of Bet-a-million Gates, came out in his private Pullman car. The first morning he strode down the main street of the town. On one side of the street were the saloons and on the other, it is said, "the ladies walked." To every lady who said "Good morning" to Gates, he presented a $300 raccoon coat. The townspeople still talk with wonder about the Colonel's parties in the mountains. A typical hunting party included wagons loaded with liquor, cronies, and girls.

Gerard Wallop, now the Earl of Portsmouth, grew up in Wyoming where his brother still owns a ranch. When Lord Portsmouth was a child, Buffalo Bill often visited his father's ranch, on at least one occasion accompanied by Theodore Roosevelt, to discuss the establishment of a game preserve for the vanishing bighorn sheep in Goose River Canyon. Once, on a more festive day, Buffalo Bill and Portsmouth's father turned up at the ranch in an old spring wagon, driving a couple of broncs, "greatly to the hazard of the wagon, the

Colonel Cody always wore a Stetson made especially for him. Picture from Stetson advertisement in the early 1900s. Inset, the Buffalo Bill Hat (#1100) as listed in the illustrated catalogue.

Col. Wm. F. Cody

Buffalo Bill was one of the greatest American scouts. Reclaimer of waste land, pioneer in irrigation, pony express rider.

broncs, the outstanding gateposts and himself." In the back of the wagon was a case of Scotch. The two merry ranchers settled down to it, forgetting they had a small boy watching from behind the sofa.

After they had consumed a large amount of the Scotch they decided to stage an old-time shooting match. They started by shooting the ace of spades out of each other's hands. To make it more exciting, they tried shooting tin cans off each other's heads. The Earl of Portsmouth continues the story as he recalls it:

"I was spellbound with excitement. We had a turkey gobbler, the only one on the ranch, and it represented our future Christmas dinner. My father, in his mood of elation, suggested that he and Buffalo Bill shoot for the gobbler. Buffalo Bill had first shot with a rifle when my father tossed up a silver dollar. Buffalo Bill missed it first shot but got it the second shot. I can hardly describe to you my immeasurable relief when my father got the dollar that Buffalo Bill threw up first time and the gobbler remained on the ranch for Christmas dinner."

But Wyoming was not entirely the scene of relaxation and fun for Cody. He was seriously interested in agriculture. The agricultural potentialities of the Shoshone River Valley were first explored by the early Mormon settlers about 1890. They constructed some crude irrigation works and successfully tilled a fertile area where the river was broad enough to permit a simple development.

The greater project was sponsored by Buffalo Bill, Nate Salsbury, George T. Beck, and the company which they formed. After establishing the town of Cody they began building the Cody Irrigation Canal, which still serves the immediate vicinity around Cody. It was the pioneer unit of the day.

However, the original group realized that the need for greater water resources demanded a much bigger project with government financing. It was then that the U.S. Reclamation Service was organized, which developed the Shoshone Reclamation Project. Buffalo Bill and his associates relinquished their rights to the government service. They did so on the condition that the canal, then known as the Highline Canal, be built as soon as the dam was finished.

The dam was built by the government solely because of the urging of Colonel Cody and his group. The Shoshone Reclamation Project was authorized by the Secretary of the Interior on February 10, 1904. Four months later actual work was started on the dam, which was later named the Buffalo Bill Dam. Water was delivered to the first unit on June 1, 1908.

Buffalo Bill Dam is a concrete and rubble structure 328 feet high, and creates a reservoir with a capacity sufficient to supply water to a depth of two and a half feet over each acre in the project of about fifteen thousand acres. It is located in the Shoshone Canyon, just west of Cody.

Colonel Cody also founded the first newspaper in the town, the *Shoshone Valley News*. The first issue appeared on Thanksgiving Day 1896. Later, in 1899, he brought a printing press from Duluth which had originally belonged to the Duluth *Press*. He persuaded Colonel J. H. Peake, whom he had met in Washington, to edit the paper. The first office was in a log cabin.

Mrs. Peake later wrote an account of the trip to Wyoming for the Cody *Enterprise* special birthday edition in 1939. The Peakes were met at Alliance, Nebraska, by Louisa Cody and her daughter Arta Boal and the Boal children. They then went to Red Lodge, Montana, where the Colonel's secretary Okey Snyder and John "Reckless" Davis met them. "They had provided stagecoaches of the old western type. I asked Mrs. Cody if the new town of Cody was as large as Red Lodge, to which she hesitantly replied, 'No, Mrs. Peake, I don't think it is,' and I began to have a sinking feeling." Cowboys came out to meet them and escorted them along the road over very lonely country—not a ranch, a person, or an animal to be seen. They stopped at the Sirine Ranch overnight and slept on the floor. When they finally reached the town of Cody, Mrs. Peake inquired when they would get there. The driver answered, "This is Cody." That was before the Irma Hotel was built, and the only overnight accommodation was run by a gambler called "Cold Water Bill" Prante.

Buffalo Bill enjoyed himself most when entertaining his friends, but the TE ranch house was small, so he sometimes had many guests camping in tents. The TE Ranch was chiefly for privacy, for resting and relaxing.

Mrs. Betty Isham, his cook there for six years, from 1903 to 1909, worked for the Colonel while her husband was a cowpuncher on the ranch. Those were her happiest years, she told a reporter for the Cody *Enterprise*. The guests she remembered best were Johnny Baker, Billy Sweeney, leader of the cowboy band in the Wild West Show, and Iron Tail, a member of the troupe.

"The Colonel's appetite was that of a true westerner," she said. "His favorite foods were wild meat, fresh eggs, soft boiled with bacon, and coffee and toast or sourdough and hot cakes. Also chicken and dumplings, fried chicken, and broiled kidney. His favorite dessert was custard pie."

It was traditional to serve chicken on the Colonel's birthday, and Mrs. Isham told how each year she would raise some late chicks so they would be just about right for February 26: "The Colonel would go out, and when the flock were on the run, he would take aim and shoot the required number of friers, hitting each one in the head without a miss."

She also told about how Colonel Cody was chided for carrying a shabby gunmetal watch, whereupon he pulled the watch out of his pocket, pressed something on the stem, and showed that inside the gun-metal case he was carrying the famous King Edward watch, studded brilliantly with diamonds. He said, "You know I'm an easy touch, and I love this watch and that's the only way I dare carry it when I'm going around the country."

In 1907 the unruly Ute Indians, tired of

life on the reservation, dashed into Wyoming to enjoy the freedom of the open spaces as their ancestors had. Colonel Cody received a wire from General Miles asking him to go out and meet this band and persuade them to return to their reservation without making trouble.

The Colonel invited George T. Beck and Hank Fulton of Cody to go with him. They had only one rifle among the three, as they didn't want to give the impression that they were heavily armed and precipitate a skirmish. After several days they found the runaways. The Colonel talked with them and told them it would be much better if they returned to their homes on the reservation in Colorado. He also suggested in

A drawing by Baden-Powell, founder of the Boy Scout Movement, friend and admirer of Buffalo Bill.

BUFFALO BILL LOVED CHILDREN, and they loved him.

a friendly manner that it would be just as well if they didn't kill any more cattle than was absolutely necessary on their way back. There had been considerable complaining from the cattlemen that the Utes had been helping themselves to their stock. After a pow-wow the Indians decided to behave as the Colonel suggested.

There was an intimate relationship in spirit between Buffalo Bill and the whole world of scouting, expressed concretely and practically in the Boy Scout movement. In his later years Colonel Cody was much interested in the Boy Scouts and, when talking with boys, he always told them that if he were a boy again he would join the Boy Scouts. He helped Dan Beard by writing articles and making suggestions when Beard edited the magazine *Recreation*.

Through this magazine Dan Beard organized a society of scouts, then known as the "Sons of Daniel Boone," in which boys were to be identified with Daniel Boone. He took this organization with him after *Recreation* was sold and he went to the *Woman's Home Companion*. Finally he formed a strong link with Sir Robert Baden Powell, and developed the Boy Scouts in the United States. Beard adopted the cowboy sombrero or famous Stetson, such as Buffalo Bill made popular, as his trade mark and the typical Cody kerchief around the neck. These were also adopted by Baden Powell in England.

In 1907 Dan Beard went to Washington to see President Theodore Roosevelt and to discuss plans with him for the Boy Scouts. "Whom have you?" Teddy Roosevelt asked.

"I told him," Beard relates in his autobiography (page 355), " 'John Muir, Joaquin Miller, and John Burroughs.'

" 'Who else?' he asked, to which I replied, 'Buffalo Bill.'

" 'Bully!' cried Roosevelt, bringing both fists down on the table with a bang."

Buffalo Bill from then on was a kind of lively patron saint and hero of the Boy Scouts of America, holding with Teddy Roosevelt an equal place in the affections of the boys.

Baden Powell, who, like Dan Beard, was a gifted artist, visited Buffalo Bill on two occasions, and later drew an illustra-

239

tion for his autobiography from a photograph taken with Cody in Winnipeg in 1912. Beard, who had illustrated some of Mark Twain's early books—including *Huckleberry Finn*—often delighted in telling an anecdote about Twain's pride in being mistaken for Buffalo Bill by a Boy Scout on Fifth Avenue during the period when Twain was wearing his gray hair longer than usual.

Although Cody did not see a great deal of Theodore Roosevelt, the two men had much in common and admired each other extravagantly. Both were outdoorsmen and lovers of the West, both lived and advocated the strenuous life; while these two Americans were alive they occupied a position of influence and inspiration in the minds and imaginations of the boys of America such as no two great public figures have occupied before or since. Both men still seem very close to all boys.

After the Colonel died in 1917 the Cody *Enterprise* asked Annie Oakley to write some of her memories of him. She said, "He was the kindest, simplest, most loyal man I ever knew. He was the staunchest friend. He was in fact the personification of those sturdy and lovable qualities that really made the West, and they were the final criterion of all men, East and West. Like all really great and gentle men he was not even a fighter by preference. His relations with everyone he came in contact with were the most cordial and trusting of any man I ever knew.

"I traveled with him for seventeen years —there were thousands of men in the outfit during that time, Comanches, cowboys, Cossacks, Arabs, and every kind of person. And the whole time we were one great family loyal to him. His word was better than most contracts. Personally I never had a contract with the show after I started. It would have been superfluous.

"He called me 'Missy,' almost from the first, a name I have been known by to my intimate friends ever since. In those days we had no train of our own. No elaborate outfit, not even any shelters, except a few army tents to dress in. Among ourselves it was more like a clan than a show, or a business performance. Major North, one of the famous old pioneers, and Buffalo Bill, his two hundred friends and companions, a bunch of longhorns and buffalo, would come to town and show what life was like where they came from.* That was all it was. That is what took—the essential truth and good spirit of the game made it the foremost educational performance ever given in the world.

"It may seem strange that after the wonderful success attained that he should have died a poor man. But it isn't a matter of any wonder to those who knew him and worked with him. The same qualities that insured success also insured his ultimate poverty. His generosity and kind-hearted attitude toward all comers, his sympathy

---

* Annie Oakley joined the show after Major North's death; but obviously she is here reporting on the early atmosphere when Col. Cody referred to North as if he were still with the troupe or at North Platte.

240

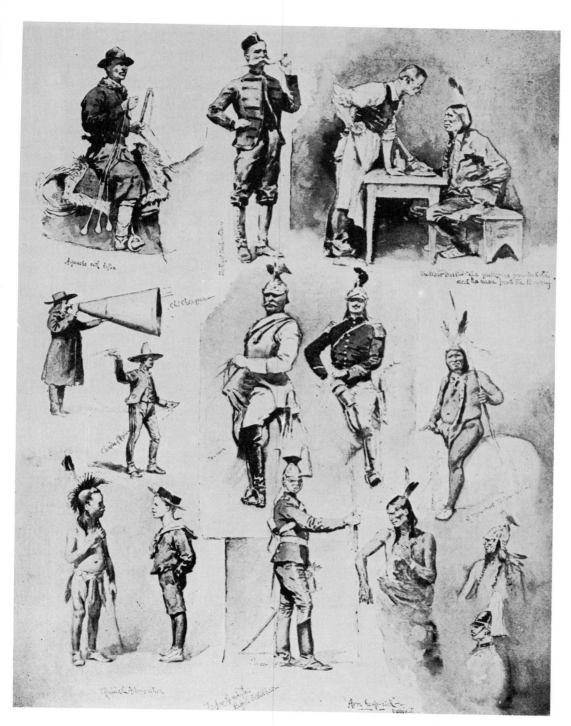

Sᴋᴇᴛᴄʜᴇs ʙʏ Fʀᴇᴅᴇʀɪᴄ Rᴇᴍɪɴɢᴛᴏɴ behind the scenes at Wild West Show.

241

and his broad understanding of human nature, made it the simplest thing possible to handle men, both in his show and throughout the whole world. But by the same token he was totally unable to resist any claim for assistance that came to him, or refuse any mortal in distress. His philosophy was that of the plains and the camp, more nearly Christian and charitable than we are used to finding in the sharp business world he was encountering for the first time. The pity of it was that not only could anyone that wanted a loan or a gift get it for the asking, but he never seemed to lose his trust in the nature of all men, and until his dying day he was the easiest mark above ground for every kind of sneak and gold-brick vendor that was mean enough to take advantage of him.

"I never saw him in any situation that changed his natural attitude a scintilla. None could possibly tell the difference between his reception of a band of cowboys and the train of an emperor. Dinner at camp was the same informal, hearty, humorous, storytelling affair when we were alone, and when the Duchess of Holstein came visiting in all her glory. He was probably the guest of more people in diverse circumstances than any man living. But a tepee or a palace were all the same to him, and so were their inhabitants. He had hundreds of imitators but was quite inimitable.

"His heart never left the great West. Whenever the day's work was done, he could always be found sitting alone watching the sinking sun, and at every opportunity he took the trail back to his old home. The sun setting over the mountain will pay its daily tribute to the resting place of the last of the great builders of the West, all of which you loved and part of which you were."

Annie Oakley died in Greenville, Ohio, November 3, 1926. In the fall of 1901 she was severely injured when the Buffalo Bill show train crashed in a head-on collision near Lexington, Virginia, but she recovered sufficiently to resume her career and she traveled with the show in 1912, the last year that Colonel Cody headed his own show.

Poster representing Annie Oakley, star of show for seventeen years.

Sketches by Charles Dana Gibson, done at
Wild West Show. Man at lower left is Curley, a
Crow Scout, the only man in Custer's Command
who escaped at the battle of the Little Big Horn.
At upper right is Rain-in-the-Face, who is said to
have killed Custer.

244

Chapter 15

Last Days of Buffalo Bill

BY 1912 Buffalo Bill, then sixty-six, was a tired and occasionally disenchanted man. The pounding of the saddle for nearly sixty years, the hounding he faced for money from all sides, had aged him severely. Always more money was needed to pay the mounting debts. The more money he made, the more he needed. Not one of his investments—ranches, hotels, the stock market, mortgages, loans, real estate—had paid off. It was almost more than his spirit could endure.

Since he had teamed with Nate Salsbury he had always had a business man-ager to attend to the financial details of the show. After Salsbury died in 1902 James A. Bailey had managed the show, had seen it through reverses and disasters, and had kept it solvent and on the road. Bailey died in 1907, leaving the show slightly in debt. The Colonel had neither ability nor strength sufficient to carry on alone. His wife provided no comfort; his occasional female intimates were more interested in taking than in giving; and nearly all of his old pards of the early days were occupied with their own projects, retired, or dead. The movies had brought

COLONEL CODY drove these horses in show when he could no longer ride in 1912.　　**245**

the magic of the West to every crossroads hamlet, since film traveled lighter and faster than buffaloes. Buffalo Bill, who had shown America the amazing saga of the frontier, was as gallant and heroic as ever, but not any longer a fresh and surprising contemporary of the dynamic young generation of the future. He had seen the astonishing transformation of the West by the railway, the telegraph, the telephone, the tractor, the plow, and the barbed-wire fence, and never imagined that he would be "fenced in" by the technical progress that had overtaken the land whose history he had represented nearly all his life.

His old friend Pawnee Bill—Major Gordon Lillie—who had helped him procure Indians for his first Wild West Show, came to Colonel Cody's rescue. Lillie had a show of his own which he called the Far East Show. He suggested that they organize a "farewell tour" together, one that would take three years, and visit every town and city in the United States and Canada. Buffalo Bill leaped at the idea. Lillie bought out the Bailey interest, and the two shows were combined. The first season, 1911–12, was successful because the crowds believed that this was a genuine farewell. In the second year business began to fall off. There were profits, but not enough to keep Buffalo Bill ahead of his creditors.

Early in 1913, while visiting his sister in Denver, Colonel Cody met H. H. Tammen, who, with his partner Fred Bonfils, owned the Denver *Post* and the Sells-Floto Circus. Harry Tammen seemed a friendly sort of man, and when Cody told him that

Colonel Cody took Major Gordon W. Lillie (Pawnee Bill) as partner in 1910, made farewell tour with him.

he needed twenty thousand dollars to get clear of his debts, the newspaper proprietor said he would lend it to him, taking a six months' note on the show property as collateral. To Buffalo Bill this seemed the solution of his most pressing problems. Tammen then pressed Buffalo Bill to leave Pawnee Bill at the end of the season and to appear with the Sells-Floto Circus the following year. Colonel Cody reluctantly agreed to do so.

The deal was announced by the Denver *Post* on February 5, 1913: "The most important ever consummated in American amusement enterprise . . . The Sells-Floto Circus shall continue and the Buffalo Bill

Exposition of Frontier Days shall be preserved with the circus. . . . The strongest combination ever formed in the history of American amusements, if not in the world."

During the spring the Pawnee Bill-Buffalo Bill combination did very poorly. Bad weather, bad luck, and small audiences meant that they owed money to everybody. Their route took them back through Denver in July. Feed bills had piled up, and the printing and lithographing company which did their posters demanded payment on a debt of sixty thousand dollars.

Harry Tammen met Buffalo Bill in his private car as the train pulled into the Denver railroad yards. Tammen seemed full of confidence and good feeling. With effusive heartiness he asked the Colonel, who was sleepy and shaky after the journey, how things were going. Cody tried to bring himself out of his melancholy mood. As he talked to Tammen, he began to suspect the latter's affability, and a sense of disaster overwhelmed him. Feeling that something terrible was about to happen, he called for drinks.

When Buffalo Bill finished his highball the newspaper proprietor reminded him of the note. Nothing had been paid on it, not even the interest. Colonel Cody summoned his courage, promised to do something about the obligation. Harry Tammen smiled agreeably. Perhaps everything would be all right, thought Buffalo Bill, but he had a nervous feeling in the pit of his stomach. Maybe another drink would dispel it.

The next morning as he was trying to stir himself awake, four men from the sheriff's office appeared at the show grounds. Buffalo Bill saw them, guessed who they were. He sent a man to grab the cash box before it could be attached, but he was too late. The sheriff's men announced that all the property of the Wild West and the Far East Show had been attached for debt.

Lawyers explained the situation to Cody. If the United States Lithographing Company could not get a sizable payment a move would be made to put the properties up for auction. The Colonel thought of the friends he had once had in Denver. Some of them were bankers. He told Lillie he would go see them, raise some cash. Lillie shook his head. "We'll never get help in Denver," he said. The alternative was bankruptcy, and there seemed no escape from it. The tents would have to be folded.

What Buffalo Bill did not understand was that he had gotten involved with a man who wanted a big circus that could compete with Ringling Brothers. When Harry Tammen decided he wanted the Buffalo Bill show, he went about getting it in the only way he knew how. His methods were direct, legitimate, and not irregular under the tenets of business practice. What Colonel Cody could not conceive was that Tammen was determined to make him, Buffalo Bill, his personal, private property.

As Gene Fowler, the author and historian of Denver in this period, tells the story, Harry Tammen was always looking for new toys. When he decided he wanted a circus, Bonfils told him to study nature —there were 405 species of birds in Colorado. "Birds, hell!" Tammen said. "I want elephants."

So he got elephants—after he had begun with dogs, calling his first show the Floto Dog and Pony Show. The Denver *Post* sports editor was named Floto, and never owned a single share of the show. As the circus grew, Harry wanted another name to add to the title of the show, so he hired a relative of the Sells family and called it "Sells-Floto." This annoyed the Ringling Brothers because they had already bought the Sells Brothers Circus. From then on it was a battle, with Buffalo Bill caught in the middle.

For a month Buffalo Bill tried frantically to raise cash to save his show and to get out of the clutches of Harry Tammen. None of his friends responded; none could help him in the generous way in which he had always been so ready to help them. All the promises of "If you ever need anything, Colonel, just call on me" suddenly evaporated. As the days passed, Buffalo Bill knew that everything would go under the auctioneer's hammer.

On the day of the auction one old friend appeared, Colonel C. J. Bills of Lincoln, Nebraska. He had come to bid on Isham, the last of the series of many horses Buffalo Bill had loved. It was a colorful and tragic occasion. Mirrored wagons, steel cages, broncos, horses, oxen, mustangs, cattle from India, and camels went up for sale to the highest bidder. Even the show train was sold.

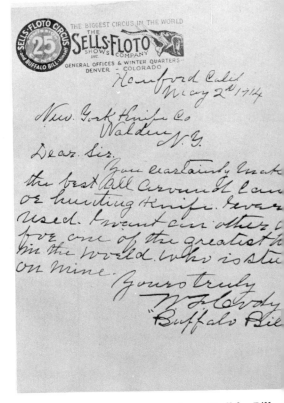

TYPICALLY GENEROUS LETTER from Buffalo Bill when he toured with Sells-Floto circus in his last days.

Pawnee Bill's lawyers tried to stop the sale at the last minute, but Tammen's lawyers were alert, and watching for some such move. All that Lillie could do was to have handbills passed out: "Warning! Let the buyer beware!" Nobody paid attention to these. The auctioneer went ahead on schedule.

When the bidding started on Isham somebody said the horse was just an old, flea-bitten nag. Yet it was still the great white horse which had carried Buffalo Bill proudly around the area. Colonel Bills bit into his cigar. If he couldn't buy the horse, he said, he'd steal him from whoever did buy him. Whatever happened, he would see that Buffalo Bill got his horse back. Finally Isham was sold to "the gentleman from Lincoln" for $150. Colonel Bills ordered Isham shipped to the TE Ranch in Wyoming to stay there the rest of his life.

Two days later, Colonel Cody, heartsick at the thought of such an ending to his career, took the train to the town in the Big Horn Basin that he had founded. He worried and frankly wept about his show people, and how they would get home. Never before had his people been stranded; not in thirty years in show business had they ever gone without the pay they had earned.

As he rested at the ranch Buffalo Bill began to think of what he might do. Tired though he was, his mind was restless with new plans. He was sixty-six, but he wasn't

through. He'd show the world that he could make a comeback. Little by little his strength returned, his optimism rose once more. He would start that super dude ranch his friends had been urging him to do. He would go into the hotel business in a big way. A London booking agent cabled him a tempting offer: $2,500 a week. Colonel Cody thought it over and then asked for more. He never heard anything more from London.

He sat under the trees at his ranch and his eyes wandered over the mountains. He could almost see the Indians creeping out from the trees. That was it. Why not a movie that would tell the whole story of the Indian wars, the epic struggle for the West? If movies were replacing the theater and the art of live showmanship, why not keep abreast of progress and go into the movies? Who would finance the venture? Again he pored through the list of his rich and successful old friends. There was nobody who could put up the capital except Tammen and Bonfils. Maybe they would help him make enough money so that he could liberate himself from them. He took the train back to Denver.

The eyes of Harry Tammen lit up when the Colonel told him of his idea. "You're a wonder, Bill," he said. He and his partner would talk to the Secretary of War, get his co-operation, use the U.S. Army and its equipment. The picture would be a historical record of the great Indian battles. Perhaps General Miles could be persuaded to act in it.

A film company was organized with the

Buffalo Bill in the movies, a shot from the only movie he ever made.

249

BUFFALO BILL'S WILD WEST
COMBINED WITH
PAWNEE BILL'S GREAT FAR EAST.

Phila—
Sept 27

Dear Stay,
Will take nearly $70.000 here this week. Guess 101. Ranch. Wish they had never got ahead of us.
Say keep me posted on their business this week
Send me a few dozen cheap small photos of my self to give away
Yours
W. F. Cody

help of Essanay of Hollywood. Colonel Cody would have a one-third interest for supervising it. His spirits soared as he traveled to the Pine Ridge Indian reservation in South Dakota. There he found old Iron Tail, the Indian chief who had toured with his show, and before long a number of Indian villages had been constructed along the creek at Wounded Knee. The technicians and their movie cameras moved in. The plan called for the battle to take place right over the Indian graves, which seemed

to the Sioux a horrible desecration. General Miles could see nothing wrong with the idea, however, for that would make everything historically accurate. Johnny Baker came to join the Colonel. He understood how the Indians felt, and talked to them.

Nevertheless the Indians were resentful, remembering how the white soldiers had massacred their tribesmen and the women and children. Iron Tail came to Buffalo Bill's tent and warned him there would be

250   LETTER FROM COLONEL CODY while touring with Pawnee Bill.

trouble. Colonel Cody told him to call together the old men of the tribe. Short Bull and No Neck came to the council. Buffalo Bill told them how hopeless it would be to turn this movie battle into a real one, to shoot real bullets at the white men, for the Indians would be pursued and caught, and probably tried for murder. The Sioux warriors finally saw his point, and the following day the sham battle went before the cameras. No one was hurt.

In the fall Buffalo Bill went off again, this time with the Sells-Floto Circus, as he had agreed. It hurt his pride to be displayed as a sort of freak, the chattel of Harry Tammen. No longer did he have the strength to ride his horse, but instead drove a team of white horses hitched to a phaeton. Whatever people might say, he was still in show business. He was paid a hundred dollars a day by Tammen plus 40 per cent of the gross over three thousand dollars a day. In his contract he agreed not to take more than three drinks a day. He didn't, but he had the whiskey served to him in oversized beer mugs. Yet, as his creditors pressed him for old bills, he needed to borrow more money from Tammen, advances on his salary and his prospective share of the gross.

BUFFALO BILL WITH HIS DEADWOOD COACH in days when he was putting on weight.

In those days he was a familiar figure in the city of Denver. Gene Fowler remembers that period: "The Colonel had a baritone voice that rang out in the arena; nor did he tone it down much in private. When he was pressed for money, which was often, for he was open-handed and careless in monetary matters, he used to come down to the *Post* to touch the owners of the newspaper." Fowler was a reporter on the *Post* at that time. "They humored him. I often was assigned to interview him.

"As you no doubt know, a newspaper office sometimes was noisy, but two noises were looked down upon: loud conversation or whistling. Indeed, whistling was regarded as a most terrible breach of newsroom manners. I mention this because when I first interviewed Cody in the office I pretended that I had gone deaf. I liked to hear him speak in stentorian tones. The result was that he roared the answers to my questions, and everyone in the city room became mad as hell, and if the bosses had not been interested in his name and property in their show, he might well have been thrown out."

Soon after this, while working in the Sells-Floto Circus, Buffalo Bill began to suffer painfully from rheumatism and neuritis. What was more serious was prostate trouble, which could have been relieved by an operation. Yet he put it off, postponed it from month to month, until it was too late for the surgeons to help him. When the doctors said he needed a long rest he would shake his head; he'd keep going as long as he could. He was only a name now,

but it was a glorious name and he would live up to it as long as he had the strength to stand.

Although friends urged him to go into personal bankruptcy, he would not listen to them. Back at the TE Ranch he dreamed of the money he would make when the new Cody Road was built—today the Buffalo Bill Highway, one of the most beautiful scenic drives in the world, from the town of Cody to the majestic east gate of Yellowstone. Wapiti and Pahaska overnight lodges were on that road; he owned them, and visualized big profits from them. The Irma Hotel in Cody would have more business than it could handle. However, the road wasn't finished until years later. What Buffalo Bill dreamed of would come true in the age of automobiles for every family—but too late for him.

Colonel Cody, irritable because of illness, complained constantly to Tammen about the slovenly atmosphere of the show. He said that the ropes that held the tent were worn out and that someday the canvas would crash on the spectators. He quarreled about money, how much was owed to him, how much had already been deducted from his salary and percentages. He wanted more than anything else to get free of Harry Tammen.

They finally parted company at the end of the 1914 season. But Buffalo Bill had no intention of giving up show business. He talked of buying another show: Ranch 101, owned by the Miller brothers, which was featuring Jess Willard, the boxing champion. With the stimulation of interest pro-

The Irma Hotel in Cody, Wyoming, in 1908. He built it in 1902. Stagecoach in foreground took tourists to Yellowstone National Park, fifty miles away.

vided by the war in Europe the Colonel thought he could turn it into a military spectacle something like the ones he had produced with Salsbury.

However, he was unable to raise the capital to buy the show, and in the end merely joined it. At the age of sixty-nine he pulled himself into the saddle again and was once more shooting at glass balls. The show was prosperous while he was with it. But people kept after him, harassing him with demands to be paid for old bills which he had forgotten. Tammen annoyed him with demands. Major Lillie sued him.

Desperately he tried to sell everything he could, even Scout's Rest in North Platte. At the end of the season he had overdrawn so much from the Miller brothers that he barely had train fare back to Wyoming.

Still, there was no rest for him. In the winter he went on a lecture tour with the movies of the Indian battles. He talked while the pictures were shown. In the summer of 1916 he went on the road again with the 101 Ranch. Although he was seventy, he didn't miss a parade or a performance. At the same time he discussed with William Randolph Hearst writing a series

253

of articles for *Hearst's Monthly* magazine. And he never ceased plotting big schemes for the Big Horn Basin.

After Johnny Baker had a season in London he returned to be with the Colonel on his final tour with Ranch 101. The old man still mounted his horse and shot at the glass balls; he still led the grand parade around the arena. Sometimes he feared he would collapse in the ring. Baker would help him onto his horse. He would slump there, trying to gather his strength as he waited for the signal. When the curtains parted, Johnny would say, "Ready, Colonel!" and Buffalo Bill would raise his chin from his chest, although he was breathing heavily, and straighten his back as the pains seemed to be killing him. By sheer will power he would sit in the saddle, ride out before the spectators, doff his big Stetson, and bow while the crowd cheered.

When it was over he would ride back again through the curtains, his head still erect, with fear clutching at his heart, the fear of dying "before all those people." Unable to control himself, he would slide from the saddle into the arms of Johnny Baker. That painful routine continued all summer and into the autumn. When the show reached Portsmouth, Virginia, on November 11, 1916, the Colonel's chest was congested with a cold. It was his last appearance. He set out for home.

At Chicago he hoped to talk with some rich men who might provide fresh capital for him to start over again with his own show. He saw them, but he was too weak to get down to business. He went on to Denver, stopping off to see his sister May who lived there.

She urged him to stay with her, for she was alarmed by the state of his health. He shook his head: he would continue on to Cody. Once back among his friendly mountains he felt better, strong enough to attend a dinner held in his honor at the Irma Hotel early in December. Though he tried to be gay, some of his friends noted the look of death in his eyes. Determined not to give up, he said he must go back to Denver on business. As long as there was a spark of life left in him, he would make the gesture, nourish the hope he could yet recoup his fortunes.

The trip to get back to Denver was too much for him. Uremia had already set in. The doctors suggested he go to Glenwood Springs for the mineral baths and to see Dr. W. W. Crook, who might be able to ease his pains.

At Glenwood Springs he collapsed. The Denver *Post* headlines reported, "Death Feared. Colonel Cody's Mind Impaired by Illness, but Plans Big Show. Dr. Crook told reporters that Buffalo Bill would return to Denver and later to Wyoming if his condition permitted." The old man told his friends that he wanted to die in the Big Horn Basin, and to be buried there. He had selected the site on Cedar Mountain, at a place which overlooked the whole valley. Long ago he had climbed the mountain with an old friend and piled up some rocks to show the spot.

When he was in New York City a decade before he had drawn up a will. The

Last picture of Buffalo Bill with his wife; no others were taken of them together in his later years.

of which I have taken so deep and loving an interest, and to which wheresoever and to whatever parts of the earth I have wandered I have always longed to return. . . .

"I further direct that there shall be erected over my grave, to mark the spot where my body lies, a monument wrought from native red stone in the form of a mammoth buffalo, and placed in such a position as to be visible from the town, in order that it may be a constant reminder to my fellow citizens that it was the great wish of its founder that Cody should not only grow in prosperity and become a populous and influential metropolis, but that it should be distinguished for the purity of its government and the loyalty of its citizens to the institutions of our beloved country. I give to my said executors the sum of ten thousand dollars for the cost of the monument and its erection and to carefully keep the ground about it in proper order."

second clause read, "It is my wish and I hereby direct that my body shall be buried in some suitable plot of ground on Cedar Mountain, overlooking the town of Cody, Wyoming, in order that my mortal remains shall lie in close proximity to that fair section of my native country which bears my name and in the growth and development

Dr. Crook gave a statement to the press on January 5, 1917: "Colonel Cody is slowly but surely nearing the end. There is no hope whatever for him. He suffered a nervous collapse yesterday and his mental faculties are seriously threatened." Soon after the statement was issued Buffalo Bill roused himself and showed flashes of his old-time self. He told his friends that he would soon go on the road with a new show bigger and better than ever. Dr. Crook added, "We will leave with him this evening for Denver, where his wife and daughter will meet him. If possible they will take him home to Wyoming."

255

The Denver *Post* continued to report plans of the Colonel and his family for a return to Wyoming. On January 6 it carried the headline, "Colonel Cody Going Home to Old Wyoming Ranch with Death Beside Him. Doctors Say Buffalo Can Live But a Few Hours Longer. Famous Old Scout Will Reach Denver This Morning. . . . Mrs. Cody and her daughter Irma Garlow will arrive in Denver today from Cody. Another sister, Mrs. Susie Cody Goodman, arrived yesterday."

On January 8 the *Post* reported that plans had been changed. The Colonel would not return to Wyoming after all: "Buffalo Bill Arrives in Denver Too Ill for Removal to Wyoming. Old Indian Fighter Being Weakened by Moon Eclipse Attending Doctor Says. Passed a Bad Night. Kidneys in Serious Condition, Heart Action Weak. Nerves Completely Shattered. . . . Dr. East said, 'It has been known for ages that eclipses of the sun and moon influence all life on earth and especially one in ill health. I consider Colonel Cody's condition very serious as metabolism has ceased. By metabolism I mean the change of organic or life forces. . . .'"

At the home of May Cody Decker, his sister, who lived at 2932 Lafayette Street, he seemed to feel a little better after he had been put to bed and had rested. He called for Dr. East. This is the physician's account of the interview as he told it to the Cody *Enterprise*:

"Sit down, Doctor, there is something I want to ask you. I want you to answer me honestly. What are my chances?"

"There is a time, Colonel," said Dr. East, "when every honest physician must commend his patient to a higher power."

Colonel Cody's head sank. "How long?" he asked.

"I can only answer that by telling you your life is like an hourglass. The sand is slipping gradually, slowly, but soon the sand will be gone. The end is not far away."

Cody roused himself and called for his brother-in-law, Lew Decker, who inquired what the doctor had said.

"Let's forget about it," said the old scout, "and play high five."

In his private office, known as the Red Room, in the Denver *Post* building Harry Tammen waited for the end of Buffalo Bill. So did all of Denver. On January 9 the *Post* reported, "Colonel Cody Waits End Calmly at Home of Sister. Told He Can't Live Long and Shows no Emotion. He was rational for a time about ten o'clock this morning. The total lapses of memory which have been so frequent during the last week or ten days seem to have passed. This is taken to mean the approach of the end."

On the front page of the evening edition of the Denver *Post* for January 10 was the headline everybody expected: "Colonel Cody Dies at Noon After Relapse at Home of his Sister. At ten o'clock the famous old Indian fighter suffered sudden relapse. Uremic poisoning was spreading rapidly through his system."

Before he died Buffalo Bill said, "Let the Elks and Masons take charge of the funeral." Within minutes of the death,

Major Robert V. Speer of the Elks had the body removed to a funeral home. For two days it lay in state at the capitol building in Denver in a big bronze casket, the Elks forming a guard of honor.

Among the tributes published immediately after Buffalo Bill's death was one from Theodore Roosevelt: "Buffalo Bill was one of those men, steel-thewed and iron nerved, whose daring progress opened the great West to settlement and civilization. His name, like that of Kit Carson, will always be associated with old adventure and pioneer days of hazard and hardship when the great plains and the Rocky Mountains were won for our race. It is eminently fit to commemorate his gallant, picturesque and most useful career by such a monument as you propose. He embodied those traits of courage, strength and self-reliant hardihood which are vital to the well-being of our nation."

The monument to which Roosevelt referred was one that was being planned by the Denver *Post*. As soon as the Colonel died the *Post* announced a nationwide campaign of the school children of America, sponsored by the *Post*, to collect pennies to erect a monument for Buffalo Bill on Lookout Mountain, above Denver. Nothing was said about his wishes to be buried at Cedar Mountain, above the town of Cody. Another and later will was produced by Mrs. Louisa Cody in which everything was left to her, his widow. It had been signed and witnessed at North Platte.

Whose was the decision to bury Buffalo Bill at Lookout Mountain? Evidently it was decided by Louisa Cody. She paid for the funeral expenses. But the story has persisted that she was persuaded to make this decision by Harry Tammen. The Denver *Post* said it was the Colonel's wish to be buried at Lookout Mountain. Nobody, however, heard him express such a wish before his death. It was also said and believed by many people in Denver and Cody that Mrs. Cody was paid ten thousand dollars by Mr. Tammen, for the privilege of selecting, with Bonfils, the burial place.

The simple funeral services were held in the Elk's Lodge on January 15, 1917. Dr. Charles H. Marshall, Chaplain of the Lodge and Rector of the St. Barnabas Episcopal Church, officiated. Buffalo Bill's favorite hymn, "Tenting tonight on the old camp ground," was sung. Before the services eighteen thousand people braved the bitter cold in a march to the Elk's Lodge. In the parade was led an old horse, which the newspapers said was McKinley, the horse the Colonel rode in the 101 Ranch show. But it wasn't McKinley, and those who had known the Colonel knew it. It was just an old horse produced for the occasion.

The burial spot selected by Tammen was not ready at the time of the funeral, and roads up the mountain had not yet been built. So the mortal remains of Buffalo Bill were placed in a vault until the time for the final burial, a time selected by Tammen. This was June 3, 1917. It was a circuslike affair and the Sells-Floto Circus played a part in the parade up the mountain.

The banner headline across the front page of the Denver *Post* for June 3, 1917, read, BUFFALO BILL IS LAID AT LAST REST, and in big, bold-face type, "All Nature Bows in Homage as Casket Is Opened to View of Pilgrims of Sunset Trail. Thousands of Vehicles Surge over Mountain Road to Final Resting Place of Frontiersman on Lofty Peak of Rockies Standing Sentinel Over Sweeping Prairies and Scene of Birth of Wonderful West./Funeral Services are Impressive and Fitting to Life of Noted Scout and in Spirit with Career—Stars and Stripes Raised to Mark Spot to World That Will Wear Path to Tomb."

Tammen put Gene Fowler, then the chief feature writer for the Denver *Post*, in charge of the arrangements for the burial. Tammen said he thought it would be a fine thing for the circus to give Buffalo Bill a burial in a Colorado spot. He thought Lookout Mountain would be ideal.

Gene Fowler wrote the story that appeared in the *Post* that day:

"Upward for hours the pageant moved. Upward the thousands of vehicles surged. From a distant height they looked like tiny creatures climbing methodically over a long brown ribbon. Peeping buds of flowers, the dew yet clinging for the sun to drink, bowed their heads in the slender grasses. They seemed to know that a funeral cortege was passing by, accompanying a great man—one who was reaching the end of the sunset trail. Hence, they too paid homage.

"Brigadier General William F. Cody, Buffalo Bill, rests in a tomb splendid. Human hands today placed him on the crest of Lookout Mountain, on the dividing line between the wild and the tame. And such should be his sepulchre. For, was not he a bridge between the Past and the Future? There in the light of the setting sun are the memories of his achievements. There to the east, where the first grey dawn sets the wheels of commerce in motion, there lies a city, a dream come true! . . .

"The 25,000 citizens who saw them press the earth over the sleeping form of Pahaska, the trail blazer, this afternoon were touched by the romance, the thrill of it all. . . .

"It was the most impressive, the most notable funeral ever witnessed in America. No president could have been more honored by the presence of thousands. No statesman could have been interested in a crypt more ideally situated.

"To Nature and to God this afternoon we Americans of the West surrendered Pahaska to his final slumber.

"Pahaska, Farewell!"

In *Timberline*, published in 1933, years after Gene Fowler had graduated from the Denver *Post*, he wrote, "When the *Post* began speculating on what sort of memorial should be placed at Cody's tomb on Lookout Mountain the Boulder *Camera* of Boulder, Colorado, had the following comment: 'why not let the Denver *Post* proprietors determine the kind of shaft to erect over Buffalo Bill? He was their meat. It was they who brought him down after a gallant career by breaking his proud heart. Why should not the shaft be crowned with a miniature Red Room bearing this device: "Abandon hope, all ye who enter here." ' "

THE GREAT SCOUT'S LAST FAREWELL on horseback at the end of the show. **259**

A kind of transfiguration took place in the reputation of Buffalo Bill the moment he died. While he lived his last years people pitied him. They saw him, his linen immaculate, his boots gleaming, but his pockets practically empty, on the streets of Denver and at the bar of the Albany Hotel and at the Windsor where he was often found with some of his cronies. Denver has thus transmitted a paradoxical, contradictory reputation for its adopted, or abducted, hero. You will hear it said in Denver that he was a pathetic old poseur who drank too much. And yet in Denver there is that rugged, sky-topped monument over his grave at Lookout Mountain that hails him as Colorado's glorious son.

While he struggled for life in a little hall bedroom of his sister's home, he was a sad figure. Yet the moment he died the miracle of the resurrection occurred. He became immortalized as the Great American Hero. All the richness, the depth of spirit, the magnificent heroism of Buffalo Bill, man and boy, were suddenly remembered. Buffalo Bill, from a suffering human being fighting against impossible odds for his life, became in his death the legend of the West, the apotheosis of greatness, of all the qualities of adventurous self-reliance and pioneering that are most American, and that Americans most admire.

The Scout Still Rides Among the Stars

ON a wind-swept hundred-acre mesa, between Rattlesnake Mountain and Cedar Mountain at Cody, Wyoming, the twelve-foot bronze statue of Colonel Cody riding Old Smoky, a horse from the TE Ranch, faces the Rockies. Gertrude Vanderbilt Whitney completed this representation of Buffalo Bill in her New York studio in the spring of 1924, and it was unveiled at Cody in July of that year. She meticulously depicted the Scout as he was in the 1860s and 1870s, reining his mount on Old South Fork Trail and scanning the ground for Sioux pony tracks.

Not far from the monument the Buffalo Bill Museum* abounds in Western Americana, including Buffalo Bill's guns, knives, buckskin jackets, uniforms, vehicles, saddles and bridles, medals and trophies, thousands of letters, hundreds of Buffalo Bill dime novels, and a growing collection on the Old West in paintings, prints, sculpture, and photography. To these archives in the cow-town which Cody founded scholars come to study the frontier, as

---

* Colonel Cody's niece, Mrs. Mary Jester Allen, is curator of the Museum.

261

naturally as they turn to the books of Parkman, Turner, and Webb, the historians. The hundreds of thousands of acres which the Colonel once owned have proven to be rich in oil and minerals. The scenic beauty of the Buffalo Bill Highway to Yellowstone attracts a stream of tourists; during the summer there is a Wild West show every night on the Cody Stampede grounds.

THE WINCHESTER RIFLE USED BY BUFFALO BILL in his show, a gift to Buffalo Bill Museum by Colonel Walter F. Siegmund.

THE PLACE WHERE BUFFALO BILL WANTED TO BE BURIED, pointed out by guide, Ned Frost, who was with Colonel Cody when he placed the stones on this spot at Cody, Wyoming.

BUFFALO BILL'S GRAVE ON LOOKOUT MOUNTAIN ABOVE DENVER.

To the local residents the Colonel is as alive today as he was a generation ago when his hearty laugh and "Hi, old hoss!" echoed through the corridors of the Irma Hotel. They—including his descendants and old neighbors—don't worry about the lingering gossip of occasional girl friends, or a few too many drinks during the last decade of his life. They remember him as a generous man, with a hard and warm handshake, always the natural aristocrat. The courtly flourish of his Stetson was not an actor's pose, but a graceful compulsion, as unaffected as the fringes and feathers of an Indian chief. Of course, he loved beautiful women, including a few attractive Indian squaws! They take that for granted.

But he also had an eye for beauty in horses, mountains, rivers, and plains. He adored children. He was fundamentally, childishly innocent. Without knowing it, he was in the same primitively classical tradition as Benjamin West who, upon seeing a nude statue of Apollo Belvidere, exclaimed: "Ah, a Mohawk!" The rhythmic Indian nomenclature sanctified his special projects and possessions all his life.

To the world outside the Wild West, Buffalo Bill is a character in a great procession of legendary heroes, ranging from Robin Hood, Don Quixote, and D'Artagnan to Davy Crockett, Kit Carson, and Teddy Roosevelt. Yet despite the fact that he knew, and was known to, as many people of high and low degree as any individual of his time, no one ever penetrated his inner personal life. He gallantly concealed the anguish of his domestic unhappiness even in his intimate letters to his sister Julia. He strove, with all the stubborn integrity of poet or artist, to convey, first to his comrades, then to the world, how romantic a man could be in a simple frontier setting. Beneath the trappings, the gregariousness, the showmanship, lay a tragic sense of the unattainable, of the vanity of exhibitionistic youth in a shrinking and maturing world. A loquacious man surrounded by press agents and tellers of tall tales, he quickly became part of the folklore of his own time—Mr. Everyman in the wilderness; Leatherstocking plus modern polish; a pre-atomic Superman endowed with the grace of the Great Spirit of the Indians. Always a Scout, he understood long before he crossed the Great Divide into the Happy Hunting Grounds that like the Indians he was engaged in a race with the enclosing fence of progress.

Boy and man, saint and sinner, he symbolizes the picturesque heritage of the American frontier more forcefully today than he did at the many, many peaks of his earthly fame.

IBLIOGRAPHY

THE AUTHORS and their researchers have studied the general literature (books, magazines, and monographs) and the newspapers, in the West and abroad, ranging from Kansas, Colorado, Nebraska, and Wyoming to Great Britain, France, Germany, and Italy. They have also had permission to study personal correspondence, even when it might not be quoted, such as the so-called "love letters" in the Piatt Collection of the Denver Public Library. United States Government reports on the Great Plains, from the Frémont period to the resource and ecological surveys, and Indian reports of the past two decades have been consulted; and scores of living men and women who knew Buffalo Bill have been interviewed. The authors have frequently visited the Cody terrain in the West, and in addition to their study of written material, published and unpublished, have viewed thousands of photographs, maps, drawings, posters, and paintings, the most interesting of which are reproduced as illustrations, with sources carefully and gratefully noted in the acknowledgment or notice-of-copyright pages of this volume.

The bibliography which follows is limited to the specific books and publications dealing with William F. Cody, his family and associates, the Wild West, and the Wild West Show.

THE LIFE OF THE HONORABLE WILLIAM F. CODY, Known as Buffalo Bill, the Famous Hunter, Scout and Guide, by William F. Cody. Hartford, Conn.: F. E. Bliss, 1879.
The classic autobiography; exaggerated; illustrated; rich in anecdote and background on life as a youth, scout, guide for dudes—and the early days on the stage.

BUFFALO BILL'S LIFE STORY, An Autobiography of Buffalo Bill (Colonel W. F. Cody). Illustrated by N. C. Wyeth. New York: Rinehart & Company, 1920.
Anecdotal, this is the last of several 'autobiographies' written for Cody. It has been edited for easy reading and contains the best known of the many stories about him.

THE STORY OF THE WILD WEST AND CAMPFIRE CHATS by William F. Cody. Charles C. Thompson Co., 1888.

LIFE AND ADVENTURES OF BUFFALO BILL by William F. Cody. Chicago: John R. Stanton and Co., 1917.
Incorporates the best of the autobiographies, goes into more detail than BUFFALO BILL'S LIFE STORY. Obviously contains much fiction.

BUFFALO BILL FROM PRAIRIE TO PAL-
ACE by John M. Burke. Chicago: Rand,
McNally, 1893.
Written by his press agent; contains much in-
formation about Colonel Cody's career up to the
time he went to England in 1887.

LAST OF THE GREAT SCOUTS by Helen
Cody Wetmore. New York: Grosset &
Dunlap, 1899.
Reminiscences by Colonel Cody's sister, sen-
timental and incomplete.

LETTERS FROM BUFFALO BILL. Edited,
with comments by Stella Adelyne Foote.
Published by Stella A. Foote, Billings,
Montana, 1954.
Letters written by Colonel Cody to his sister,
Julia Cody Goodman. They give an insight into
his marital and financial trials and tribulations.

FOUR YEARS IN EUROPE WITH BUFFALO
BILL by Charles Eldrige Griffin. Aldia,
Iowa: Stage Publishing Company, 1908.
An account of Griffin's trip to Europe; con-
tains information about the show abroad from
1904 to 1908.

MY LIFE WITH BUFFALO BILL by Dan Mul-
ler, with illustrations by the author. Chicago: Reilly and Lee, 1948.
Written by a friend of the family who lived
within the Cody family circle during his boyhood and youth and then traveled with the show,
these reminiscences also tell of Colonel Cody's
last days.

THE GREAT SALT LAKE TRAIL by Colonel
Henry Inman and William F. Cody. Topeka, Kansas: Crane and Co., 1898.

THE OLD SANTA FE TRAIL by Colonel
Henry Inman and William F. Cody. Topeka, Kansas: Crane and Co., 1897.

TRUE TALES OF THE PLAINS by William
F. Cody. New York: Cupples and Leon,
1908.

THE CODY FAMILY ASSOCIATION DIREC-
TORY, 1952. Descendants of Philip and
Martha at Beverly, Massachusetts, 1698.
By Ernest William Cody and Ella Jean
Cody. London, Ontario, 1952.

MEMORIES OF BUFFALO BILL by Louisa
Frederici Cody in collaboration with
Courtney Ryley Cooper. New York: D.
Appleton and Co., 1920.
A sentimental story, told from the point of view
of the widow. It contains much more or less legiti-
mate fictionalizing.

THE MAKING OF BUFFALO BILL, A Study
in Heroics, by Richard J. Walsh in collaboration with Milton S. Salsbury. Indianapolis: Bobbs, Merrill, 1928.
A critical biography, based on material left by
Nate Salsbury, Colonel Cody's partner; gives the
somewhat cynical Salsbury point of view.

BUFFALO BILL, The Legend, the Man of Action, and the Showman, by Rupert Croft-
Cooke and W. S. Meadmore. London:
Sidgwick and Jackson Ltd., 1952.
An objective but uninspired biography; gives
the story of Colonel Cody's friendship with Katherine Clemmons.

THE STORY OF BUFFALO BILL by Shannon
Garst. New York: Julian Messner, 1948.
Written primarily for children, this is excellent
for dates; contains a chronology.

ANECDOTES OF BUFFALO BILL by De Witt
Winget. Chicago Historical Publishing
Co., 1927.
A collection of all the anecdotes this editor
could find attributed to Colonel Cody. Not all
of them are authentic.

266

THE TRUTH ABOUT BUFFALO BILL, Westerners Brand Book 1945–46. Chicago, 1946.

BUFFALO BILL AND HIS HORSES by Agnes Wright Spring. Printed for the author by B & M Printing Co., Fort Collins, Colorado, 1953.
Anecdotes about the horses of Buffalo Bill.

THE STAGE CAREER OF BUFFALO BILL by Jay Monaghan. *Journal of the Illinois State Historical Society,* vol. XXXIII, no. 4 (December, 1940), pp. 411–33.

TEN DAYS ON THE PLAINS by General H. E. Davies. New York: Crocker and Co., 1871.
A precise account of the hunting party with the dudes by one of them.

INDIANS OF THE AMERICAS by John Collier. New York: New American Library, Mentor edition, 1948.
The story of the American Indians from the Paleolithic Age to the present.

HANDBOOK OF AMERICAN INDIANS by Frederick Webb Hodge. Published by the U. S. Government Printing Office, Washington, D.C., 1910.
Indispensable for the student and researcher on Indians. Contains information on such subjects as scalping not to be found elsewhere.

WARPATH AND COUNCIL FIRE by Stanley Vestal. New York: Random House, 1948.
The story of the warring Sioux.

SITTING BULL by Stanley Vestal. Boston and New York: Houghton Mifflin Co., 1932.
A superior and highly informative biography of a great Indian.

MY FRIEND THE INDIAN by James McLaughlin. Boston and New York: Houghton, Mifflin, 1926.

PERSONAL RECOLLECTIONS AND OBSERVATIONS by General Nelson A. Miles. Chicago: The Werner Co., 1896.

THE DUEL WITH YELLOW HAND by Stanley Vestal. *Southwest Review,* vol. 26, no. 1 (Autumn, 1940).

THE DUEL ON THE WAR BONNET by Don Russell.
American Military History. The most meticulous account of the death of Yellow Hand and the scalping of the Cheyenne chief by Buffalo Bill.

QUANTRILL AND THE BORDER WARS by William Elsey Connelly. Cedar Rapids, Iowa: The Torch Press, 1910.
A detailed history of the border wars between Kansas and Missouri and William C. Quantrill's part in them.

BLEEDING KANSAS by Alice Nichols. New York: Oxford University Press, 1954.
Colorful description of early days in Kansas.

WARPATH AND BIVOUAC by John Frederic Finerty. Chicago, 1890.

MY LIFE ON THE PLAINS by General George A. Custer. New York: Sheldon & Co., 1874.

THE OVERLAND STAGE TO CALIFORNIA by Frank A Root and William E. Conelley. Topeka, Kansas: published by the authors in 1901.

THE LAST AMERICAN FRONTIER by Frederic Logan Paxson. New York: The Macmillan Co., 1930.
Standard work on the development of the fron-

tier by one of America's foremost historians. Gives the background of the scene.

FRÉMONT'S EXPEDITION by Brevet Captain J. C. Frémont. Washington, D.C.: Blair and Ives, Printers, 1845.

THE FRONTIER IN AMERICAN HISTORY by Frederick Jackson Turner. New York: Henry Holt and Co., 1920.

THE GREAT PLAINS by Walter Prescott Webb. Boston: Ginn & Co., 1931.

THE OREGON TRAIL by Francis Parkman. New York: G. P. Putnam, 1849. The New American Library, Mentor edition, 1950.

MEMOIRS OF GENERAL PHILIP SHERIDAN, vol. II. New York: D. Appleton Co., 1904.
Tells of the famous Buffalo hunt with Grand Duke Alexis.

SHERIDAN THE INEVITABLE by Richard O'Connor. Indianapolis: Bobbs, Merrill, 1933.
Gives details of the hunting party with the dudes. A very lively biography.

BUFFALO LAND by William Edward Webb. Chicago: E. Hannadord & Co., 1872.

CAMPAIGNING WITH CROOK by Charles King. New York: Harper & Brothers, 1890.
Gives some details of the Yellow Hand duel.

SEVENTY YEARS ON THE FRONTIER by Alexander Majors. Chicago: Rand, McNally, 1893.
Tells about the pony express and the wagon trains.

THE THRILLING AND TRUTHFUL HISTORY OF THE PONY EXPRESS by William Lightfoot Visscher. Chicago: Rand, McNally, 1908.
A good description of the pony express and how it operated.

TENTING ON THE PLAINS by Elizabeth Bacon Custer. New York: C. L. Webster and Co., 1887.

ACROSS THE PLAINS WITH THE FIFTH CAVALRY by George Frederick Price. New York: D. Van Nostrand, 1883.

THE STORY OF THE PONY EXPRESS by Glen Danford Bradley. Chicago: A. C. McClurg and Co., 1913.

FAMOUS FRONTIERSMEN, PIONEERS, AND SCOUTS by E. G. Cattermole. Chicago: Donohue and Co.

HEROES OF THE PLAINS by James William Buel. Philadelphia: Historical Publishing Co., 1883.

VIRGIN LAND, The American West as Symbol and Myth, by Henry Nash Smith. Cambridge, Mass.: Harvard University Press, 1950.

ANNIE OAKLEY OF THE WILD WEST by Walter Havighurst. New York: The Macmillan Co., 1954.
An excellent, slightly sentimental biography of "Little Missie."

ANNIE OAKLEY by Courtney Riley Cooper. New York: Duffield & Co., 1927.

WILD BILL HICKOK by Frank J. Wilstach. New York: Doubleday, Doran, 1926.

PASSING OF THE WILD WEST, A Chapter in the History of American Entertainment, by Winifred Johnston. *Southwest Review* (Autumn, 1935).

THE GREAT RASCAL NED BUNTLINE by Jay Monaghan. Boston: Little, Brown & Co., 1952.
Tells of Buffalo Bill's stage debut and early years on the stage.

LIFE AND ADVENTURES OF NED BUNT-LINE by Frederic Eugene Pond. New York: The Cadmus Book Shop, 1919.

THIS WAY TO THE BIG SHOW by Dexter Fellows and Andrew Freeman. New York: The Viking Press, 1936.

CIRCUS by George A. Hamid (as told to his son, George A. Hamid, Jr.). New York: Sterling Publishing Co., Inc., 1950.

ANNALS OF THE NEW YORK STAGE by George Clinton Dinsmore Odell. Volumes XI, XII, XIII. New York: Columbia University Press, 1938–42.

R. D. BLUMENFELD'S DIARY, 1887–1914. London: William Heineman, Ltd., 1930.

DIARIES 1881–1901, Lord Ronald Sutherland Gower. London: John Murray, 1902.

PROCESSION by R. D. Blumenfeld. London: I. Nicholson & Watson, Ltd., 1935.

THE LIFE OF SIR ROBERT JONES by Frederick Watson. London: Hodder & Stoughton, 1934.

THE LETTERS AND FRIENDSHIP OF SIR CECIL SPRING-RICE. London: 1929.

THE BUCKING HORSE, with a History of the American Mustang, by P. Frenzeny. London: printed by Buffalo Bill's Wild West Show.

PICTURE MAKER OF THE OLD WEST by Clarence S. Jackson. New York: Scribners, 1947.
(The Life of William Henry Jackson.)

THE SUNNY SIDE OF DIPLOMATIC LIFE by Lillie de Hegermann-Lindencrone. New York: Harper & Brothers, 1914.

LESSONS OF A LIFETIME by Sir Robert Stephenson Baden-Powell. New York: Henry Holt & Co., 1933.

HARDLY A MAN IS NOW ALIVE: The Autobiography of Dan Beard. New York: Doubleday & Co., 1939.

THE WILDERNESS HUNTER by Theodore Roosevelt. New York: G. P. Putnam, 1893.

THE BUFFALO HUNTERS: The Story of the Hide Men, by Mari Sandoz. New York: Hastings House, 1954.

TIMBER LINE by Gene Fowler. New York: Covici Friede, 1933.

PICTURE CREDITS

NOTE: BBM indicates pictures from Buffalo Bill Museum (Buffalo Bill Memorial Association) Cody, Wyoming; photographs by Jack Richard Studio.

YALE indicates pictures from William Robertson Coe Collection, Western Americana, Sterling Library, Yale University.

DPL indicates Denver Public Library, Western Collection.

A indicates pictures from Col. Cody's 1879 autobiography.

For purposes of space and simplicity pictures from the Bettman Archive are credited: *Bettman;* Brown Brothers: *Brown;* Culver Service: *Culver;* Mercaldo Archives: *Mercaldo.*

Schreyvogel's "Breaking the Circle," *C. R. Smith collection;* Sioux capture UP train, *Brown;* Gen. Crook, *Mercaldo;* Wild Bill Hickok as Scout, A; Hickok later, *Mercaldo;* Gen. Carr, *Mercaldo;* The golden spike, *Mercaldo*

Chapter 6

Cody with ladies, A; Buntline, *Mercaldo;* Cody as Scout, *Mercaldo;* Grand Duke Alexis, A; Custer and Alexis, *Mercaldo;* Buffalo Bill in New York, BBM; James Gordon Bennett II, *Brown*

Chapter 7

Posters that brought the crowds, YALE; Buntline, Buffalo Bill, and Texas Jack, BBM; Mlle. Morlacchi, *Mercaldo;* He-Nu-Kaw, May Cody, and Prairie Waif posters, YALE; Kit Carson Cody, BBM

Chapter 8

Section of Yellow Hand poster, BBM; Buffalo Bill in Mexican costume, *Mercaldo;* Sioux version Little Big Horn battle, *Käsebier;* Maps of War Bonnet engagement and photograph of terrain, *collection of Robert F. Canaday, from American Military History;* First scalp for Custer, *painting by Robert Lindneux,* BBM; Generals Merritt and King, *collection of Robert F. Canaday*

Chapter 9

Buffalo Bill in Indian dress, Captain Jack Crawford, and Major Frank North, *Mercaldo;* Welcome Wigwam, *Mercaldo;* Arta Cody, *Mercaldo;* family group, BBM; Dr. Carver, *Mercaldo;* first Wild West Show poster, YALE; "Arizona John" Burke, *Mercaldo*

Chapter 10

Car from special train, DPL; John Nelson, *Mercaldo;* Wild West poster, DPL; Annie Oakley, *Mercaldo;* Sioux tepee, *Käsebier;* Annie Oakley's dressing-room trunk, BBM; Prentiss Ingraham's dime novels, BBM; Sitting Bull with Buffalo Bill, *Mercaldo;* Short Man, *Käsebier;* High Heron and Has-No-Horse, *Käsebier;* Deadwood Coach at Madison Square Garden, *Bettman;* Willie-Spotted-Horse, *Käsebier;* Red Cloud, Buffalo Bill, and American Horse, DPL; Layout of show abroad, BBM

Chapter 11

Queen Victoria and Red Shirt, *London Graphic;* Troupe in London, DPL; Exhibition grounds in London, *London Illustrated News;* Deadwood Coach in London, *Mercaldo;* sketches of Indians and Cowboys at Earl's Court, *London Illustrated News;* Prince and Princess of Wales, *Brown;* Col. Cody and Old Charlie, *Mercaldo;* sketches of command performances, *London Illustrated News;* Distinguished visitors, BBM; Company forming in line, *London Illustrated News*

Chapter 12

Buffalo Bill with Braves in gondola, *Mercaldo;* Rosa Bonheur painting Buffalo Bill in Paris, DPL; Rosa Bonheur's portrait of Buffalo Bill, *W. R. Coe estate;* poster on European tour, BBM; Col. Cody in Europe, *Mercaldo;* Cody shooting glass balls, and race between Indian cowboy and Vaquero, *drawings by Carl Henckel;* King Ludwig of Bavaria at Wild West, *Mercaldo;* German dime novel, *Mercaldo;* Emigrant train and buffalo chase, *drawings by Carl Henckel;* the Czar's gift to Cody, BBM

272

Chapter 13

Complimentary ticket to the big show, BBM; meeting with General Miles, *Mercaldo;* Pine Ridge peace meeting poster, YALE; Mrs. Cody with Irma, *Mercaldo;* Nate Salsbury on tour, *Brown;* Show poster, YALE; the Cody family, BBM; advertisement of Wild West Show, *New York Public Library;* pages from Route-Book, Buffalo Bill's Wild West 1899, *collection of Henry H. R. Coe;* Candid glimpses of side show, top going up, the cowboy band, and children entering show, and Col. Cody shooting glass balls, DPL; Has-No-Horse, Indian Chief, Whirling-Hawk, Flying-Horse, Samuel Lone-Bear, Two Bulls, and Kills-First, *Käsebier;* Col. Cody with Chief Joseph, *Mercaldo*

Chapter 14

Branding iron of the TE ranch, BBM; Panorama of Scout's Rest Ranch, *Cody Enterprise;* the Col. relaxes in his tent, *Mercaldo;* Katherine Clemmons, *Mercaldo;* Teddy Roosevelt as a rancher, *Brown;* Stetson advertisement and the Buffalo Bill hat, *John B. Stetson Co.;* Baden-Powell's drawing of Buffalo Bill with Indian and boy scout, *Henry Holt and Co., Inc.;* Buffalo Bill surrounded by youthful admirers, BBM; Remington sketches of Wild West Show, *Life;* exotic Bailey influence on show, *Brown;* Annie Oakley poster, *Mercaldo;* Charles Dana Gibson sketches of the show, *Life*

Chapter 15

Col. Cody driving, not riding, in 1912, *Bettman;* Cody and Pawnee Bill become partners, *Mercaldo;* a generous letter from the Col., BBM; Buffalo Bill in his only movie, *Mercaldo;* letter requesting more photographs to give away, *Mercaldo;* Buffalo Bill with the Deadwood Coach, *Library, State Historical Society of Colorado;* the Irma Hotel in Cody, 1908, *Brown;* last picture of Buffalo Bill with Louisa, *Mercaldo;* the Great Scout's last farewell on horseback at the end of the show, *Brown*

Epilogue

The Gertrude Vanderbilt Whitney statue at Cody, BBM (*Jack Richard Studio*); Buffalo Bill's grave on Lookout Mountain, *Denver Convention and Visitor's Bureau;* the spot at Cody where Buffalo Bill wished to be buried, *Jack Richard Studio;* Buffalo Bill's old Winchester rifle, BBM

INDEX of Principal Names and Places

BUFFALO BILL *and the* WIL